ADVANCE PRAISE

"Matt Bellace takes a fresh and humorous look at how adversity can be the quickest way to learn resilience and resilience builds high performing neuropathways. In an age when the norm is to shield ourselves and our kids from the discomfort that simply comes from being human, Matt uses his training in neuroscience to demonstrate that such shielding behavior only delays the potential for the personal growth we ultimately strive for. Bravo, Matt! For a truly bold and fulfilling life, load up on challenge!" **DAVID PACKHEM**, Executive Producer, "Voices of Hope...The Rugged Road to Recovery"

"Since the first time I met Matt years ago on the comedy scene in New York City, his focus has been on bringing humor to serious topics. He has done it again in this book on disappointment! It's part memoir and part self-help, but fully engaging." **GUY WINCH, PhD**, Author of *Emotional First Aid: Healing Rejection, Guilt, Failure, and Other Everyday Hurts*

"*Life is Disappointing... and other inspiring thoughts* is an important (and yes, sometimes funny) look into how challenges and pain are opportunities for personal growth, even an essential part of a full and meaningful life. A must-read for young adults and the young at heart—reimagining how we process, adapt, and grow stronger from trauma and adversity...something we all need now more than ever emerging from a pandemic-scarred world." **DOUG BRATTON**, Executive Director, Partners in Prevention

"My life is way more disappointing after reading this book! At least I can post the front cover as a review." **BLAKE**, college student (not a fan)

Life is
Disappointing

... and other inspiring thoughts

Matt Bellace, Ph.D.

Wyatt-MacKenzie Publishing
DEADWOOD, OREGON

To all those who have caused me pain, loss and failure,
both intentionally and unintentionally.
Thank you.

Also by Matt Bellace

A BETTER HIGH
Inspired by the nationally renowned youth program
"How to Get High Naturally"

**Life is Disappointing
...and other inspiring thoughts**

Matt Bellace, Ph.D.

ISBN: 978-1-954332-22-5

Cover illustration by Karolina Madej.

Wyatt-MacKenzie Publishing
DEADWOOD, OREGON

ATTENTION SCHOOLS & BUSINESSES:

This book is available at quantity discounts with bulk purchase for educational, business, or sales promotional use. For information, please contact **Matt Bellace, Ph.D. Presentations, LLC** at matt@mattbellace.com

CONTENTS

INTRODUCTION

Life is disappointing. What an uplifting message from a motivational speaker to start an introduction! It's true. On a regular basis, there are moments that are emotionally crushing. There are times when the human condition feels unbearable. The most positive outcome I can imagine from pain, loss, and failure is that you get to decide what to do with those emotions. If you channel the energy in a negative direction, more pain and distraction can follow. However, if you're inspired to put those emotions back into the world as positive energy, you win. We all win.

This book will examine the process of disappointment, from the initial insult to the later stages, and mining the emotions for inspiration. Everything good in my life has come from something that initially didn't go well. My journey to getting a PhD started with a failed test. My youth athletic career began with the loss of a loved one. My actual career, professional speaking, formed during periods of loneliness and social isolation. We all live through disappointment, but learning how those moments can propel us forward is empowering.

I completed a rough draft of this book a few weeks before COVID-19 shut down the entire world. As a speaker who used to work primarily in schools, talking to large audiences, I would brag to my wife, "I've got over a hundred bosses a year. For me to lose my job, they'd have to shut every school in the country!" Cut to March 12th, 2020 and my work disappeared faster than you could say super spreader. In three days, I went from jet setter to mediocre homeschool teacher. It was terrible! At least, that's what my kids wrote on their teacher evaluation of me.

In a matter of days, I found myself feeling sad and stuck in a way I had never experienced. My way of making a living had been taken and I didn't know when I might get it back. Well-meaning, but empathetically-challenged friends were quick to dismiss my feelings and tell me to "switch to doing online stuff." For weeks, there was no hint of any demand for such a thing. To make matters worse, my days were filled with just trying to get my kids to focus on virtual learning. When I did get a little free time, I walked or biked outside as long as I could to try and forget this nightmare.

Despite all that was taken from me during the pandemic, I was the fortunate one. I got to sit in the safety of my home. In the months before the shutdown, I used to say, "If I could just hit the pause button on my life, I could complete this book!" This was my chance. The pandemic was a master class in disappointment and I was an inadvertent student. Eventually, I chose to focus not on what was taken from me, but what I can take from it.

As I examined disappointment in my life and others', I noticed an interesting pattern in most stories. There was an initial expenditure of energy on ruminating about fixing it or recreating what happened. The anxious brain took over, seeing the world in a myopic way and focusing on worst-case scenarios. What seemed to help many people, including myself, was to be surrounded by positive support. People who served as a buffer against the worst of it, like a protective coating on an electrical wire in the rain. The next step was to find an outlet to express the feelings. Sometimes it wasn't even a conscious choice, like being hungry and searching out food. When people found the activity that made them feel good, they also got better at it, much better.

This book is personal. I lived the lessons I'll be describing. I used the techniques I'll be presenting in these pages. The book is funny at times, hopefully very funny. They best stories and jokes seem to come from negative events. The book is also serious at times. Relevant findings in neuroscience and psychology are presented to back up some of the statements.

If you're going to read one book on resilience and this is the one you've chosen, I promise it won't suck. In the words of a high school student who watched my assembly at his school, "If we have to listen to someone talk about that stuff, he's definitely the best at it." For a seventeen-year-old, that's a ringing endorsement.

CHAPTER 1

The Most Beautiful Waves Come From the Biggest Storms

"In surfing, success is determined by the ability to be poised and present as the elements break apart around you."

~ Narrator in ESPN's *30 for 30* on Kelly Slater

In 2017, I was speaking at a juvenile detention center in Northern California, and it was not going well. The flop sweat on my neck would say I was bombing. My plan was to start the presentation with a demonstration of support, using four chairs and having volunteers sit down and lean back into the lap of the person behind them. If it worked, the audience would be immediately engaged and the program would be off to a good start.

As I was setting up the chairs in the unusually cold gymnasium, a guard approached and asked, "What's up with the chairs?"

A little taken aback, I said, "It's going to be great! They'll lean back, and I can pull their chairs out. It's about support."

He responded sternly, "They can't do it. The kids can't touch. It's against the rules here."

As boxer Mike Tyson once said, "Everybody has a plan until they get punched in the mouth." As the audience filed in, about 100 young men in khaki jumpsuits with heavy work boots, I felt like I had gotten punched in the mouth. They wore flat and angry expressions on their faces, and I began to sweat despite the glacial temperature in the room. A guard quickly introduced me and pronounced my name wrong. It's always a bad sign when the guy who asks in advance how to pronounce your name instantly mispronounces it. If he can't listen to me, how can he listen to them? If they don't feel heard, why would they listen to me? He might as well have said to the audience, "I know you'd all rather be somewhere else right now, I know I would, but we have a speaker for you." A superintendent introduced me that way at a back-to-school night once. It did not go well.

There was a polite smattering of applause, like a mediocre golfer teeing off in a small tournament. The guard handed me the mic, and I was so flustered that the first thing out of my mouth was, "So thanks for being here!" What's the worst thing to say to teenagers in prison? That's it. Thank them for being there. Yuck!

I struggled, and it showed. Every joke fell flat, and I started losing them. I felt uncomfortable, like I was up there wearing oversized clothes. When I asked for a volunteer to come up and guess a few song titles, I assumed no one would raise their hand. Mercifully, a tall, slender young man with a kind face volunteered. His name was Eugene, and if I saw him on the street, I never would imagine he would be in detention. He was tall and innocent looking, like he would be the class president. It turned out he was also a singer songwriter. After the music demonstration, I took a risk and asked if he wanted to sing one of his songs for us. To my surprise, he agreed without hesitation.

Eugene grabbed the mic and delivered one of the most heartfelt songs I've ever heard. It was about his life, how his parents didn't love him, how he smelled so bad no one would hug him, and now he's locked up, incarcerated, and stuck. His song gave me the chills. It was a whole-body tingle, like the first time I heard The Roots song "My Shot." When he finished, the crowd went wild! They were cheering and yelling for him. When he finished, there was a standing ovation, which I'm sure was against the rules, but who cares? In about two minutes, he changed the mood of the room and the fate of my presentation.

After Eugene sat down, the audience treated me like I was a different person. They listened and laughed. It was almost as if they were saying, "Okay, you let that happen, now we'll listen to you." When I was finished talking, I was supposed to field questions, but instead I brought Eugene back up for an encore. He performed again and crushed again. When Eugene finished, I asked him, "How did you create such powerful music?" He told us he had always loved performing, but that being in detention gave him the time and opportunity to write.

I didn't expect Eugene's answer. I assumed that being in juvenile detention would be the worst experience of his life, one that would stifle his creativity. It was quite the opposite. The structure of his day allowed for multiple opportunities to sit quietly and write. In addition, the feedback from teachers and peers gave him the kind of guidance he lacked at home. It's a credit to Eugene that he turned the energy from his personal pain and incarceration into powerful music.

I've thought a lot about Eugene since that moment. In over twenty years of bringing volunteers on stage with me, I've never seen anything quite like it. Sure, I've witnessed talented people do something special and get a round of applause; however, Eugene's circumstances were among the most difficult I'd ever heard, and his talent was the best. I'm convinced those two things are related. In the darkness of his life, he found a way to harness those negative emotions into powerful lyrics and a moving performance.

I love surfing, and the sport taught me that the most beautiful waves come from the biggest storms. I believe that's how life works, too. That relationship between struggle and inspiration is worthy of examination. How do people take pain, loss, and failure and turn them into energy that propels them to greatness? Perhaps an even more relevant question is: how can people take minor annoyances, microaggressions, and everyday setbacks and harness them as vehicles to become more inspired, effective, and resilient?

This Book

This is a book about disappointment, and it took me forever to write because so many disappointing things kept happening! Each new crisis required another chapter. I knew I had to finish it because you can't quit a book about resilience. That would be pathetic.

I started the book in 2017 BC (before COVID, as comedian Juston McKinney says). Once the pandemic hit, everything was on hold. Businesses were halted. School years were altered. Celebrations were canceled. Most importantly, lives were lost. You know all this—I'm just writing it down for the next generation who'll soon be here asking, "What's COFFID?"

My professional life was also completely upended. After high school, I earned four degrees. The last one was a doctorate in clinical neuropsychology. I had advanced training in the assessment of cognitive impairment and was preparing for a career working with brain injury patients in a hospital or teaching at a college. Then I decided to do something radical. I followed my dream. I created a professional speaking business (yes, that's a thing), which integrated my education with a passion for stand-up comedy. I traveled the world (okay, United States and Canada) for over a decade and spoke to more than one hundred thousand people a year. I was such a big deal. When I pulled up to a venue, sometimes they had saved a parking spot for me. Of course, my mom didn't want me to pursue speaking. She was afraid I'd end up at home writing a book about my disappointments. I showed her.

Before pandemic hit, I was the main "breadwinner," which sounds like a term that's about to get canceled, but it's true. A decent amount of my identity was wrapped up in providing income for my family. We live in Princeton, New Jersey, a well-to-do lively suburban town where I'm told there's a great university. I was one of the lucky ones and not a day goes by that I'm not thankful. For over a decade, I got paid to do what I love most: speak to a crowd. I used to stand in front of large audiences and perform. In a matter of days, those events became known as super-spreader events, and my entire calendar was wiped clean. Fourteen years of cultivating relationships and it felt like they were all gone.

I went from being a busy provider to a mediocre homeschool teacher. My kids were ages ten and seven at the time, which might be the worst ages for remote learning. They were old enough to have assignments but not old enough to do any of it independently. Throw in some legitimate anxiety about their parents losing work or getting sick and you've got a recipe for them never leaving me alone.

When my kids were in remote learning, I could focus on my stuff for about a minute until one of them would interrupt with a question. It's like child-induced attention deficit hyperactivity disorder (ADHD). I don't entirely blame them. It must have been weird to go from a certified teacher to an unshaven sad father who gets tons of sleep but always looks tired. One morning early on, I had a *Captain Phillips* moment (great movie, by the way) when they were trying to ignore my instructions for their schoolwork. I said loudly, "Look at me! Look at me! I'm the teacher now!"

As my daily planner became the most useless purchase of the

year, I never faced that kind of economic fear. The good news was my wife's practice in clinical psychology immediately doubled, which prompted an unappreciated joke in my house: "Where was this ten years ago?" She saved us, along with family who helped out and some clients who paid me in advance. We survived thanks to her, and a day doesn't go by without me thinking about that. I did all I could do. I applied for every federal and state aid program available, but for two months, I heard nothing. I called the New Jersey Unemployment office, but back then, the phone wouldn't even ring. It just went to silence. I guess, so at least you could just scream.

I was feeling so down the first two weeks that it felt like someone had stolen my career. I finally understood the lyrics to the Talking Heads song, "Once in a Lifetime." I found myself living in a beautiful house with a beautiful wife, and I asked myself, "How did I get here?" I couldn't travel or work. I spent my free time looking for disinfecting wipes. This was not my beautiful life. All I remember thinking was, "How can I make it through two weeks of this?"

In the two months leading up to the shutdown, I had taken eleven flights, crossing the country four times, visiting Costa Rica once, and staying in eight different hotels: I was sure I had the virus. When things shut down, I woke up each night and played a fun game called, "Is this chest pain from coronavirus or a panic attack?" Thankfully, it was just the panic of losing everything.

I did make sure to go for a walk around the neighborhood each afternoon. I was like Andy Dufresne in *Shawshank Redemption*, pacing the prison yard and planning my escape. The only difference was that every time I shook my pant leg, it wasn't to deposit rubble from the tunnel I was digging. I was just itchy from not showering.

As the weeks turned into months, it was settling in just how bad things were for the country. The television news was so awful that one night my wife exclaimed, "This is horrible!" I replied, "Could you be more specific?"

I had a distant cousin pass away, as well as the father of a high school friend, but neither family could have a funeral. The New York City hospital where I trained needed to put up a tent in Central Park to treat all the extra patients, while the hospital down the street needed refrigerated morgue trucks for all the bodies. I felt selfish for being so down about my situation because at least I was still healthy. At the same time, I was a victim of the economic fallout, which exceeded 20 million lost jobs in the first two months, and it hurt.

The pandemic has been like a master's class for experiencing disappointment. In the midst of my struggles, I noticed that the one thing that I kept looking forward to was finding time to write. This had happened before when a good friend passed away. I was pulled toward the book because it felt like the only way to express myself. It happened again later on when my dad had a terrible accident, and I took to writing with a renewed sense of urgency. This is remarkable because I don't normally love writing. It takes me a long time. I don't just burp out content like a machine making stuff.

It was almost as if the pain and suffering I experienced made the process of reflecting and creating more rewarding. I went through mini versions of what Eugene did, and I'm better for it. Don't get me wrong, if I could have stopped all these negative circumstances from happening and not finished the book, I would choose that outcome every time. However, I don't have the option. There is only one path in this life, and it's forward.

As the book's title suggests, disappointment can be inspiring, if you choose to use it that way. However, it's also about other inspiring thoughts connected to the theme of pain, loss, and failure. Each chapter features a saying that has motivated me at crucial times in my life, along with stories, jokes, research, and techniques to help you cope. I'm part motivational speaker, comedian, and clinical psychologist. I think all three will come out in these pages. I hope you'll enjoy reading this book as much as I hated writing it.

Perspective Shift

One morning at breakfast, about two weeks into the shutdown, all of my self-pity about the pandemic hit a wall. My brain started producing thoughts about young people who didn't have a parent at home struggling to teach them. What about the kid who has two working parents? What about the parents who are essential front-line workers, risking their health, and their kids are at home at night wondering if mom and dad will get sick? What about the kid who is living with a mentally ill or chemically dependent parent and can't get away?

What about the kid who has an abusive parent and they're unsafe? I realized how privileged I was to be able to sit at my table and grouse about my problems. I was overwhelmed by empathy for all the pain and suffering taking place in homes across the world. The psychologist part of my brain had finally turned on.

My perspective continued to change with each passing day. I suddenly wanted to focus more on what I could do than what I couldn't do. Then one evening around sunset, I was out biking with my kids when I looked up the block and saw the most miraculous sight. Kids were playing outside. They were rollerblading, walking, and biking like it was the 1970s again. I kept looking for bell-bottom jeans and butterfly collars. The normal hyperactive routines of suburban families had been replaced by this throwback of community togetherness. It was almost as if the virus was taking us back to a time when all that mattered was playing outside until the street lights came on.

The pent-up energy of anxiety over the virus plus being stuck inside had inspired kids to do the one thing parents failed to do in recent years: get them outside! Of course, that's how it looked. Inside, parents were still prying them away from screens to get them out the door.

As long as you were socially distant, being outside was the best place to be. In New Jersey during the first two months of the shutdown, it seemed the only thing you could do was exercise around the neighborhood. The added bonus was watching spring unfold up close and personal. It was almost as if, for those spared the worst of the pandemic, certain aspects of life had gotten better.

Disappointment can focus the mind on making transformational changes that we wouldn't have otherwise. Getting back to nature or being more physically active sounds easy, but for some people, it took a pandemic to do it. For me, the pandemic shifted my mindset from the deprivation mentality of losing work to the abundance mindset of embracing tons of outside time with my kids and in my garden. Once I made the mental shift, my mental health began to improve.

Heckler

I was speaking to an audience of about five hundred high school students in Upstate New York when a kid in the front row started heckling me. He was being very disruptive, talking loudly to his friends, shouting at inappropriate moments and just constantly making noise. I found it hard to concentrate, and as a result, I was losing the crowd. After a few nonverbal attempts to engage him, I stopped the program, started walking in his direction, and said, "Do you realize what you're doing? I'm a comedian with a microphone. I'll make fun of you and enjoy it."

The crowd laughed as I continued, "And the audience will love me for it. They'll scream, 'Dude, make him cry!'" The crowd roared with laughter and applause. Then I followed it with, "But I'm not here for that! I just want you to listen to me, is that okay?" I figured it would be because it has worked many times, but it didn't work this time. The young man continued to be disruptive, but I ignored him.

I learned years ago that you don't poke the bear. I was in Tacoma, Washington, speaking in a gym to nearly two thousand high school students, when a kid way in the back just kept yelling words that I couldn't hear well. I tried to make a joke about how he was so far away it was hurting his heckling. That didn't work; he just yelled louder. I even kidded him about how he was acting like a tough guy "from the mean streets of Tacoma." Turned out he was in a gang, so that was a mistake.

Eventually he got kicked out, and as he was leaving, I continued, "You seem so angry. I think you're going to meet me in the parking lot!" And he did. He never took a swing at me, but he put his fists up. He got expelled from school that day, and I felt partly responsible. I vowed from then on to give hecklers less attention.

In the first story, the heckler ruined my presentation, but afterwards, a tall young man sitting near him approached me and said something that blew my mind. He said, "I just want to apologize. He doesn't represent our school. We loved you."

I was pleasantly surprised. Putting on my psychologist hat, I said, "Wow, thank you for saying that. He probably has a tough home life. That's why he comes here and does that."

The young man responded, "He does! I live across the street and see him fighting with his parents all the time."

I nodded. "That's what I mean."

"Yeah, but my life is much tougher than his."

Exasperated, I looked at him and said, "How could you say that about someone else's life?"

He stood there for a second, never breaking eye contact, and said, "I lost both my parents in a car accident when I was ten. We were eating at a diner when a car crashed through and killed them both."

My mouth dropped open, and my shoulder sunk as I said, "I'm so sorry. I'm so sorry for you."

He stood very still, looked at me calmly, and said, "Yeah, well, I didn't disrupt your program." Then he walked away. In my head, I was thinking, "Who is that? Is he a superhero?"

Turns out he was a student leader at the school, a good athlete, and someone who was well regarded by others. What fascinated me most was how he dealt with unspeakable pain as a child. A loss of such magnitude didn't seem to destroy him; rather, he found a way to use it and become more mature. He apologized to me! In addition, he pursued a life dedicated to being a role model and positive influence at school.

The heckler had also used his pain, but it motivated him to be disruptive and get negative attention. For him, it was better than nothing, but it was maladaptive. It wasn't working for him or anyone else. An administrator at the school told me his behavior was problematic every day. Which made me think, "Wow, thanks for the heads up."

I was told they were going to use the assembly as a teachable moment for the kid and have a meeting with him. I hope it led to some positive change for him, but for me, there was an important takeaway. We all have a choice about what to do with our pain. We can use it to make us better students, better athletes, better parents, better citizens, or we can use it to disrupt ourselves and everyone else every day of our lives.

I've seen teenagers convert pain into positive behavior before in my travels. In 2019, I spoke at Newtown High School in Sandy Hook, Connecticut, in front of ninth graders, a third of whom had survived the shooting at Sandy Hook Elementary. I was told it was a "quiet school" with no bells or slamming doors due to the trauma these students suffered.

There were definitely students in my audience who appeared

emotionally fragile, understandably, while I talked about dealing with pain and loss. However, I also met the opposite. A friend of mine had given me the name of a student there who was his cousin. As I finished my first of two presentations, I was mentioning his name to the school's vice principal when the young man appeared out of nowhere! It was one of those memorable coincidences that I'm convinced was fate because he had no idea of the connection.

We talked more about his life since the shooting and how he dealt with the everyday stress of being a teenager. It felt like I was talking with a colleague since he seemed so mature. He was thoughtful and had insight beyond his years. I would have done anything to erase that event from his life, but clearly it had shaped his personality in a way that was working for him.

Productive Disappointment

Disappointments happen. They're a part of life. We can't prevent the emotions produced by them, but we do have a choice with what to do with the emotions. A machine wouldn't respond at all to a setback. It would just continue plugging away. A benefit to that response is efficiency. Humans have the advantage of fueling their response to disappointment if they know how to use the emotions effectively. It can be a productive disappointment if the response is adaptive. We can use the energy produced by life's negative moments to inspire greatness.

As humans, we tend to do a poor job of predicting our emotional reaction to negative life events. We assume we'll never recover from the big stuff and underestimate the impact of the smaller stuff. It turns out we have sort of a psychological immune system that kicks in, especially for those intense adverse experiences. Gaining an understanding of the process can help you be stronger than you think you'll be when the unexpected happens.

—·—

Brain Matters:
Psychological Immune System

These sections of the book—**Brain Matters**—will allow me to nerd out a bit.

I like to tell stories and jokes, but when I make reference to some scientific or psychological study, this section will give me space to expand on it a bit.

There is research that suggests human beings are not very accurate at predicting their emotional future.[1] The reason is we tend to focus too much on a single aspect of an event and how it will make us feel about our lives. We assume the good event will improve how we feel dramatically only to find out it doesn't. We assume the bad event will push us into a depression but are pleasantly surprised when things go better than expected.

The theory behind why we do such a poor job predicting our feelings when something negative happens is that our psychological immune system kicks to stabilize us. Similar to the lymphatic system, which steps in to rid the body of toxins, the psychological immune system fires up when needed to handle pain, loss, or failure.

A study on emotional reactions to being treated poorly found that participants predicted recovery from mistreatment would last longer if they were hurt a lot. They also predicted that minor transgressions would be handled quickly and forgotten. However, the results found just the opposite. It was the minor negative interactions that produced the longer lasting recovery.[2]

In the study, nearly one hundred college students completed questionnaires asking them to imagine their reaction to a range of specific hypothetical situations. For example, asking for a date and being politely turned down, meeting a person and be ignored by them a short while later, catching someone trying to break into their gym locker, or having a best friend have a romantic encounter with a former girlfriend or boyfriend. Participants were asked to rate the intensity of their reaction in the moment and predict how they would feel one week later. The results showed that participants consistently reported the more intense situations would be felt a week later compared to the less intense ones.

The study also examined reactions to actual experiences of rejection, in the moment and a short while later, by creating scenarios in the laboratory. They found that small negative interactions had more of an emotional impact over a longer period of time, suggesting the psychological immune system had not yet kicked in.

The concept of a psychological immune system might be new, but it appears to bear some similarity to our actual immune system. Small reactions can fly below the radar, but can turn into chronic problems. Larger reactions are detected by the system and dealt with immediately.

—·—

Kids Today

One day I was working from home, and I got a frantic phone call from my wife. "You forgot to give the kids their water bottles!"

It was a really hot day, but I asked, "Don't they have water fountains in schools anymore?" My question didn't seem to affect her goal. She wanted me to interrupt my busy workday and go back to the school to drop off two water bottles filled with ice cold water. As I trudged down to the school, I tried to imagine what would happen if I didn't do it. Would the school call and say, "Mr. Bellace, I'm sorry to inform you that your son tragically passed out from dehydration. He was trying to get to the water fountain, which I know was only fifteen feet away, but he didn't make it. If you had only brought water bottles like your wife asked you to do, none of this would have happened."

As I entered the building, I tried to imagine how my father would have reacted to such a phone call during his workday. I think he would have said, "Louise, how did you get this number?" My father could have worked at my school and would've done nothing. As a kid, I broke my wrist playing football, and my hand was bent inward at a ninety-degree angle. I said to my dad, "I think I broke my wrist. The coach says I need to get an x-ray." He responded, "Why do you need an x-ray if you already know it's broken?"

I don't know if I'm angry or jealous at how little my dad did back then. One thing is for sure, parents today invest so much more time and attention into their kids' lives. In many ways, it's amazing, because having adults take an interest in kids is a protective factor for them. Where it goes off the rails is when well-meaning parents intervene too much and stifle development.

Obviously, I'm as guilty of coddling my kids as anyone, but it can be reversed. It starts with reminding children and teenagers that they are stronger than they think. Telling them that we can't always prevent them from being hurt in this sometimes-unfair world, but instead we can help build up their psychological immune system by allowing pain, loss, and failure to happen. We need to embrace the struggle when it visits our kids. I guess what I'm saying is, I don't want to drop more water bottles off for my kids.

Montclair versus Randolph

Sports are a laboratory of disappointment. Every game has a winner and loser. Every season crowns a champion while the rest miss out. My junior year at Montclair High School was special. Our football team was ranked as high as #1 in the State of New Jersey according to *The Newark Star Ledger* and #6 in the country based on the *USA Today* list High School Football Top 25. We weren't good, we were great. The radio station Z100, based in nearby New York City, jokingly mentioned our team one morning, "Montclair High could probably beat the New York Jets!" The Jets lost ten games that season, but it was still a ridiculous statement. We definitely could have beaten them.

If you had told me at the beginning of the season that my team would play in what the *Newark Star Ledger* "Greatest High School Game Ever Played," I would not have believed it. If you had told me then that our final game that season would be listed as *Max Prep's* #3 Most Memorable High School Football Game of All-Time, I would have asked, "What is Max Prep's?" By the way, it's a website that displays scores and stats from high school sports across the United States.

That the New Jersey State Championship between Montclair High and Randolph High was such a highly regarded game had little to do with me. I was the backup quarterback. If you saw me, you wouldn't believe I even played football since I'm built more like a reader.

The two teams were undefeated, ranked #1 and #2 in the state respectively and we faced off in the final game. Montclair was heavily favored. We were much bigger than Randolph. In addition, we had been #1 in the state for most of the season and ranked #6 in the nation during the week of the championship. However, if Randolph won, they would break the state record for wins at 49. They had been undefeated for years playing against smaller schools, so that season they moved up to our group. Oh, and their coach died two weeks before the game! His son, Jack Baur Jr., took over the team. I heard that he took the team to his dad's grave site the day of the state championship. If that happened in a movie, you probably wouldn't believe it.

The game was close from start to finish. There was about a minute and half left in the fourth quarter and Montclair lead 21-19. However, Randolph had the ball and was marching down the field. They were threatening to score, deep in our territory, when they fumbled. We recovered! The fans went wild! All Montclair had to do was take a knee a few times and the game would be over. After the third straight down of our quarterback taking a knee, the scoreboard clock ran out and the crowd rushed on to the field. We did it! We won! I got kissed by a girl I didn't even know. We were sizing our fingers for rings. It was a beautiful day!

In the midst of our celebration, the referee's whistles were blowing and the announcer was encouraging fans to return to the stands. The officials met and announced there was time left on the clock. They put seven seconds back on the scoreboard. Our offensive coordinator, who was also a math teacher, argued it should only be two or three. His protests went nowhere, the clock was set to seven seconds. On fourth down, our talented quarterback Lamont Ponton stood with his back to our end zone and punted the ball. He was such a calm, cool guy and a talented athlete, but something went wrong. The punt only went eleven yards past the line of scrimmage. Randolph received the ball and quickly sent their kicking team onto the field. We were in shock. I can remember thinking, "He won't make it. It's just too far and there's too much pressure." We called time out just to set up a defense and the tension was palpable. Randolph snapped the ball, the holder got it down and their kicker booted a 37-year field goal with one second left on the clock. It was good. Randolph won. We were robbed or as Randolph fans would forever know it, The Miracle at Montclair.

The Randolph kicker, who happened to be their quarterback, Mike Groh, went on to become the offensive coordinator of the Philadelphia Eagles. Whenever I saw him on television, I'd yell "Screw you Mike Groh! You ruined my life!" But did he, really? No. I wasn't going on to play football in college. Heck, I didn't even play in that game.

Today, I feel lucky to have lived that sad moment. If I could wave a magic wand and change the outcome, I would. But I would never want to erase the lesson that in life there will be times when your hopes and dreams are dashed. There will be times when you feel like you got robbed and were treated unfairly. Watching that game on YouTube recently made me realize that the intense feelings of that loss have subsided. It looks like just another old game now. What remains in my mind is the scar tissue and callouses that made the next time I was handed a big defeat a lot easier to swallow.

In athletics, as in life, your greatest ability is your availability. When you show up and work hard, good things happen. Do not underestimate the power of your presence. Being there, mentally and physically, puts you in a position to achieve things that absence does not. There will be times you fail, but you are stronger than you think. You are capable of more than your talent should allow, but you have to show up.

The Greatest Game: Beautiful Waves

Coincidentally, the same week I started writing this chapter, a lengthy article came out on *NJ.com* about the 1990 Montclair-Randolph game titled, "The Day That Changed Everything: They lost the biggest N.J. high school football game ever played. Can one agonizing defeat destroy a life?"[3] It was a deep dive into the reaction of our head coach and quarterback/punter after the game. The author suggested that losing the game sent both men into a downward spiral from which they never recovered. I have a different perspective. There were others players who went on do great things inspired by that game. Of course, that was never mentioned.

Garland Daron Thornton was a guy who led by example and didn't make excuses. He was definitely one of my favorites on that team. He nearly blocked the field goal that gave Randolph the win. There's an iconic photo of him lying on the ground beneath two celebrating Randolph players. It looks like he's been devastated.

Garland made sure that his senior year would not be the final memory for him on the football field at Montclair High School. He shared with me that the state championship loss motivated him to get a college degree and eventually work for the Recreation and Cultural Affairs Office in Montclair. That job allowed him to pursue a dream that he had had since that Randolph game, to became an assistant football coach at Montclair High School. Since being part of the coaching staff, he has helped them win five state championships! Those events are definitely related.

My memory of Steve Baffico at the Montclair-Randolph game was in warm-ups, when the second team got to run a few practice plays. I always felt a little pressure because Coach Davies wanted to see everything run perfectly right before the game. The play we ran that day was a belly pass, which meant I would hike the ball, fake the handoff to the running back and then roll out to my right and throw a pass to one of two different receivers. I usually threw a quick five-yard pass to ensure a completion, but not that day.

I remember rolling out and throwing a deep pass to wide receiver Steve Baffico. He caught it about twenty-five years away in stride, though in my mind it was like forty yards! By some estimates, there were more than thirteen thousand fans there that day and at that point there could have been a few thousand already. When Steve made the catch, I heard the crowd cheer like it was a big play in the game. I got the chills all throughout my body.

Steve was a senior, but was not a starter at Montclair. He was a good athlete, but like me, was surrounded by excellent athletes so he had to wait for playing time. Steve graduated and attended the University of Wisconsin. Amazingly, Steve decided that losing to Randolph would not be his final football act. "It just left this black hole," he told the author of the *NJ.com* article.

Steve's inspiration was to "walk on" for the Wisconsin football team and he made it! In the 1993 season, Wisconsin went 10-1-1 and won a share of the Big Ten title. He played on special teams, and when Wisconsin outlasted UCLA in the 1994 Rose Bowl in Pasadena, California, he got a ring. To put it into perspective, out of the 130 or so players on a big-time college football team, only a couple unrecruited walk-ons make it. Even fewer get to play. Steve did both and I suspect filled that black hole from the Randolph loss.

The most highly awarded player on our team in 1990 was All-State Wide Receiver/Tight End, Jason Curry. He was a big, sure-handed kid with a cool temperament. As I recall, his mom only started letting him play football in ninth grade, but he was so good that he suited up for varsity that season.

Based on his comments nearly thirty years later, Jason was perhaps plagued the most by the Randolph game. "It's always stayed in my mind, even to this day," said Curry. "It's not a week that goes by that that game doesn't at least pop into my mind at some point." He's now an accomplished attorney living in California, but his football talents earned him a football scholarship to Rutgers University in New Jersey. He had three touchdown receptions in his career and even played against the University of Notre Dame during legendary coach Lou Holtz's final game.

I remember watching Jason in the Notre Dame game in the fall of 1996. I was at Bucknell, packing to leave for a trip to Washington D.C. with the game on in the background. Then I heard the announcer call his name. He had dropped a pass around mid-field and the commentators were criticizing him for it. It didn't bother me; I was just proud to say I had played with someone who was on that field. But I do remember thinking, "He's going to feel bad for dropping that pass, but he's dealt with disappointment before. He'll be fine."

Finally, there's the legacy of Lamont Ponton (our quarterback in the infamous loss to Randolph), and his brother Derek. He was a slightly taller version of his brother, but bore a striking resemblance. I met him my senior year while during a peer leadership program where seniors would mentor freshmen. At one point, I remember talking with him one on one about making good choices, especially around alcohol and other drugs. He acknowledged wanting to avoid the mistakes he'd seen his brother make.

Three years later, Derrick was a senior quarterback for the Mounties with a talented squad of players around him. Wearing his brother's number 12, he led the team on a memorable run to the state championship. Who did they play? You guessed it, Randolph. On an unseasonably warm December day, 10,000 fans packed Randolph's stadium, named after their late coach John Baur, Sr.

It was an exciting game again, coming down to the wire. Randolph was in front, 12-7 with 1:57 remaining in the fourth quarter. Derrick Ponton dropped back, pump faked and threw a high arcing pass to the back of the end zone. His receiver hauled in the 19-yard pass and fell to the group for a touchdown! It was perfectly timed and proved to be the winning score. Derrick avenged the disappointing and controversial loss from 1990. The beautiful wave had come in and the Mounties rode it to victory.

SPOTLIGHT
Cat's Story

Despite the political division in the United States during and after the 2016 Presidential election, there was one movement worth applause. According to the Center for American Women and Politics at Rutgers University, a record number of women candidates ran and won seats in 2018 in the House and Senate. By the time they were sworn into the 116th Congress, more than one hundred women won seats in the House of Representatives, which shattered the previous record. In fact, more women and people of color were seated than ever—including the first two Native American women and the first two Muslim women.

The historic results in 2018 were not by accident. I suspect a significant number of those candidates were upset by what they perceived to be displays of misogyny, stoking of racial tension, and contempt toward women and minorities by Donald Trump during the 2016 Presidential campaign. You don't have to agree, but if you put yourself in their shoes, you can understand what motivated these women and minorities to take action

It's been said that all politics is local, so I met a woman who had been motivated by the 2016 Presidential election events to run for her town council. Her name is Catherine "Cat" Gural, and it was the first time she had ever run for any office. As the mother of a special needs child, she watched in disgust as Donald Trump mocked a disabled reporter and then went on to win the election. She felt it should have cost him the race and feared that his win was an acceptance of bullying culture in America.

The morning after the presidential election, Cat drove to work and sat in the parking lot feeling "tremendous sadness and disappointment." She said, "He has no respect for women! This is an open assault on my personal values." She decided to take off work for a much needed mental health day. She went home and started sending emails to her state and local politicians to see what she could do.

"I wrote to Cory Booker and Bonnie Watson Coleman (senators in her state of New Jersey), and I searched for my county elected officials, sent them emails, and they wrote me back!" The Democratic Party took an interest in her story. She is an amazing mother, who in addition to struggling with multiple sclerosis and having a child with a disability, overcame a first marriage deci-mated by her spouse's opiate addiction. At one point, she even applied for welfare to get her through the toughest times.

As a result of reaching out, she entered a six-month training program to instruct candidates how to campaign for themselves. "It was every Saturday from 9-5, so I had to miss being with my family," she said. "It sucked, but I just looked at my young daughter and knew it was the right thing to do." Most people in Cat's position might have suppressed the emotions, hoping that some external force would come along and fix things. Instead, she took a proactive approach and turned out to be an ideal candidate.

"For me, I felt a call to service. I felt compelled to do it. I felt motivated to make time for this to show my kids that you have to be the person who makes change," she said. Cat Gural won her election for Township Committee, and based on the laws of her town, will have a turn at being mayor one day.

The Jersey Shore

I've spent most of my life living in New Jersey. In fact, the first joke I ever wrote was about my home state. "New Jersey's the Garden State, because if you live here, you'll be guardin' your house, guardin' your car, guardin' your wallet."

I still live in New Jersey and vacation here. That's how much I enjoy it. I take my family to the same Jersey Shore towns I visited as a kid: Point Pleasant Beach, Manasquan, and Ocean City. My childhood summer vacations to the Jersey Shore always started the same way: wake up at dawn and sit in traffic. No matter what time of day, the two-hour drive would take almost four hours to get there, packed in the car like sardines with our luggage piled high around us. There were always sheets and towels in the car because, for some reason, The Jersey Shore had everything you could imagine, except linens.

There were no screens in the car back then. It was the horse and buggy days of personal entertainment. All I had were a few books and a handheld Frogger game that made me car sick in ten minutes. My older brother sat in the back, too, lip-syncing songs from the radio in my face with his morning dog breath. It's no wonder we would pull on to the Garden State Parkway and I'd ask, "Are we there yet?"

Despite the pain of the trip, it was always worth going because we got to hang with my cousins. I was the youngest, which meant being buried up to my chest in the sand and left for dead. I also got to play arcade games on the boardwalk, mini-golf, and eat Kohr's Frozen Custard every night. My favorite thing to do was riding the waves. Ocean City, New Jersey, in August meant one thing: big surf, at least for a little dude like me. Late summer was hurricane season, and the storms blew up the East Coast and added tremendous energy to the water. If you were lucky, it would never get close to land, but the waves would be huge.

I learned many life lessons from the ocean. The first one was about respecting the power of something that could pick you up, throw you down, and remove your suit for all the world to see. I started out afraid of the water, but thanks to my family, I got into bodysurfing and boogie boarding. One of my fondest memories of childhood was watching everyone go into the water. It seemed like everyone was happiest when we were in the ocean.

The sea is a healing place. I used to get horrendous poison ivy as a kid, but as my mother always told me, "It's nothing a few days in the salt water can't cure." It always worked. Of course, back then there could have been tons of pharmaceuticals in that water, too. I felt like the ocean also helped calm my family a bit, so it was healing in more ways than one.

Kayak Therapy

In my twenties, I got dumped by a long-distance girlfriend and took it pretty hard. I was completely miserable for almost a year. When it first happened, I had crazy thoughts. I wanted to drive three hours to her house to talk to her, or worse, call her grandmother. It turns out the brain reacts to rejection by getting obsessive, perhaps in an attempt to fix it. As the weeks passed, and it was apparent that she was not coming back, I got flashbacks of her when I would see a certain type of car or jeans. It was like she was re-dumping me at random moments throughout the day.

One weekend, I dragged myself to the beach and saw people riding waves in a sit-on-top ocean kayak. It looked like so much fun that I decided I had to have one. A few weeks later, I drove to my parents' house with a new ocean kayak tied to the roof of my car. My mom reacted like I had lost my mind. "What did you do?" she exclaimed. You would have thought I just ran over a guy, and he was still stuck to the bumper.

That kayak brought me so much joy because it gave me an excuse to go to the beach. During one of those trips, I caught a lucky break when my older cousin offered to let me store the kayak at his beach house. I understood even back then that it was quite a privilege. When he gave me his house key and told me I could use it any time, it was one of the coolest things anyone had ever done for me. I showed up so often that I hardly blame him for changing the locks.

Kayaking helped me get over the breakup. It gave me an excuse to travel to the ocean. It was beach therapy for the brokenhearted. When summer turned into fall, I got a wetsuit so I could continue going out. In fact, one warm November day, I decided to drive down to Ocean City after my graduate school class in psychology let out. Before I left, a classmate named Dara (who I was interested in at the time) heard I was going kayaking and started asking questions. She seemed intrigued, like having a small boat made me an international man of mystery. Dara later shared that it made me seem "independent," like I was a person who was forging his own path in life. A short while later, we started dating. A few years after that, Dara and I were married!

To recap, the breakup was a loss that hurt. I took the pain and pursued kayaking because it looked like fun, and the ocean has always been a healing place for me. That healthy activity drew interest from someone who would go on to become my wife. That wonderful woman gave me two beautiful children who have continued to enrich my life. During the pandemic, that same kayak served as a socially distant way to get my kids outside. Yes, we all fit on it! We spent countless hours looking for turtles and fishing from the kayak in the scenic waters near my house. So to the girlfriend who dumped me and moved on, thank you! You were the storm that has produced so many beautiful waves in my life I've lost count.

Brain Matters:
Blue Space and Forest Baths

Spending time in nature positively impacts our mood. Outdoor air contains negative ions, highest at the beach and in the mountains, and has been shown to reduce symptoms of depression.[3] In a systematic review of the literature on the impact of outdoor blue spaces (e.g., oceans, lakes, rivers) on human health and well-being, 12 of 35 studies showed improvements in mental health and well-being when participants were exposed to blue space[4]. Thirteen of the studies also showed increases in physical activity as an incidental benefit of being near water. This is consistent with the fact that people go to great lengths to live and vacation near the water and in the mountains.

In Japan, scientists have been studying how walking in the forest impacts stress hormones in our body. They refer to it as "forest bathing," which sounds like a cross between a hike and streaking through the park. More accurately, forest bathing isn't about taking a bath in the woods, it's more about walking with no destination in mind. It involves slowing down and being mindful of the sights, smells, and textures that green space can provide.

In 2011, researchers investigated the effects of taking two walks in the forest, both morning and afternoon, for two hours a piece.[5] That is a lot of walking for most people, but they needed a big dose to demonstrate the largest effect in size. Blood pressure, as well as blood and urine samples, were taken before and after each hike. Compared to walking down a city street, exposure to green space significantly reduced blood pressure. Previous studies had shown a reduction in the level of the stress hormones adrenaline and noradrenaline, but this study also found a depletion in dopamine levels. Taken together, it suggests that green space decreases sympathetic nervous system activity, which is responsible for the fight or flight response, helping to calm people.

The next time you're feeling down, rate your mood on a scale of 1 (lowest ever) to 10 (highest ever). Then make a point to spend at least 60 minutes either near blue space or forest bathing. If you can't get there at the time, then the next time you can, mentally revisit what happened to you when you were first feeling down. Bring back the memory of the difficult event and breathe deeply as you look out at the vastness of the ocean, lake, mountains, or forest. When your trip is over, rate your mood again. Has there been any improvement?

Homo sapiens evolved to survive outdoors. For tens of thousands of years, we spent more time outdoors than we do today. As a result, happiness and a sense of peace are more apt to be found in nature. It's not surprising mental health problems are higher in places with less access to nature and more pollution. According to a 2017 review study, the risk for some major mental illnesses (e.g., anxiety, psychotic, mood, or addictive disorders) is higher in cities than in rural areas.[6] In several Asian and Latin American countries, there were higher rates of anxiety disorders in urban versus rural areas. They also found a similar relationship for psychotic disorders like schizophrenia in large cities in Europe and China.

By 2019, half of the global population was living in a city. The pandemic of 2020 could shift the trend away from living in cities, and even if it doesn't, there are still activities we can do. It just requires more time and energy dedicated to seeking out green and blue space. I lived in New York City for almost a decade, and nearly every day, I biked or jogged to a nearby park. If you don't know the city, you might not realize that biking in Central Park can make you feel like you've left the city or how jogging along the Hudson River can inspire you with the skyline in the background. Of course, it's still New York City, so the sound of someone yelling is never far away. The point is, it's essential to make getting to green and blue space more of a priority when you live in a city. It's extra effort, but if the window of your apartment looks out to a brick wall, like mine did for many years, you need it!

— · — · — · — · — · — · — · — · — · — · — · — · — · — · — · — · — · — · — · —

Lessons from Surfing

My go-to blue space is the ocean, preferably with waves. Over the years, I've attempted to surf hundreds of times, from Maine to Florida and California to Costa Rica. I've been in water so warm I hardly noticed it was there and water so cold even my wetsuit was shivering. I've ridden mellow waves into the sunset, hoping it would never end, and I've flailed in ferocious pounding surf when I felt like my time was up. I'm not a good surfer, but as a sign on the pier in Cocoa Beach, Florida, reads, "The best surfer out there is the one having the most fun."

Learning how to surf combines the calming effect of the negative ions with the excitement of trying to catch waves. There are physical and mental skills to master, especially when it comes to managing anxiety. The first thing I learned is that **getting crushed** by waves is part of the sport. Just like in life, getting slammed to the ground happens and should be expected. The second is after the waves thrash you around a bit, the best thing to do is find a calm spot, **sit on your board**, breathe, and recover. Sitting and feeling your emotions is an important part of figuring out what went wrong and how you might make changes. The final step is to use the energy from all those failed attempts and **ride the wave** when the opportunity arises. If you can summon the emotion from all the times you got pounded, focus your attention like a laser beam, give it everything you've got, good things are bound to happen.

Step One: Getting Crushed

On a speaking trip to schools in Southern California, I had a free afternoon, so I decided to surf in Newport Beach. The weather was incredible, blue skies with a light onshore breeze. I paddled out and soon found myself in a set of the largest waves I'd ever seen. Okay, I've *seen* bigger waves on Instagram, but I've never been *in* bigger waves. At one point, I ended up in the break zone, a dangerous spot where a large wave could break your board or your nose. I've done that last part twice. Fortunately, I've got a bulbous Sicilian nose, so nobody really noticed.

What got me in trouble that day was getting knocked off my board by a wave and then pulled under. Being held against my will by nature is a lot like being drowned by my older brother, except without knowing Mom would totally ground him for it. The wave eventually let me up, and I managed to find the leash attached to my ankle to retrieve my board. From the time my head popped up, it felt like I had about two seconds before the next wave hammered me. I was determined not to vomit from anxiety, so I focused on getting back on the board and out of harm's way. As my head emerged, I saw the third wave cresting and bearing down on me. There was no time! I got hit and tumbled over and over. I didn't know which end was up. I reached for my leash, and it went completely taught. If it snapped, I was chum. I pulled the cord until I found the board and hugged it like my baby blanket, which I still own (don't judge).

When I resurfaced, I saw the largest swell coming right at me. At that moment, I'll admit, my mind kind of gave up on me. It was the opposite of movies like *The Perfect Storm* where the crew fights the wave until the bitter end. Nope. My brain was all, "Well, it's been a good run." I didn't even think about signaling to a lifeguard—I just assumed it was over.

My thoughts totally betrayed me, which is ridiculous when you consider I was attached to an eight-foot flotation device! In life, some people are prone to catastrophic, worst-case scenario types of thinking. Apparently, I'm one of them. It reminded me of meeting a student at one of the most selective private schools in the country. She had just earned a B on a biology test and exclaimed, "All hope is lost!" I remember thinking, "You go to one of the best schools in the world. Even the worst student here is going to be fine." Her perspective was like mine in the ocean that day. All I could see were huge waves bearing down, not my proximity to shore. All she could see was a grade that wasn't perfect, not the amazing education she was receiving.

Getting crushed is part of life. It can be quite scary because our lives rarely expose us to life-or-death decisions. In the weeks following the COVID-19 shutdown, every day brought more cancellations for my business. It was understandable. My clients couldn't hold events, so they needed to cancel. From my perspective, as my spring work disappeared, I feared running out of money and losing our house. I began watching the local news about New York City each night, something I hadn't done for years. As awful as it was to hear nightly updates of deaths from the virus, it gave me perspective on what mattered. I was okay. My family was okay. We had our health, which meant we could work on everything else.

Choosing to surf and being forced to deal with the economic collapse caused by a pandemic doesn't seem like fair comparisons. However, the primitive emotional parts of the brain don't differentiate existential threats well. Whether the threat is drowning in water or debt, you may feel scared, vulnerable, and insecure. It's the rare individual who can prevent the fight-or-flight alarm from going off.

When you're bombarded by the emotion of fear, it's important to do a reality check with yourself. If you're intact and still functioning, you can respond. You have the ability to restore balance to the situation. Once things are stable, your limbic system will eventually restore calm to your nerves. Remember, the opposite of fear is trust. Trust yourself that you can see it through, and trust others to help you when it matters most. Resilience begins with trust.

Brain Matters:
Catastrophizing

When you're in distress, the network of brain regions that processes emotions, called the limbic system, is activated. The brain structures involved in this system are the amygdala, the prefrontal cortex, the cingulate cortex, basal ganglia, and the hippocampus. The hippocampus plays a major role in memory, but it's also involved in processing emotions. This is important because when we're in distress, we're likely to be reminded of other times in our life when we were in distress. The current situation might be completely different, but the emotions could feel the same. This part of the body's strategy to stop what were doing and try something else, but avoidance might not be the best strategy. This could make us less likely to persist in the activity.

One of the ways our mind can work against us is by becoming irrational and overly negative. Our past trauma can influence our future reactions, and we find ourselves assuming the worst-case scenario will play out. Psychologists refer to this phenomenon as catastrophizing. It's a cognitive distortion that can lead to severe anxiety or depression in some individuals, but there are ways to counteract it.

It's important to remember that everyone catastrophizes from time to time. If you receive a text from someone you're in a relationship with that says, "We need to talk," you might justifiably start thinking the worst. However, it becomes a problem when you start to use it on a regular basis as a reason to avoid everyday activities, like getting on a plane or driving a car.

Psychologists often use a form of therapy called Cognitive Behavioral Therapy to bring awareness to the person experiencing the catastrophic thoughts. Many times, just hearing yourself express internal thoughts, the quiet part out loud can cause a person to catch the distortion and realize the problem. The next step is to intervene and counteract the irrational thoughts. For example, you might convince yourself that you'll fail an exam, never get a degree and be out of work. In this case, it might be helpful to remind yourself that many successful people have failed exams and that failing a test is not proof that you'll never find a job.

The human brain has an estimated fifty to seventy thousand thoughts per day. That makes me think, "Who counted?" Probably some poor undergraduate student who needed extra credit. Our thoughts are automatic and unfiltered, which means they could turn anxious and irrational anytime the emotional part of our brain takes over. However, we don't have to listen to the thoughts like they are chiseled in stone. You have a choice of whether to accept or reject the thoughts your brain produces.

If unchecked, catastrophic thinking can lead to cascading failures in our secondary response. In other words, we become less resilient. Referring back to my surfing story, it would be like becoming untethered to the board, crippled by fear of drowning, and forgetting how to swim. Charles Darwin, best known for his natural selection theory of evolution, once said, "It is not the strongest of the species that survives, nor the most intelligent, but the one most responsive to change." We don't want to allow our thoughts to ever cripple our response.

–·–

Step Two: Sitting on Your Board

From time to time, life knocks us down. When I was a kid, I heard adults say, "You got your head handed to you." That's a pretty violent thing to tell a child after they lost a kickball game. In surfing, sometimes you get knocked off your board, which is a visceral reminder that the ocean is more powerful than you. Regardless of what form it takes, when you've suffered a disappointment, it's an opportunity to pause and breathe.

Surfers often go out with a buddy or a group, so connecting with others after navigating rough waters is easy. In life, we sometimes feel disconnected, like we're the only one out there. In that case, it's beneficial to have positive social support in the form of friends, family, and maybe a therapist to lean on. When you finally get to the moment of truth, be as specific as you can about describing how you feel. Don't expect everyone to be good at responding to you. Many people in our lives cannot tolerate sitting with our negative emotions. They love us and don't like to see us in pain, or they are so overwhelmed by their own lives they have little capacity to help us.

When the pandemic shutdown hit my business, I recall two kinds of people in my life. Those who could sit with me in my grief and fear, and those who were very quick to dismiss my negative feelings. I'm sure the second group meant well, but I heard statements like, "You'll just do your thing on Zoom," or my favorite, "Have you thought of going remote?" Of course, I had thought of it; I could think of nothing else as I stared at my empty calendar. There wasn't a quick fix. However, I noticed those who let me vent helped me realize what next steps might work. I do recall one family member who was so uncomfortable with my bad news that she always seemed to want to get off the phone. She would say, "I've got to go." And I thought, "It's a quarantine. There's nowhere to go!"

Crisis reveals character. After you've been metaphorically crushed by life and you've survived, it's time to do the difficult work of processing and expressing your emotions. Identify the good listeners in your life and approach them for a long-form conversation. In the conversation, use words that are descriptive and nuanced. You may perceive yourself as sad, but there is likely a specific description of what is going on for you. This conversation will likely leave you feeling better, and you will be more likely to make healthier decisions later that day.

TRY THIS: **Use Emotionally Granular Words**

It sounds like an assignment for a first grader to "use your words," but it can be remarkably difficult to do when we're upset. Use "I" statements to describe how you feel. Take responsibility for what you think and what you need. Most importantly, be as specific as you can when labeling your emotions. Emotions are like spices on your shelf: it's hard to use them if they're not labeled.

When we develop a more finely tuned language to describe our feelings, psychologists refer to it as using "emotional granularity." This isn't so much about having a depth of vocabulary as it is about describing your experience with more precision. Instead of using words like "sad" for everything that gets you down, decide if you're really feeling "ashamed" or "inferior." It tells a more nuanced story. It might seem like all you've done is added a thesaurus into the mix, but it does convey a different degree of displeasure.

The positive impact of using more targeted language to represent your feelings include being less likely to explode out of frustration when you're upset. You might be less likely to turn to what psychologist Terry Reale called "misery stabilizers," alcohol and other drugs, gambling, or other risky behavior. Emotional granularity might allow you to defuse a situation as you engage the frontal lobe, thinking of better ways to describe what you're experiencing.

Brain Matters:
Simple Breathing

A technique that works well on adolescent inpatient psychiatric units is called the "5-minute rule." Giving someone a little time to calm down and breathe is helpful with more than just teenagers. It can be hard to give ourselves permission to do it, but there is a neurological rationale for the method.

Breathing is intimately related to mental functions. Taking a few minutes away to breathe also gives the emotional centers of the brain time to deactivate. This allows the more logical part of the brain in the frontal lobe to come back online and begin to take over the decision making. Research suggests there is a distinction between the "hot" and "cold" brains in teenagers, namely they are mediated by different neural circuitry.[78] This dynamic also exists in older brains to some extent, so taking time to breathe will help to switch from a "hot" to a "cold" cognitive state.

The next time life crushes you, and your "hot" brain starts to take over, give yourself a time out. During that period, close your eyes and take a deep breath. Notice your breathing. Feel the air truly filling your lungs. If it feels good—and it will—take a few more deep breaths. Notice that it seems to clear your mind, if only for a few seconds. After five minutes of sitting and thinking about breathing, your brain has had some time to deactivate the "hot" and switch over to the "cold" neural pathways.

An empirically backed breathing technique, created by Dr. Andrew Weil, is called the 4-7-8 Breathing Exercise. You can do the exercise in any position, but try it first by sitting with your back straight and putting the tip of your tongue behind the front of your teeth. Keep it there for the entire exercise. You'll be exhaling through your mouth around your tongue, so pucker your lips a little to help. Here are the steps:

- Exhale completely through your mouth, making a whoosh sound.
- Close your mouth and inhale quietly through your nose to a mental count of **four**.
- Hold your breath for a count of **seven**.
- Exhale completely through your mouth, making a whoosh sound to a count of **eight**.
- This is one breath. Now inhale again and repeat the cycle three more times for a total of four breaths.

When I started doing it, I noticed right away how calming the exhale felt. I got a little light-headed. Remember to inhale quietly through your nose and exhale audibly through your mouth. The tip of your tongue stays in position the whole time. Try this twice a day for a week during times when you're feeling activated and see if it helps.

—·—

Step Three: Riding the Wave

In the ocean, when a wave finally makes it to shore, the swell might have traveled hundreds of miles. The best waves arise from a hurricane or typhoon occurring far offshore, extreme wind near the eye of the storm, pushing the water out in all directions. If you're lucky and you time it right, you can capture the energy from that storm days later by riding the final few seconds of the wave.

Each wave represents an opportunity. If you're positioned correctly and paddle hard at the exact moment you should, your speed will eventually match the speed of the wave and you'll catch it. If you're not positioned correctly, the opportunity will gently pass you by, and you'll hardly even notice.

If you react at the right moment, you'll know it because your surfboard will suddenly feel stable on top of the unstable water. As you feel the force of the water pushing up on your board as your speed matches the wave, that's when you can pop up. It's a split-second move. If you land on your feet, placed shoulder width apart and perpendicular to the board, you just might be able to ride the cresting wave. It may take hundreds, if not thousands of attempts to get it right, but in a flash you go from lying down to standing on your feet, and you will feel the natural high of surfing. It's like hitting a home run, nailing a piano piece, or winning a bid for your dream house. It's skill and luck all at the same time.

In life, when we see someone performing at a high level, we don't see all the practice that went into it. We're not privy to all the other times they failed. We don't see the passion it took to master the moves. We don't get to see the pain that leads them to repeatedly return time and time until they get it right. We just see a beautiful performance and marvel at their achievement. In some ways, we're missing half the beauty of the accomplishment. It's the repeated failure that creates a context to truly appreciate the success.

People don't walk around with swords anymore, not unless they're leaving their parents' basement for Comic-Con. However, the process of hardening or tempering a sword is an age-old skill. From what I understand, it involves improving the characteristics of steel by heating it to a high temperature, but not to the boiling point, then cooling it. This process occurs over and over again: metal pounded with a hammer each time, making it more resilient. Life works the same way. We emerge better after the struggle: not despite the pounding, but because of it.

Life is incredibly disappointing sometimes, which means when things go our way, we should enjoy it. Joy is so fleeing that we need to embrace the moment when it arrives. When you've suffered the most, for a long period of time, the pleasure is heightened. Look at the iconic photos of soldiers returning from World War II and see the expression of happiness in their eyes.

We don't have to risk our lives at war to take pleasure in the everyday joys of living. It does require that we're mindful of the fact that life is incredibly disappointing, often without warning. It's precisely the fact that life lets us down so much that celebration is warranted when things go well. I remember on a trip to Key West, Florida, I had taken part in the nightly ritual of celebrating the sunset. It was beautiful to be surrounded by so much water, watching the colors change every few seconds as the sun disappeared over the horizon. Listening to the people cheer was also fun, but I realized I could be doing this more often. There are so many sunsets that go by unappreciated when they could be celebrated. Each day involves riding the wave. Some days it works out, and some days it doesn't; but you made it, and it's worthy of a smile.

Treehouse Novice

A year or so after we moved into our new home, my son asked me to build him a treehouse. Trying to appease him, I said, "Sure buddy, I'll build one for you." He quickly responded, "If you don't do it now, you're never going to do it." Taken aback, I considered saying, "How are you reading my thoughts?"

That night, I purchased an ebook called *The Complete Guide to Treehouses*. I read the book and quickly realized I was in way over my head. The book showed how involved the process was, and I convinced myself that I couldn't do it. The book had crushed me. My next move was to procrastinate and hope he would forget, which of course, he did not. My son, like most kids, has a radar for adults who aren't living up to their promises.

A few weeks later, I saw something rare on my calendar: a week off in early November. I thought if I could just get started, maybe I would catch a lucky break and wake up competent in building stuff. Nothing magical happened, but a kindhearted neighbor had built a treehouse the prior year. He was inspiring as he showed me his work and told me I could pull it off. Suddenly, momentum was building.

As the big week approached, I realized that most people in my life assume, given my travels for work, that I'm never home. I know this because they say things like, "Are you ever home?" It's not true, but despite telling them that, the thought persists.

I am home *a lot*. Not like quarantine level a lot. But I'm home a lot more than I'm away. I'm telling you this because once I realized that this treehouse would be a symbol of how involved a father I am, which I am, it motivated me. I wanted to give it a shot, if for nothing else, the next time someone stands in my house and asks, "Are you ever home," I could just point to the treehouse.

Day One of the Build

On the first day of the build, I went to Home Depot and purchased four nine-foot beams. Driving back home, I felt like I was back in my 20s with a kayak strapped to the roof of my car. These beams were so long, they went from the front console out the back hatch.

I also naively thought, "It won't take long for me to screw these beams into the trees. I'll be done by lunch." It took me all day. First, I drilled holes into the beams, then the trees, and I had to use all of my body weight to crank the nine-inch lag screws through the branches. When I was finished, I sat on a nearby stump, exhausted. I stared at the beams on the trees and thought, "This is a disaster. I'll never finish at this rate." My brain started working against me. "This is in my yard! People will see it! I'm a failure on the first day." It was like learning to surf and getting crushed all over again.

I felt completely overwhelmed. There was no way I could build a treehouse, let alone have children walk around on top of it. Now I understand why humans haven't lived in trees for a few million years. I was ready to quit and walk away. The only thing that saved me was that I did technically finish the first step.

In my moment of tremendous self-doubt, I took a deep breath. Then another one. I sat on a stump, closed my eyes, and focused on my breathing until my nervous system calmed down. I remember thinking it would be cool if one day I could meditate in the treehouse. I noticed that my brain felt rested a bit, and my mood was up. At that moment, I was visited by some very strong emotions. I even teared up. It might have been allergies. No, I cried.

My father would never have done this for me. I love my dad, but despite getting a degree in engineering, he was not a handy guy. Even if he was a handy guy, he was too busy working when I was a kid to do this kind of project. Even if he had the time, he never would have attempted a treehouse. Even if we had had a tree in our yard that could work, which we didn't, he never would have even bought a book about building a treehouse. What I'm trying to say, without hurting my father's feelings, is that he wasn't as involved in my childhood as I would have liked.

It would have been nice to have him take more time in my day-to-day life, but life is disappointing that way sometimes. My dad probably would have never been as successful at work if he had more time, and his work paid our bills and gave us a comfortable life. But as a result of my experience, when I became a dad, I vowed to be an involved father with my kids.

I had always thought of myself as involved, but that question of, "Are you ever home?" was weighing on me. On that day, sitting on that stump, I realized this was my shot to end those questions, in my mind at least. Besides, I couldn't stop now, not after screwing those beams!

Getting in touch with my emotions helped me focus on why I was building the treehouse. The energy that those emotions created pushed me to keep going even when times got tough. I never looked back. I hit a few snags along the way but never gave up.

The pairing of the emotions with the activity created inspired work. The entire project took me six weeks working off and on around my schedule. My son had sketched what he wanted the treehouse to look like, and it was remarkably close to the finished product. He dreamed up two platforms with a footbridge connecting them and a roof to hide underneath. He also wanted a trap door, but that wasn't going to happen. I could just see his little sister falling through on her head.

The first day of construction.

Three weeks into the project.

Now it's done!

Just kidding! Here's the finished treehouse.

My son Roy enjoying his creation, before begging me to go inside
and play video games.

My dad, mom, and daughter Sidney with me up in the treehouse.

I was overwhelmed by the reactions of everyone in my life to the treehouse. They were so positive, almost like they knew how much feeling went into it. I rode the wave of childhood issues to create something that my kids and their friends love. I didn't expect building the treehouse to bring up strong emotions, but I suspect it was a necessary step in the process. It's possible that I could have stopped on day one without the benefit of those childhood experiences.

If I had a magic wand that could be used to revise my childhood, giving me a father who was more interested in spending time with me, I would have used it. However, trying to reimagine the past is not a productive mental exercise. Besides, my emotions about my childhood party inspired me to build the treehouse. This is true of so many disappointments in life, when I'm left with one thought, "What does it inspire?"

Disappointment Is Inspiring

I learn something each day that makes me feel a little sad. It could be about a friend in pain, the loss of a family member, failure of government, or finding out my kid broke that heirloom I loved. As I write this paragraph, I just found out I need over a thousand dollars of plumbing work on my house; it needs to be done tomorrow, which is also my birthday. Happy birthday to me! As I experience these sensations, I take a deep breath. Then I take another and another. I practice the research-based techniques that have reliably helped patients in hospitals for years. While I do this, I remind myself that life is disappointing. I also ask excitedly, "What is this disappointment going to inspire?" Sometimes I don't have an answer. I may need to wait before I can catch the wave off those feelings.

Life is disappointing for everyone. You know how it ends, right? It's hard to remember that when you're the one who is disappointed. We can't escape the down moments. Okay, maybe Tom Brady can escape them. The guy is like the *Highlander*. "There can be only one!" If you're under a certain age, you have no idea what I'm talking about but should Google it. Great movie.

I find that reminding myself of this relationship between disappointment and inspiration is helpful because it reminds me that pain is a necessary part of the formula. From a presentation I gave in Upstate New York, here are a few examples of how disappointment fueled inspiration. I love reading these because they remind me that I'm not the only one.

"Unplanned pregnancy while in college. Planned on placing the child for adoption, but once I heard her cry, I could not do it. Best choice I ever made—to bring her home and raise her. She's now 25 years old, graduated from college, and living a happy life."

"After struggling with chronic exhaustion for years, I was diagnosed with a sleeping disorder. The medications didn't help, and [the] side effects were horrible, so I used that as motivation to push forward [without them]. I've since gotten into the best shape of my life, teaching fitness classes and eating right. Now I help others who are struggling and empower them to live a healthy, fulfilling life."

"My dad decided not to be a parent. My mom was an amazing single mom. Now I am following my calling of being a foster parent, and I know I can do it, even though I'm single."

RECAP

The most beautiful waves come from the biggest storms, but your psychological immune system is prepared for the big stuff. It's the everyday smaller agitations that fly below the radar and wear you down. Whether you're a teen in juvenile detention, a rock star, or a dad trying to build a treehouse, you have the ability to harness your emotions and create inspired work. There are so many stories of individuals who used pain, loss, and failure to their advantage—this entire book could be filled with them.

These chapters intend to go further, not only telling stories but analyzing the valuable life lessons we can take from them. You don't have to be gifted and talented or famous to benefit from the storms of life. However, you do need to be willing to try different coping skills and see which works best for you. You should explore the benefits of blue space, green space, self-talk against catastrophizing, and simple breathing techniques. Whether you use them all or just one, this book will help you fill your tool with ideas that are backed by research.

Life is profoundly disappointing at times. It can feel like it has crushed your soul. However, at some point, after you've processed your emotions in granular detail, you're going to be ready to ride the next wave. If you've done the work, you'll be in the right place, mentally and physically, to capitalize on it. As you're riding that beautiful wave, you'll almost want to thank the storm for putting you on the journey. So the next time you get crushed, hopefully at some point you'll ask, "So, what will this inspire?"

CHAPTER 2

Find the Suffering You're
Okay with in Life

"My doctor says if I don't drink, don't smoke, and take excellent care of
myself, one day I'll get very sick and die."
~ Rodney Dangerfield

My favorite quote by comedian Jerry Seinfeld isn't even funny, "Find the torture you're comfortable with and you'll do well. You master that, you've mastered life." He said it in an interview while talking about his legendary work ethic. I often mangle Seinfeld quotes, so I've paraphrased it to, "Find the suffering you're okay with in life." To me, it means there's no career path in this world that doesn't involve struggle, but if you find the hard work you can tolerate, you'll be fine. I think it's a great motto that can apply to many aspects of life, especially school and work.

In college, I found the academic suffering I was okay with during my first year. I was never a straight-A student, more of a "Bs get degrees" kind of guy. I went to class and studied, but I didn't know what it meant to study hard. My major was undeclared, but I really wanted to study biology, so I was dipping my toe in the subject with a course known as "Baby Bio." I'm guessing "Bio for Dummies" wasn't allowed. It was time for the first exam, and I recall studying by passively reading and hoping the information would magically stick in my brain. When the grades came out, I got a 38. Out of 100! I was turning the page like, "Maybe it's an 83!" Oh, no.

The guy next to me got a 68. He stood up immediately and swore out loud, "F this, I'm dropping this class!" Meanwhile, I'm staring at my incredibly low and inadequate grade, wondering how Baby Bio was kicking my ass. That's when I decided to do what any entitled kid would do: I met with the professor and whined. In high school, I looked down on students who did that, but with a 38, I had few options left. I guess it worked. I got some points but walked out with a score somewhere in the higher end of failing.

In the aftermath, I did some real soul searching. Life had crushed me, and I was taking a few minutes to metaphorically sit on my surfboard and breathe a little. I called my mom for empathy but got the "This is your rude awakening" speech. She had been saying it would happen for years, and this was her big moment. She wasn't wrong. I had blown it and felt terrible about myself. I thought I knew how to study, but clearly, I had a lot to learn.

What did that moment inspire? I decided that I really loved biology and wasn't going to quit because of one grade. I wasn't going to ignore a passion of mine just because I had no chance of getting a perfect grade. The simple concept of accepting imperfection was a huge moment of insight. I could work tremendously hard and strive for perfection, but I knew deep down that wasn't going to happen. When I inevitably came up short at the end of the semester, hopefully with at least a "B," I was okay with it because I was studying what I enjoyed.

The suffering for me was completely reworking my approach to studying. I studied for Baby Bio every day for the rest of the semester. I studied on Saturday nights and twice on Sunday. I studied harder and smarter than I ever had before. When it was all over, I ended up with a B minus. To that guy who dropped the class and had an F-bomb, that grade was garbage. To me, it was a badge of honor that I didn't give up. I failed a test, and the world didn't come to an end. It's amazing how freeing it was to allow intellectual curiosity to lead me rather than perfection for perfection's sake. I graduated with a Bachelor of Science in biology and a Master of Science in biology, but it was inspired by failure.

Brain Matters:
Grades, Success, and Perfectionism

Research suggests that grades do not predict career achievement.[1] A study examining a wide range of careers, including scientists, physicians, and business managers, found that decent grades (e.g., Bs) were enough to get jobs and do well. In fact, there wasn't much of a relationship between grades in school and accomplishment on the job. That doesn't mean terrible grades predicted achievement in the workplace but neither did amazing grades; the conclusion being that getting at least decent grades plus possessing skills beyond the report card matters most.

A 2014 survey of more than 10,000 middle and high school students from 33 schools found that a large majority of youth, across a wide spectrum of races, cultures, and classes, appear to value achievement and happiness over concern for others.[2] When youth were asked to rank what was most important, achieving at a high level, happiness, or caring for others, more than 80 percent of youth picked high achievement or happiness as their top choice, while the rest chose caring for others.

Happiness and achievement are important values, but when youth and their peers do not prioritize caring and fairness, they are at greater risk of harmful behavior. Over 50 percent of high school students admit cheating on a test, 75 percent copy someone else's homework. Interestingly, 80 percent of the students feel their parents are more concerned about achievement and happiness than caring for others, agreeing with statements like "My parents are prouder if I get good grades in my classes than if I'm a caring community member in class and school."

Adolescents with high levels of perfectionism set excessively high standards for performance and can be their harshest critics. A study of high school students found that striving for perfection was actually a positive predictor of behavior, as it was associated with higher levels of motivation, better grades, and improved well-being.[3] However, it was the reaction to imperfection that brought about the fear of failure and depressive symptoms. In addition, if there was perceived parental pressure, imperfection was related to complaints of physical symptoms, known as somatic complaints. Interestingly, figuring out the mental game of striving for perfection, but having compassion when the inevitable disappointment of imperfection arrives, is the key.

Try This: Certificate of Failure

At Smith College in Massachusetts, there's an initiative called "Failing Well," aimed at destigmatizing failure. The belief is if you're more comfortable with the idea of setbacks in the classroom, then coping with everyday problems won't seem so tough. I love the idea, so on the next page, you will find your certificate of failure. You have my permission to copy it. Feel free to get a 38 on a test (hopefully just one) or get dumped by the person you thought was "the one" or completely mess up at work and get let go. It's okay. Life is disappointing. Someone should write a book about that.

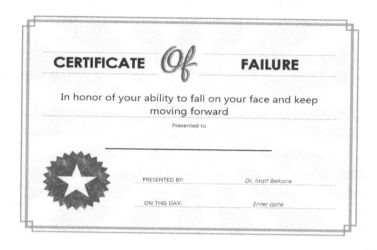

Stepping In It

"There are no shortcuts to any place worth going."

~ My daughter's fortune cookie

In my junior year of college, long after my experience in Baby Bio, I was a fully declared biology major looking for interesting courses to take. That's when I read about a course in the psychology department called physiological psychology. It sounded like an oxymoron, like fresh cafeteria food. I thought psychology was talking about your feelings, the opposite of talking about physiology. It turns out the class was about the neurochemistry of behavior. I was hooked. It was next level interesting for me.

When the semester was over, I doubled my major to add psychology because I love Saturday nights in the library. I don't remember the exact moment I decided to apply for a PhD, but I do recall the ritual of reading the book about graduate school programs over and over like it was the Dead Sea Scrolls. The next step was building up the courage to speak with the dreaded graduate school advisor. Her job was to review my transcripts to give a critical assessment of how I stacked up. I knew that didn't sound good. I preferred a Pollyannaish reading of my grades. "Oh, look what we have here! It's a B minus in Baby Bio. Awww, that's so good!"

I really hoped she would see my hard work with the double major, my passion for the subject matter, and look past my average grades. When I walked in, she was sitting on an exercise ball chair, which she told me was good for her back. I felt like I was being grilled by a Pilates instructor. She asked to see my transcript, and I handed it to her, which she reviewed for about a minute. I studied her face to see if I could judge by the slightest movement of her eyebrow what direction my future would take. As she put the papers down, she said firmly, "You should NOT apply to graduate school. You'll never get in." That was it. She handed it back to me like I was Ralphie in *A Christmas Story* asking for a Red Ryder BB gun. "You'll shoot your eye out kid!" Boot in the face.

I was devastated as I left her office. I moped around in a haze for a while and noticed that my mind kept trying to replay the story, but script a better ending. It was pathetic. It reminded me of that hilarious *Saturday Night Live* sketch where Chris Farley auditions to be a Chippendale's dancer. The judges reject him because he's up against Patrick Swayze and not exactly Chippendale's material, but after he's rejected, he keeps dancing a little more to see if he can sway their vote. At least I never returned to her office to see if I could dance a little more.

A few weeks passed, but for some reason, I didn't give up on the dream. I realized that it might take me a bit longer, but I was not going to give up on the PhD. Just like Baby Bio. I figured I needed better grades, so I applied for a master's degree in biology at my current school, and much to my surprise, I got in. The bad news was I had to pay for it myself. My parents had picked up the tab for my undergraduate degree, for which I'm eternally grateful, but any additional school would be on me. When I saw the cost of one semester, it almost stopped me in my tracks. It was a risky proposition. I could easily be strapped with debt and never get into a PhD program.

What happened next can only be described as having a stroke of luck. As my cousin likes to say, "You stepped in it!" It's an odd phrase because stepped in poop usually doesn't mean anything good. A student who I did not know was offered one of the coveted graduate school scholarships but decided not to attend. He didn't even tell anyone he wasn't coming. He just didn't show up. On the first day of classes, the head of the program came up to me and gave the scholarship to me! I felt like one of those walk-ons at a big-time football program who earns a scholarship and gets a bucket of Gatorade dumped on his head.

Master's Degree, This First Time

The next two years were bittersweet. Staying on campus immediately after graduating felt like being punished. I sometimes saw old professors, and they asked, "You're still here?" I did enjoy it, though. I lived in my own apartment and got really into researching biology and neuroscience, fell in love with cooking, dated, and was able to spend more time with the student group on campus that I had created as a sophomore. Life was good.

The hardest part of the program came during the final semester of the second year. My thesis research wasn't going as planned, meaning the experiment I designed wasn't yielding the results that I had anticipated. As a result, I had to stay on campus and work through holidays and weekends while my mind kept daydreaming about traveling across the county. I thought about California so much, like the Golden State was trolling me. I guess what I'm saying is I was suffering, but it was suffering that I was okay with because I knew I was investing in myself.

Brain Matters:
What Predicts Resilience?

In 1989, the results from a longitudinal study on a group of nearly 700 children found that not all children react to stress the same way.[4] Two-thirds of the children came from happy and stable backgrounds, while the remaining kids were considered "at-risk." The study determined that two-thirds of at-risk children developed "serious learning or behavioral programs by the age of ten," but the remaining children progressed to become competent, confident, and caring adults.

The children were followed consistently for over 30 years, and the study found that several elements predicted resilience in the most "at-risk" group. For some, having the good fortune of having a supportive teacher, parent, or other mentor played a significant role. However, for others, it was how the children responded to their environment. Early on, resilient kids would show the ability to be more independent and exhibit pro-social behaviors. They also saw themselves as the one responsible for their own fate. They didn't leave it in the hands of someone else. These successful at-risk youth were not described as "gifted," but rather able to use whatever skills they had to effectively navigate their environment.

The takeaway from this study is that resilience begins from within. Even in individuals who are fighting against external obstacles, such as poverty or institutional racism, adopting an internal locus of control is the best. This concept will come up later in the book, but it's the perception that your life is primarily the result of your actions. It may or not be the reality, but you are likely to be more resilient if you perceive yourself that way.

— · — · — · — · — · — · — · — · — · — · — · — · — · — · — · — · — · —

Unusually Persistent

As I was working on my master's thesis, which was a long research project and paper on Sertoli cells in the testicles of rats, I was pondering my next move. I was hoping to finish the program, get my degree, and start a PhD program in clinical neuropsychology the following fall. I had dedicated four years of my life to undergraduate studies and now two more years, so I felt like I couldn't afford to waste more time.

By the way, I did not tell the unsupportive graduate school advisor that I was applying to seven PhD programs. Would you? I applied to seven schools, and a few agonizing months later, I received five rejections, a deferred admission, and one acceptance. One, and it felt amazing! It was like being vindicated. The next day, I returned to the graduate school advisor's office to share my news. I wasn't there to brag (maybe a little) but I definitely wanted to see her reaction. When

I told her about the acceptance, she just sat back in her desk chair, with this half-smiling, half-disapproving look on her face, and she said, "Wow, you're unusually persistent."

Unusually persistent? I guess that's a compliment if you say it with a positive tone of voice. However, she said it in a, "Are you kidding me?" tone. I guess I made the mistake of assuming that an advisor, someone who is supposed to be helpful, would be supportive of me. Instead I got someone who sounded like she was rooting against me. It's an example of why life is disappointing sometimes. It's also why I feel so grateful when things work.

Hahnemann Oh

After getting accepted to that PhD program, it might surprise you to learn that I decided not to go. The cost would have topped two hundred thousand dollars in student loans, and besides, their clinical neuropsychology program was small. It was a tough decision, given how long I had waited, but I ultimately decided to wait another year and reapply. I was hoping to get in somewhere better and more afford-able, but it was a risk. My life would be in limbo for another year.

I went back to reading that book on graduate programs in clinical psychology and trained my sights on a school in Philadelphia called Hahnemann University. It's pronounced "Ha-na-man," not "Hominem," as my friend Andrew used to say. The elites from the University of Pennsylvania used to call it "Hahnemann Oh." They would ask, "Matt, where are you doing your graduate studies?" I would say, "Hahnemann," and they would say, "Oh." That's an old joke. Not sure where it came from, but it still makes me laugh.

A Second Master's Program

I just knew the PhD program at Hahnemann Oh was perfect for me. They had a medical school and a University hospital where students trained. In addition, there were grants and teaching assist-antships available to help pay for it. I was so thirsty, as the kids say, that I called the school, spoke to a professor, and asked for advice on getting in. He told me to enroll in their master's program in clinical psychology that fall. My heart sank. I thought, "I can't do that again! This isn't Monopoly where four houses equals a hotel, and a second master's degree doesn't give me a doctorate."

After the initial shock wore off, I thought about my ultimate goal and decided to pursue it. Again. A second time. Twice. Double the fun. I am certain everyone in my life thought I was crazy. My buddy Doug asked, "Are you just going to be a student until you retire?" What was my option? A gap year back then meant actually working at the Gap.

I submitted an application to the master's program and a month later was confused to receive an acceptance letter—for the PhD program! I was exasperated. "Did they reconsider?" I had a fantasy that they saw my application and thought, "We overlooked his brilliance. This kid belongs in the doctoral track!" No, it was a clerical mistake. They sent me the wrong acceptance letter. My letter was supposed to be for the master's program. I thought psychologists were supposed to prevent trauma, not create it!

The disappointment over receiving the wrong letter inspired me to prove myself at my new school. On the first day, I was introduced to the head of the department at a group meeting with all the students. She asked me, "Are you a master's student?" I responded, "Not for long!" Yuck. My ambition was so transparent. That year, I walked around every day thinking about how to position myself to get into the PhD program. Looking back, it's the opposite of living in the moment. I was caught up in the future every day, and I was rarely happy. True joy comes from being in the moment, and when your mind is stuck elsewhere, you're suffering. Despite everything, it was still suffering that I was okay with and that would be rewarded someday.

Brain Matters:
Distraction and Unhappiness

In the early days of the smartphone, researchers used a data collection technique called experience sampling to gather information on thoughts and moods during everyday activities. At random times throughout the day, their iPhone would make a sound and up would pop a brief questionnaire about their activity and mood. They found that 47 percent of the time, participants thought about something other than what they were doing and that these distractions were making them unhappy.[5] Interestingly, the mind wandering occurred during presumably enjoyable activities, such as watching television or having a conversation. It didn't seem to matter what the person was distracted by, and even pleasant thoughts made people less happy.

The opposite of being distracted is being "present in the moment" or mindful. Research suggests that individuals differ in their tendency to get distracted in everyday life, but those with higher levels of mindfulness tend to have less distress and greater well-being.[6] To build up your ability to be present in the moment, practicing mindfulness meditation regularly has been shown to significantly lower internal distractions such as rumination, thought suppression (e.g., when you consciously try to stop thinking about a particular thought), and fear of emotion.[7]

—·—

Hahnemann No!

My first year at Hahnemann turned out to be more tumultuous for the school than for me. The Allegheny Health conglomerate, which ran Hahnemann University and Hahnemann Hospital, filed for bankruptcy.[8] It's a complicated story, but the CEO, whose name I refuse to learn, stole medical research money and used it to buy himself a jet plane and other toys. This is illegal, and fortunately, he went to jail. As a result, Hahnemann's medical and graduate schools were in jeopardy of closing; going belly up, which is a lot like folding. That's right, the school I had purposely gone out of my way to attend, the place I delayed my life for, was about to no longer exist!

You're Done When You're Finished

At the risk of boring you with all the trials and tribulations of my nerd journey, I wanted to show the uncertainty involved in pursuing a graduate degree and how the experience can be an emotional roller coaster. It was definitely suffering that I was okay with because I love learning, and the people I met were (mostly) good to me. When I got overwhelmed and burned out, I remembered a quote from a yoga instructor I once had in class: "You're not done when you're tired, you're done when you're finished."

My personal struggle in those final years of school was managing my anxiety in the face of uncertainty. The thoughts that kept floating to the surface of my mind were, "Would Hahnemann fold? Would I ever get into a PhD program again? If I failed, could I move home and become a *mammone* (Italian man who lives with his mother)?"

I had a friend who was in medical school at the time, and when I told him what I was going through at Hahnemann, he urged, "Get out immediately! Transfer!" He was so dismissive. He said it without any regard for what I had been through to get there. It reminded me of that kid in Baby Bio who dropped out the day he got a bad grade. I didn't listen to him either. I decided to stay at Hahnemann until the bitter end if necessary, and re-applied to PhD programs. My first two applications went out to Hahnemann and the crosstown school Drexel University.

"Every success story involves some luck," my very successful and admittedly lucky businessman Uncle Bob once told me. I had already been lucky to be born into a financially stable, hardworking family in New Jersey. I was fortunate to go to a university with a good reputation. Earning that scholarship for my first masters didn't hurt either. My next lucky break came from Drexel University, who decided to save Hahnemann University and buy their medical and graduate schools. Drexel's bold President, the late Constantine Papadakis and his team of lawyers, who had to spell the name Hahnemann correctly on all the legal documents, purchased the school for a Philly cheesesteak. I'm not sure about that last part.

What happened to me? My application to Drexel's PhD program was rejected. However, my application to Hahnemann's program was accepted! Weird, because a month later, Hahnemann became Drexel, so I may be the only student to ever start at a school after being rejected by *that* school.

I finally did it! I got in. I had reached my goal. It took a tremendous amount of work and some luck. I needed at least average intelligence along with some unusual persistence. I suffered from uncertainty and rejection, but I was okay with it. Of course, once I got in, everything from there on out was super easy. Yeah right.

PhD Program – seven years of my life

It would take seven years for me to get a PhD. Many people describe the process like running a marathon. To me, it felt more like running a marathon in a wet sock. At first, you think you can handle it, but by the end, it's all you can think about. Call it unusual persist-ence, grit, or resilience, I just felt like once I got my foot in the door I wasn't going to be denied.

To recap, I went through twelve years of grade school, four years of college, two years of a master's program, and seven years to get the PhD. I spent more years in school after high school than I did before, which sounds super depressing. Each one of those PhD years had ups and downs, with moments when I wanted to give up.

One low point involved me falling asleep on the floor of our apart-ment while studying, and my wife walked in and found me lying on the floor. She actually checked to see if I was alive. Any time the song *You Found Me* by The Fray comes on, I love to remind her of that moment.

- -

Brain Matters:
Grit and the Brain

Over the past decade, the personality trait "grit" has emerged as a major player in the study of achievement. It is further defined as passion and persistence for goals over months or years. It is considered different from conscientiousness and self-control because it includes overcoming obstacles as a key element.

Several studies have demonstrated that grit is predictive of academic achieve-ment, work engagement, and even sticking to an exercise regimen.[9,10,11] A 2017 study found that people with high levels of grit and academic performance have higher resting-state activity in their brain.[12] The use of resting state imaging is fairly new, emerging over the past fifteen years or so, to measure brain interactions that occur while the brain is quiet. The study included 234 students, mean age of 18.6 years, who were enrolled in a long-term study to measure health in Chengdu, China. Each participant answered an eight-item survey on grit, called the Short Grit Scale (Grit-S). In addition, their scores on the China's National College Entrance Examination (NCEE) were used to assess academic performance.

The Grit-S and NCEE were used to assess individual differences in grit among the healthy adolescent students. Researchers compared the self-reported grit scores and academic performance with the brain response at rest. They found that activity in the right frontal lobe, an area called the dorsolateral prefrontal cortex, was associated with higher Grit-S scores and stronger academic performance. This was the first neural link between grit and academic performance.

In the past, the dorsolateral prefrontal cortex has been shown to be associated with self-regulation, planning, goal setting, and critically reflecting on past failures. It is now also correlated with grit. An important next question is, can we improve grit through training activities targeting the dorsolateral prefrontal cortex? Will academic performance improve if that brain region is stimulated? Activities, such as meditation, have been shown to stimulate frontal lobe connections, improving decision making.[13] More on that later in the book.

--- --- --- --- --- --- --- --- --- --- --- --- ---

Reject the Suffering You're Not Okay With

I was willing to go through anything to get my PhD, except when I wasn't. There were definitely things I wasn't willing to compromise on. When is it okay not to be okay with suffering? There should still be boundaries, even in pursuit of your dreams. I always believed that my lifestyle needed to be sustainable. If I was pulling all-nighters once or twice a week and eating garbage food, I wasn't going to last long. I wasn't a rock star who could die young, but still look cool on an *E! True Hollywood Story*. "He did therapy by day and chased his demons at night. He left us too soon, but we'll always have his therapy notes."

Reject Skipping Meals

"The Chinese don't trust the way we work. They look at the way we work, like we look at the way the Europeans work. We look at Europeans like, "You take the whole month of August off for vacation? You close your shops from two to seven for lunch? We eat lunch at our desk!" China looks at us like, "Lunch? Whoa, Mr. Lunch!"
- Colin Quinn

A recent *New York Times* article about the eating habits of Silicon Valley entrepreneurs highlighted a common practice of skipping meals to be more efficient. More specifically, they reported on software engineers who make protein shakes consisting of water, macadamia nut oil, and a bag of protein powder called Schmoylent. I don't know about you, but my mouth is watering already! A Schmoylent sounds more like a guy in charge of a Bris than a delicious drink.

The concept behind these drinks is simple. Instead of physically getting up from your desk and moving your body, which will improve your mood, you prepare the protein shake the night before and gulp it at your desk. Of course, you could prepare a nice lunch for yourself and eat that at your desk, too, but there's nothing more efficient than just gulping it down. That way, the only breaks you'll need are for the bathroom and to cry.

I assume the people who do love drinking Schmoylent are okay with that type of suffering. I had a roommate in college who was an engineering major with a very utilitarian view of eating. "Food is just fuel," he said. He usually said it in a defensive way because I was making him defend himself over why his food choices were so boring. One morning, he had an exam and had to eat fast. When I got up, I noticed his plate was out and there was a half-eaten English muffin with green mold growing on it. Yikes! It doesn't take a biology major to understand that consuming mold isn't the best "fuel" for your body.

In graduate school, I always had the reputation of bringing the best lunches. I often prepared a sandwich of roasted turkey, cranberries, and goat cheese on sourdough. Whoa, Mr. Lunch! It was no Schmoylent, but I liked it. Good food kept me going, so it was a worthwhile investment of the little money I had. Food was like a good coach after a bad game, patting me on the back and saying, "It's okay. You'll get 'em tomorrow."

Reject Burning Yourself Out

A high achieving local school district near my home conducted a survey of mental health in their middle and high school students. The kids reported being stressed out and hating school, so the superintendent responded by reducing the homework load and focusing more on engagement rather than grades. The surprising part was that many parents pushed back. They felt the initiative was watering down their kids' education and holding them back.[14] There was a cultural component to the story, as many of the parents pushing back were recent immigrants to the United States. It highlighted how work ethic and achievement can mean different things to different people.

In the achievement arms race, at some point, you've got to ask, "At what cost?" If you burn out before graduation or quit your job after a few years, what's the point? It's great if you can get into an Ivy League college, but that's not going to matter if you're so stressed out you can't make it through. The hallmark of "Bs get degrees" is about being engaged in the work. Remember, you've got to be okay with the suffering.

In high school, my way to prevent burnout was to get in bed by 10 pm. My mom worked at the high school, which meant I had to drive with her to school at employee hours, so I was never late. She refused to miss a day, too. In elementary school, I remember being sick a few times, but my mom took me to school anyway. She knew I was going straight to the nurse, but at least she could get credit for showing up to work and not lose a day off. If that happened during the pandemic, you might be looking at prison time. It definitely taught me to show up every day and get to sleep early.

In college, my goal was to never pull an all-nighter. I did once, and I felt miserable. Plus, handing in a paper with drool on it is not a good look. I went to bed at a "decent hour" for college, like midnight or so, and I never got sick during those years. In graduate school, I prevented burnout by protecting some time on evenings and weekends just to chill. I could've worked day and night, seven days a week, but limits are important. I always found a little time to watch *Seinfeld* or talk to a friend on the phone. I just wanted something mindless to relax my neurons from all the thinking.

Reject Thoughts to Self-Harm

Suicide is one of the leading causes of death in the United States; nearly fifty thousand people took their lives in 2019. It is also one the most avoidable causes of death. Talking about it helps. If your life has become unmanageable and you're thinking of ending it all, please seek help. You can call the toll-free National Suicide Prevention Lifeline at 1-800-273-TALK (8255), available 24 hours a day, 7 days a week. The service is available to anyone, and all calls are confidential.

Rejecting People Who Mistreat You

There is a vulnerability to someone wanting to achieve great things. They're willing to do what others won't in order to reach a goal. The Me Too movement exposed how powerful men exploited women for decades, mostly in entertainment and business, who were just looking to advance their careers. Through no fault of their own, they became victims and were pressured not to tell anyone. It's infuriating to abuse power in all forms, especially when someone gets hurt in the process.

When I moved to New York City in 2003 and started doing comedy in the clubs, I heard numerous stories of harassment toward comedians. The allegations against Louis C.K. were known in the comedy community, but until the Me Too movement, it was just a story someone would share. It reminded me of a booker at a club in Manhattan who thought it was hilarious to ask comedians to expose themselves in the basement for stage time. One friend of mine did it. He wasn't a seasoned veteran comedian. He was a young performer trying desperately to break into the business. Today it would have been a legal case, but back then, it was just another crazy story being told.

There were plenty of moments in my career in which I had to deal with people who treated me poorly, and I just had to bite my lip. That is a skill set that is different than targeted harassment or abuse. A supervisor or client who has the authority to fire you holds a lot of power over your life. However, when it crosses the line into getting you to do things that are unethical or illegal, it's got to stop.

Reject Family Who Mistreat You

We can't choose our family. We can choose who we spend time with in our family. If your dad says insensitive things that hurt your feelings and you still want to keep the guy in your life, you still have options. You can choose not to be as open and vulnerable around him knowing that he will likely say something hurtful. He didn't earn that level of intimacy. There are people in my family who I treat like salt in cooking. A little bit of them is okay, but too much will leave a bad taste in your mouth.

If your mother says things that make microaggressions feel like macroaggressions, fear not, you have a choice. You still love her, but if it's hard to be around her for long, you have a choice. You can't control what she says, but you can control your reaction. You don't have to blow up and get into an argument every time she irritates you. It sends a stronger message when you simply stay quiet and change the topic. You could also go a step further and assert yourself by saying, "If you continue to say hurtful things, I'm going to leave, and we can talk later." Removing your attention when someone is behaving poorly is like depriving a fire of oxygen. Eventually it burns out.

If your sibling is stressing you out and you can hardly take it, the next time they text you, text back, "New phone, who dis?" I'm kidding. Assuming you want to keep your sibling around to help with your aging parents or at least for the birthday present each year, then choose one or both of the options suggested for your parents. If neither seems to work, it's okay to take a break sometimes. Missing an annual family vacation or even a holiday and telling them why will send a powerful message. In that time off, putting yourself in the presence of people who care more about you and your feelings is therapeutic.

The point is, I'm okay with the normal wear and tear of interacting with family. However, when it rises to the level of conflict regularly and the emotions are distracting you from your day-to-day life, something has to change. Too often we can assume that just because "it's always been that way," nothing can change. That's not true. Mistreatment from people who are supposed to love and support you is suffering I'm not okay with.

Buddhism and Suffering

This entire chapter is essentially about suffering, when to embrace it, and when to avoid it. Some of the best writing on suffering can be found in the teachings of Buddhism. A central tenet of the non-theistic (without a creator) religion is that desire for material things is at the root of all suffering. I've been there. I remember trying to buy a home in 2014. When it started, I didn't know the difference between a colonial house and a colonial soldier. Six months in, and I was feeling sad at the idea we might not end up on a certain block. Buying a home is the most material thing people do in their life, and it was filled with suffering. By the way, everything worked out great.

In the Buddhist teaching I've read, it seems any time you have a desire, like achieving a goal, it will come with some suffering. It might bring you a lot of agonizing, but if you're okay suffering that way, then you'll be fine. If it's a kind of suffering you're okay with, but you want to tolerate it better, you might wish to change how you think about it. Buddhists would probably recommend daily meditation so you can stop desiring it, but that's a discussion for a different book.

Brain Matters:
How to Deal with Pain Better

In 2018, a research group at Colorado University at Boulder examined the effect of expectations on perception of pain. The study was launched after one of the researchers noticed that even when participants were repeatedly shown that something wouldn't hurt badly, some still had strong expectations it would. They found that if you expect it to hurt, it probably will, even if it really isn't so painful. In addition, the second time around, people anticipated a high level of pain to occur even if they knew better.[15]

In the study, 34 participants were taught to associate one image with low heat and a different image with high and painful heat. Then each participant was placed in an fMRI to measure for neural activity while being shown the cues for low or high pain (e.g., symbols for low or high, words low heat or high heat). They also rated how much pain they expected. Then varying degrees of painful heat, but not damaging, were applied to their forearm or leg—the hottest temperature was the equivalent of holding a hot cup of coffee.

When the participants were asked to rate their pain, they were unaware that the heat intensity was not actually related to the cue they were shown. The results suggested that when participants expected more heat, brain regions associated with fear and threat were more activated in anticipation of the pain. As expected, when participants received the actual stimulus, regions of the brain associated with the generation of pain were more active, but participants reported more pain associated with the high-pain cues, regardless of how much heat they received. It was as if their expectations played an oversized role in their perception of the pain.

The takeaway message for those who are dealing with any type of suffering would be to be mindful of the actual sensation of pain when you receive it. For example, if you've been dreading a presentation you have to give, assuming it's going to hurt, but then it goes well, remind yourself of that the next time you have to give one. You can expand the type of suffering you're okay with in life if you're mindful of the actual pain you experience from events you thought would hurt.

—·—

9/11

On the morning of September 11, 2001, I woke up in my apartment in Collingswood, New Jersey, and decided to bike into Philadelphia for work. It was a seven-mile ride, and my favorite part was the downhill side of the Ben Franklin Bridge. I remember that morning well, looking at the cloudless light blue sky and thinking, "Wow, summer is really over." It had been hot and hazy for weeks, so the crisp air against the clear sky was a welcome change.

When I learned of the first plane hitting the Twin Towers, I was working in a windowless room administering neuropsychological tests to a very bored-looking teenager. My supervisor came in to get me, asked me to come into her office, and told me what had happened. I wanted to leave immediately and start calling family and friends, and a good boss would have let me do it. However, she was one of those supervisors who teaches you what not to do, so she wanted me to finish the testing. I went back in for a few moments but quickly realized that my attention level was worse than the kid's, so I needed to leave.

My dad was working in downtown Manhattan, and my brother lived five blocks from the World Trade Center, so I needed to check in with them. Fortunately, I was in Philadelphia, so I was safe.

Cell phones didn't work for hours that day, so I had to wait a while to make sure my family was okay. I had never experienced that kind of dread before, as I imagined the worst. I was able to get through to my mom, and she had already spoken to my brother. He wasn't working, and when he heard about the first plane, he walked from his apartment to the Trade Center to "see if he could help." That's the kind of guy my brother is; he has a big heart. He didn't know that a second plane would hit or that the first tower would fall while he was there, but I don't know if that would have stopped him anyway.

He has video footage of what happened to him. As the first tower fell and a plume of white dust and debris engulfed him, a police officer saw him hiding behind a big concrete planter and pulled him out. He was incredibly lucky to be alive. My family knew people who lost their lives that day, and it would have been heartbreaking to add him to the list. In my opinion, it changed him forever. It was certainly traumatizing, but it also seemed to make him more mature. He seemed to focus on his health after that, and he had a new-found respect for the police and firefighters. He even wanted to join the military, though he was too old at that point.

The evening of 9/11, I stayed with my girlfriend in her apartment, looking at a view of an oddly quiet Philadelphia sky. I remember talking a lot about the fragility of life that evening. Those poor people went to work and never came home. They left a spouse, children, and pets—never to return. Life can be so cruel sometimes.

In an act of rebellion against the terrorists, I decided I needed to live life to the fullest. I don't drink alcohol, but when I get a lemon with my Pellegrino, I squeeze the life out of that thing! I'm a crazy man. Like the British during World War II, I refused to stop living. I wanted to travel by plane. I yearned to move to New York City and live in a tall building. I had never wanted that before. I also found myself wanting a family.

Less than two months later, on December 7, 2001, I made my first and only attempt at starting a family. I proposed. She had no idea it was coming. I did it at an Italian restaurant where we had gone for our first date. I gave the restaurant a CD to play during dessert so I could propose over a plate of chocolate tiramisu and Enya's "Only Time." I was so scared, I forgot to get down on one knee! I just kept eating the tiramisu, which was quite good. Oh, and she said yes!

The marriage thing has worked out pretty well. I've been married for more than seventeen years. It's been a special and wonderful ride. We have two beautiful and healthy children. It has not been easy at times, dealing with the Great Recession, my unemployment during the pandemic, and raising two kids. I'm so fortunate that she continues at her core to be an unconditionally loving and supportive person. It has gotten us through the toughest of moments. I don't know what I would do without her. My life would not be as rich and full if she wasn't with me.

When I think about our life together, I keep coming back to 9/11. I was never someone who wanted to get married or have a family. When I was a senior in college, our professor Doug Candland asked us to write an obituary for ourselves. It sounds morbid, but it was a fascinating exercise. When he handed it back, he praised me because I was the only one in the class of a dozen or so who did not get married. I'm not even sure it was a conscious choice. It was just not on my radar—not until that horribly disappointing day of September 11, 2001.

Biking to Work in New York City

In 2003, my wife and I moved to New York City to complete our clinical internships. These are one-year positions that were required for graduation. In addition to being newly married, it was going to be a challenging and stressful year of work. To make matters worse, I convinced her to live in Hoboken, New Jersey, just across the Hudson River from New York City. I thought it would be a cool place to live because of the beautiful views and excellent restaurants, but her commute was so bad that living there was nearly a marriage-ending decision. She was stuck on a bus or train for four hours a day and wanted to strangle me. When we did see each other, she sometimes got a look on her face that reminded me of a great Rodney Dangerfield joke, "My wife had a faraway look in her eyes. I asked, 'Hey honey, is there someone else?' She said, 'There must be.'"

I worked on the traumatic brain and spinal cord injury units of Mount Sinai Hospital on the Upper East Side. On a daily basis, I witnessed pain and suffering on a level that I never knew existed. My job description was to perform neuropsychological tests on brain and spinal cord injured patients, but my actual job consisted of providing comfort and support for grieving families. You know a job is tough when they make support groups mandatory for the interns. It was so stressful that I broke out with a nasty case of eczema, which included fluid-filled blisters on my hands and feet. If my patients saw it, they probably wanted to ring the nurse's bell so I could get treated.

The thing that got me through that year, besides being okay with the suffering in pursuit of my PhD, was biking to work. I know that sounds crazy because New York City can be a dangerous place to bike, but the commute changed my life. For those who don't have a map of

New York City committed to memory, here is what I faced. We lived on the New Jersey side of the Hudson River, near the 14th Street ferry stop that took us off on West 54th on the West Side of Manhattan. It cost extra, but I could bring my bike on the ferry and make the five-mile trek to work. The normal fare was $8 one way, plus $5 for a bike. At $26 per day, five days a week, it would consume nearly half of my meager intern salary. There was no way I could make that work.

A few weeks into that difficult year, I got the courage to try the bike commute. I thought just doing it once would be an exciting adventure. I gathered up my work clothes, put them in a backpack, and took my bike on the ferry. What I experienced that day was the most enjoyable commute I've ever had. The trip was beautiful. I biked past huge ships at the Manhattan Cruise Terminal, then through Riverside Park along the New York side of the Hudson River. I could hardly believe how good it felt to be working out while commuting to work!

When I got to 79th Street, I turned right and biked through city streets until I entered Central Park near the American Museum of Natural History. As I made my way through Central Park, past Belvedere Castle, the Delacorte Theater, and the Great Lawn, and finally past the Metropolitan Museum of Art, I realized I wanted to do this every day. When I arrived on the East Side, I went to my gym to take a shower. I was lucky to have a great deal on a gym membership at New York Sports Clubs because it allowed me to shower up, get dressed, and look presentable. Gyms in New York City are worth it for the bathroom and shower alone. The best part was I arrived early for work! That almost never happened with a traditional commute.

On the ferry ride home that night, I struck up a conversation with the ticket attendant. He asked me about biking in the city, so I shared with him how much I loved it, but I couldn't afford it on my intern salary. What happened next was one of those "only in New York" stories. It was as memorable as the time I saw a guy propose to his girlfriend in front of the Rockefeller Center Christmas Tree, only to be upstaged seconds later by a guy who cleared the skating rink so he could skate out with a ring on a pillow in front of thousands of cheering onlookers and propose to his girlfriend. Both said yes, by the way.

The ferry guy listened to my story, walked away, and returned with a fist full of ferry tickets he had collected from passengers. He said to me, "Open your bag." Stunned, I didn't say a word. I just unzipped my Swissgear backpack and watched him shove a handful of tickets into it. I suspect that this was against ferry company policy, but somehow that got lost as I imagined a month's worth of amazing commutes. I could've hugged the guy I was so happy, but I didn't want him to reconsider.

Over the course of that year, he did the ticket thing at least three more times. I had so many tickets that we paid our last month's rent in ferry passes! Once, when I asked my guy if giving me tickets was okay, he said he was retiring anyway and wanted to help me. I felt like Matt Damon's character in *Saving Private Ryan* being told to "earn it," so I biked every day I could. I biked in the rain, snow, and fog. I biked until the Hudson River froze over, and they stopped the ferry. That almost never happens, so you know it was cold that winter. Amazingly, I arrived at work early every time I biked. There was never any traffic, unless you consider stopping on Park Avenue for Woody Allen and his kids.

Most days at work that year were emotionally draining. No matter how difficult my day, I knew that my bike ride home would make me feel better. In the immortal words of Johnny Carson, "New York is an exciting town where something is happening all the time—mostly unsolved."

Biking lets you see so many more details during the commute compared to the sensory numbing experience of public transit. Of course, smelling and hearing everything around you can be a nightmare in New York, but it forces you to use your senses. It made me feel more alive. I'd spot flowers in bloom or people watching a hawk on a tree limb, and suddenly I was reminded that there was more to life than just work. Biking along the water with towering buildings rising up around me was inspiring, like I was living in the center of the universe. That year was tough in many ways, but my marriage survived, and I made it through the internship. Biking made the suffering I went through that year okay.

Speaking to Navy SEALs

Starting in December 2011, I got the experience of a lifetime speaking to groups of Navy SEALs and their families. Most of the events were post-deployment conferences to celebrate the accomplishments of the teams, as well as support the families, and teach them about resilience. The last part sounded funny to me because who's more resilient than a Navy SEAL?

Well, it turns out that despite being modern-day super-heroes, they are still human and have problems like everyone else. For example, it's tough to go from a mission where seconds could cost you your life to dealing with a whiny toddler who makes you late because he won't get into his car seat. I totally get that last part. My kids' car seats may save *their* lives, but struggling to strap them in cost me years off of *mine*.

The first presentation I did for Navy Special Warfare was for SEAL Team Six, who famously took down Osama Bin Laden six months earlier. The craziest part was no one told me who I was speaking to until I arrived at the venue. I walked in with my wife, and actor Robert Duvall was being introduced as the keynote speaker. I immediately started sweating and wondering, "What am I doing here? I have no military experience, and I was not in *The Godfather*." I was also scared out of my mind.

The next day, I was in the ballroom waiting for another speaker to finish so I could do my talk for the SEALs and their wives when the commanding officer of the team approached me. "You see this guy on stage? He's bombing." I jumped to attention like a soldier in basic training. He continued, "I'm going to get him off stage in about two minutes."

I asked, "How are you going to do that?"

He said with a calm tone, "Don't worry. We have our ways."

As I imagined this guy putting on eye black and parachuting onto stage, he leaned in and said, "When you get up there, we need you to be funny!" It was an order!

I said, "Yes, sir!" He looked at me like, "What's wrong with you?" By the way, it's hard doing comedy for Navy SEALs. Once on stage, I asked them, "So where are you guys from?"

Someone shouted, "It's classified!"

I guess the presentation went well because I was invited to speak to almost all the SEAL Teams and their families over a period of five years. In Anaheim, California, I was speaking at a luncheon to a SEAL team about alcohol and drug abuse, and they weren't listening to me. I kicked into high school speaker mode, and I stopped everything to address it. I called them out for ignoring me and told them that they of all people needed to hear my message. I got their attention, but in the back of my mind, I was thinking, "What the hell are you doing? These are trained killers!" Their commanding officer hugged me afterward telling me how great it was that I called them out. That hug may have saved my life.

Honestly, I learned more at those events than anything else. I learned so much about military culture and Navy SEAL training. I learned that the unsung heroes for enduring hardships are the families. These highly skilled soldiers could go from mowing their lawn on a Sunday to flying to Afghanistan later that night. The family knows that dad is gone, but they don't know where he went. They know he might be in harm's way, but they don't know how long he'll be gone. They know he'll be back someday, but they have no idea what shape he'll be in, physically or mentally, when he returns. Suffering from that kind of uncertainty can be debilitating.

Navy SEALs are an inspiring example of finding the suffering you're okay with in life. They seem to tolerate difficult physical and emotional conditions as well as anyone. A psychologist who works with the teams gave me some insight into how they do it. It might be the case that they have a different threshold for pain tolerance, but they also have a tremendous amount of social support around them. The teams are a close-knit bunch. They remind me of my 90-year-old grandmother, her 93-year-old sister, and 90-year-old sister-in-law who lived within five minutes of each other and kept in constant contact. They talked every day, and literally kept each other alive. The SEAL teams seem to operate in a similar way. They know that when they're on a mission, their brothers have their back. They also know that when they're away, families will lean on each other for support. A commanding officer once told me that the best way to keep these guys focused in battle is to make sure things are stable at home.

Even Navy SEALs Cry

One of the most memorable speaking trips for the SEAL Teams happened at a Virginia Beach workshop on Father's Day. It was about twenty SEAL team members and their sons, ranging in age from nine to fifteen. My job was just to spend an hour or so working with them on father and son communication. I planned out this fun and elaborate workshop designed to get these guys to open up, and I was terrified the dads wouldn't go for it. If they failed to engage in the conversation, it would be a long day of me talking.

The workshop turned out to be surprisingly emotional. I asked the SEAL dads, one by one, to tell their sons why they chose this important and risky work. As they went around the circle, each dad got more into it. It was like they were competing to see who could be more open. Some of them got down on one knee, explaining their love of the country and family. I was waiting for one of them to pull out a guitar.

Amazingly, about half the dads said they were "not great in school" but wanted desperately to "be part of the greatest team on the planet." There were a few tears shed by the SEALs and their sons and me, but it was probably allergies. I might be the first person who can say they had a SEAL team crying on their knees.

Four Insights on Suffering from Navy SEALs

In reflecting on my time with the Navy SEALs and their families, four themes emerged on how they cope with suffering. Surprisingly, none of these involves push-ups, sit-ups, or crazy amounts of running. Instead, they focus on how to respect sleep, having the heart of a lion, not quitting until after a meal, and making sure you have a strong team around you.

1) Respect Sleep

It's odd to say that I learned to respect sleep more from the Navy SEALs, a group notorious for putting its trainees through Hell Week, where they get just four hours of sleep for the entire week! However, at almost every post-deployment conference I attended, there was an expert on the neuroscience of sleep. The focus was mostly on how trauma impacts the quality and quantity of sleep. I heard countless stories of how post-traumatic stress disorder made falling asleep and staying asleep through the night nearly impossible. I also heard about a great tip for improving sleep and how to be more mindful when you're sleep-deprived but still have to function, like when you have a newborn.

If you find the suffering you're okay with in life, you're still going to need your rest. There are three main things that interfere the most with quality of sleep. The first is light, often from screens too close to your face. When the blue light coming off those devices is entering your eyes late at night, it reduces melatonin, a hormone that is involved in the onset of sleep. The second is drinking caffeine throughout the day, which lots of people do to stay alert. Many people stop drinking it in the afternoon, assuming it won't impact your sleep. You may be able to fall asleep at night, but caffeine catches up with you because you're awakened in the morning feeling lousy and "wanting coffee" due to going through withdrawal. The third one is alcohol, which hastens sleep onset but causes broken sleep during the night. You may find yourself falling asleep quickly, but in the middle of the night, you're up and can't figure out how to fall back asleep.

Psychologist Terry Reale refers to things like screens, caffeine, and alcohol as misery stabilizers. There are many more, including gambling, drug use, and even work, that stabilize our mood in the short term, but can erode our well-being over time. For me, I love my work, but the travel can tire me out and mess up my sleep. On one trip, I walked into a TD Bank in Philadelphia in the evening to get some cash. The bank seemed empty, so I wandered up to the security guard and asked, "Is the bank open?" She looked at me in disgust, like I was some half-awake zombie, and said, "You in the bank fool." I immediately started laughing out loud, and it woke me up. Lack of sleep can make you feel like you're moving at half speed.

Former Navy SEAL John McGuire, the founder of the SEAL Team Physical Training program, was interviewed in *Business Insider* magazine about battle-tested strategies for coping with sleep deprivation.[16] McGuire said, "You can't lose focus or discipline. Self-doubt destroys more dreams than failure." In other words, you have to believe you have the right stuff to make it through the situation, even if fatigue is telling you otherwise.

McGuire's insights were helpful, because during the pandemic, there may have been more time to sleep but higher stress levels interfered with quality sleep. In my house, the kids were home all the time, and without extracurricular activities, they never seemed tired. Every night, after they finally fell asleep, the doubt would creep in. Is remote learning causing them to fall behind? Are we doing enough to keep them active? Is it too late to drop them off at the police station with a note?

McGuire also suggested to be mindful that tempers will flare when you're sleep-deprived. "You've got to work hard not to let negativity seep in." The mind game is to remind yourself that you didn't get much sleep the night before, but you want a positive outcome, so you're going to watch what you say. You might say out loud, "I'm not feeling myself because I didn't get enough sleep."

The neuroscience research on sleep deprivation has shown that even a week of partial sleep deprivation interferes with mood and other cognitive functions.[17] The study involved 60 teenagers (ages 15-19) with no history of sleep problems. The first three nights of the study, they received up to nine hours of sleep and the remaining seven nights, they got a maximum of five hours of sleep, which was the sleep-deprived condition.

The teens were tested daily on a range of cognitive functions, and the results showed significant declines in sustained attention, working memory (e.g., holding multiple numbers or words in mind) and processing speed. The decline in these areas might explain why sleep deprivation correlates with poor academic performance.[18] If you're chronically sleep deprived, you're likely a less effective version of yourself.

To assess mood, the participants completed the Positive and Negative Affect Scale, which measured both positive and negative mood during each day of the study. They found significant declines in positive mood during the partial sleep deprivation portion of the study, but no changes in negative mood.[17] Other studies of partial sleep deprivation revealed increases in negative mood, including anger, anxiety, and confusion.[19,20]

A study of adults used functional MRI to examine the response of the brain after one night of sleep deprivation.[20] The medial prefrontal cortex, which is involved in self-control, demonstrated increased activity in response to viewing emotional words and images. The brain appears to be more emotionally reactionary when we're sleep deprived, rendering us less capable to handle stress in a calm and peaceful state.

Since the release of the iPhone in 2007, there has been a significant increase in the number of sleep-deprived teens.[21] Today, nearly 40 percent of teens get less than seven hours of sleep compared to nearly 25 percent in the 1990s. Adults are also dealing with less sleep, and the CDC estimated that prior to the pandemic, one-third of adults were getting less than the recommended seven hours a night. The result is not feeling as good or functioning as well in school, at work, or in relationships. The takeaway is that deprivation might be a level of suffering you're okay with in the short term, but it's not a long-term strategy for resilience.

2) Have the Heart of a Lion

During one of my speaking trips for the SEALs, I was invited to visit their training site in Coronado, California. While there, I met an officer whose job was to recruit active-duty members of the U.S. Navy and get them to try and become SEALs. This is definitely not a situation where it's easier to get in than graduate. The average member of the SEALs spends over a year in formal training environments before being awarded the classification. The school is known as Basic Underwater Demolition/SEAL or BUD/S school. When I read about the training, the words "combat swimming" came up several times. I can imagine what that means. The most combative swimming I've ever done is a flip turn.

I asked the recruiter, "Can you predict who is going to make it through the grueling six-month training?" To my surprise, he said, "No, I'm terrible at predicting." I thought, "You're the guy who recruits them, shouldn't you know?" It turns out it's challenging because there were some who "looked like Greek gods" and make you think they'll breeze through, but tap out in a few days. Then there are others who "resemble couch potatoes" but make it all the way to graduation. It's kind of like *American Ninja Warrior*, and you just never know exactly who is going to get to the warped wall.

When I asked him, "If it's not in how they look physically, then what is it about the guys who make it?" He said, "Well, some people just have the heart of a lion and you can't really know by looking at them."

I met someone with the heart of a lion once, and it was not who I expected. I was speaking at a middle school about resilience, in front of hundreds of kids in an auditorium, when I asked for a volunteer to rap the Eminem song "Lose Yourself." A song from 1998 might not seem relevant to a teenager today, but I've found some students relate to the anger in the lyrics in a profound way.

When I asked for the volunteer, I looked toward a large group of outspoken boys in the front row, who I assumed would be the first to want to come on stage. However, the second I glanced at them, they got really quiet. I motioned to them and said, "Really, now you clam up?" A few seconds passed, and a small hand from the back went up. Henry was a small kid for his age, but there was a calmness to him. When I handed him the microphone and asked him to rap, he didn't seem nervous at all. He nailed every lyric of the song, and when he was done, the crowd roared like he was Napoleon Dynamite.

As Henry started to walk off stage, I asked him to come back because I wanted to know if music ever helped me in his life. His voice lowered, and he told me and his entire middle school that he had been bullied badly when he was younger. "There were kids who told me I sucked at baseball. They made fun of my size. I felt terrible, but music like Coldplay always helped me get through it." Some audible laughter could be heard from the row of "tough guys" in the front when Henry talked about being bullied. As he exited the stage to a standing ovation, I walked off stage, closer to the audience, and talked about what Henry had just done.

"You want to know what the heart of a lion looks like?" I announced. "There it is," I said, pointing in Henry's direction. "When I asked for a volunteer, some people who had no problem speaking up earlier wanted nothing to do with coming up here. Henry not only crushed it, but he was willing to be vulnerable and talk about his pain." As I glanced at all those boys in the front row, I repeated, "That is the heart of a lion."

I hope my validation of Henry's toughness in front of the school was helpful to him. I tried not to embarrass the other boys but did want to send them a message. I was told afterward that Henry was one of those kids who had "been through a lot," and that the moment on stage was huge for him. Does this story tell us how to have the heart of a lion? I think so. If we can face our fears and perform in front of those who doubt us, that is the heart of a lion. If we can have confidence to stand in front of our peers, that is the heart of a lion. If we can demonstrate vulnerability in front of those same peers, that is the heart of a lion. I saw all of those attributes in Henry that day, but the Navy SEAL recruiter was right: I had no way of knowing.

3) Don't Quit Until After a Meal

During yet another speaking trip for the SEALs—it was a busy five years—I got to know a retired SEAL named Wally Graves. After completing his service, he went on to create a program to support active SEALs and their families, helping them cope with the stressors of military life. I'm convinced that Wally was the reason I was invited to speak to the SEALs so many times, because he was such a fan of my work on natural highs.

The truth is, Wally inspired me. He was the one who offered to take me to the BUD/S training site. All I remember is the size of the climbing wall, which looked like a medieval torture device. It was so tall it made me queasy just to look at it. He also showed me the silver bell each group carried around; the bell acted as an escape hatch. If you want to leave, all you have to do is ring the bell, and you can go home. I can't imagine what I would do if my audience had one of those while I was performing. A joke would bomb and you'd hear *ding* followed by the person leaving the room. It would be a lot like performing on Zoom.

I asked Wally, "How did you avoid ringing that bell during your training?" He said there were many times he wanted to do it, but then he would say to himself, "Just wait until after a meal." He added, "It worked every time." It turns out that eating food is a natural high. It releases small amounts of dopamine in the pleasure center of the brain and improves your mood. In addition, eating with friends can synergize the high, especially if there are some good laughs. It was such simple advice, but so many people skip meals when they're busy and stressed out. They think they don't have time, but it actually can keep them going.

When I was in graduate school, it was a lot like training to be a seal. I don't mean a Navy SEAL; I mean an actual seal. We sat around all day long and ate raw fish. If I had a rough week back then, Grandma Rose would have me over for meatballs and rigatoni. Sicilian grand-mothers don't just make any meatballs: these were lamb, pork, and beef meatballs in a slow-cooked tomato sauce. She always had lots of pecorino cheese to "sprinkle" on top. I would call it more of a "dump-ing" when I used it because it tasted so good.

The cliché response to having a bad day is, "I need a drink!" I suggest that if your goal is resilience and you'd like to persist in the face of difficulty, try a home cooked meal with someone who makes you laugh instead. It gives you some perspective and nutrition at the same time. My grandmother, who was in her 90s, always left me with a different way of looking at life. I would come in hungry, anxious, and feeling inadequate and leave with a big smile on my face like I was the pride of the family. This is a woman who had a sixth-grade education and remembered her childhood home being heated by gas because electricity was not available in homes yet. There is no drug that could replicate the taste of those meatballs and gravy. No amount of alcohol could give you the motivational speech like a nonagenarian who knows everything is going to be all right.

— —

Brain Matters:
Eating, Socializing, Laughing, and Mood

Eating, like many pleasurable behaviors, releases the feel-good neurotrans-mitter dopamine in the brain. It's important that eating is enjoyable because it ensures that it will always keep us alive. There is evidence that multiple brain areas are involved in eating, including those regions for learning, memory, planning, and emotion. In addition, there are multiple neurotransmitters involved, including dopamine, serotonin, internal opioids, and endogenous (internal) cannabinoids.[22] Simply put, eating is a complex behavior, and it improves mood.

Social interactions, like those that take place during meals, have been shown to release the neurotransmitter oxytocin in the brain's reward center. Oxytocin, known as the love neurotransmitter, is released during social bonding, petting an animal, and holding a baby. A recent study also found evidence that oxytocin stimulates dopamine release during social interactions.[23] Interestingly, decreased brain activity in the ventral tegmental area (VTA), which is part of the reward center, is associated with a decreased social interaction.

Finally, laughter is a euphoric feeling that helps overcome stress, manage pain, and improve mental health. A study measuring blood levels and using positron emission tomography (PET) found that a person laughing showed evidence of endogenous opioid release deep in the brain, in regions such as the thalamus, caudate nucleus, and anterior insula.[24] The authors concluded that internal opioid activity due to social laughter may play an important role in forming social bonds.

Laughter also decreases hormones in the bloodstream that are associated with stress, such as cortisol and epinephrine.[25] There are types of yoga and forms of psychotherapy that integrate laughter to improve quality of life and the immune system. Laughter can also release dopamine and serotonin, which feels pleasurable and improves mood, and facilitates the release of endorphins, which relieve stress and pain.

Taken together, eating a meal, socializing with friends, and sharing some laughs might be among the most rewarding activities we can do as humans. The synergy of three natural highs coming together creates a stronger response that is experienced as an enhanced effect. The tough part is that these are natural reactions, so they don't always work. The food could be bad, there could be an argument among friends, or someone gets offended by a joke. However, the benefits of eating, socializing, and laughing far outweigh the risks, even over Zoom.

— · — · — · — · — · — · — · — · — · — · — · — · — · — · — · — · — · — · —

4) Create a Checklist for your SEAL-Team-of-Listeners

Here's a brief checklist of what to look for when choosing people to confide in. Of course, since you're not paying these people, it's probably a good idea for you to practice some of these skills as well.

1. Do they put the screen down or silence it before talking to you? Do they ever try to reduce distractions that interfere with their

ability to focus, or do they take every call, even spam, on the first ring?

2. Are they non-judgmental when you open up to them? If not, are they at least aware of what they've said and apologize for not being supportive?

3. Do they ask open-ended questions to better understand what you're trying to convey? For example, "What was that like for you?" Do they ask a question and listen to the answer, or do they ask a question and interrupt your answer to blurt out their own thoughts?

4. Do they ever reflect back on what they've heard? Even if it is days later, do you ever hear them say, "You know, I was thinking about what you said, and ..."

5. Do they respond with empathic statements like, "That's a lot for one person, how did you do it?" This requires some empathy on their part.

Study Those Who Have Suffered

Victor Frankel's book *Man's Search for Meaning* details his experience in a Nazi concentration camp and gives insights about humanity in the aftermath. The World War II movie *Unbroken* depicts the true story of Louis Zamperini, an Air Force bombardier who goes from a troubled teenager to an Olympic runner in 1936 and then a prisoner of war. At every turn, he faces unsurmountable odds and refuses to back down. Finally, there's my all-time favorite book turned movie, *Shawshank Redemption*. It's a work of fiction, but it depicts how the human spirit lives on even when it's locked up in prison.

You can spend a lifetime appreciating works of art that depict human suffering, but it's also important to talk with people in your life about suffering. We all have people in our lives who have a story to tell, but life is so busy that it's hard to sit down and listen. A 2013 *New York Times* article titled "The Stories that Bind Us" presented research by Marshall Duke, a psychologist at Emory University, who found that those who know a lot about their families tend to do better when they face challenges.

It turns out that knowing your family and community history can be a stabilizing force when you face adversity. This might explain why in March of 2020, I found myself reading about the 1918 pandemic to understand how Americans survived back then. I found the photos of men playing baseball in masks and large makeshift tent hospitals to be comforting during lockdown. I guess it made me feel like we're not alone in human history. I even went back to my family tree and noticed that all of my grandparents and their siblings, which totaled twenty-seven, survived the Spanish flu and polio!

Based on Marshall Duke's work, his wife Sara, who is also a psychologist, and a colleague named Robyn Fivush, created a measure called "Do You Know?" It's a questionnaire that asks children to answer twenty questions about their family. It turns out that being able to answer these questions is a strong predictor of emotional health and happiness.

- Do you know where your grandparents grew up?
- Do you know where your parents went to high school?
- Do you know where your parents met?
- Do you know about an illness your parents experienced when they were younger?
- Do you know the story of your own birth?

TRY THIS: **Interview Your Loved Ones**

On your next holiday or long boring car ride with relatives, why not try interviewing them using the "Do You Know?" questions. I find it intimidating to ask, "Tell me something really terrible that happened in our family." Instead, I like to ask more specific questions about how the family dealt with recessions, illnesses, and war. We've got family stories for each one, so you would need a lot of car rides to get all the information!

SPOTLIGHT:
Anthony DeVirgillo

During one of my speaking trips, I met a young man who inspired me with his poise and positive outlook, despite enduring tremendous suffering in his life. He was a senior in high school at the time, but I've followed his journey over social media ever since. Here's his online profile: "My name is Anthony

DeVergillo, I am 23 years old, and I have Duchenne Muscular Dystrophy, a muscle-weakening disease that confines me to a wheelchair. I try to find hope and inspiration in everything I do and everyone I see."

Anthony's condition is profoundly debilitating with a life expectancy in the late 20s. When I met him, he had little use of his arms and legs, and his speech was labored. Despite his physical limitations, he graduated high school and then summa cum laude from Rutgers University with a bachelor's degree in Communication and a minor in Digital Communication, Information, and Media. I can't imagine the tremendous physical and logistical effort involved in just getting through school, let alone doing well.

At a time when the major developmental milestone is independence, Anthony was forced to deal with needing others to function. Given those circumstances, I'm impressed by his ability to maintain such a positive outlook. In addition, he's pursued a career in digital communication at a pharmaceutical company. He's navigated his way through a pandemic and economic recession but continues to do well.

When I asked him if he could share some insights into how he deals with suffering and continues to be positive, he wrote the following. Keep in mind the effort involved in just writing his response.

"I live by this motto: 'Despite my disability, my abilities have no bounds!' It reminds me to be grateful for everything I have and all that I am able to do, instead of what I do not have or what I am unable to do. When I am having a tough time, I repeat that motto over and over in my mind. This motto can be helpful to anyone—even if you are not disabled, you still have barriers and difficulties you need to overcome to live your life to the fullest!"

Anthony's motto reminded me of when I was an intern working at a spinal cord injury unit of a hospital in New York City. My patients were mostly young men who lost their mobility in the prime of their lives. Even if two patients had similar injuries, their psychological outcome depended on their ability to view their new life as a challenge rather than a sentence. If they saw it as an opportunity to do things they had never done before their injury, such as learn to ski, surf (yes, surf), date, or skydive, then their outcome was better than if they focused only on what they couldn't do. This was similar to what I learned during the pandemic. Focus on what you can take from the experience, not on what's been taken from you.

ℝ𝔼ℂ𝔸ℙ

Jerry Seinfeld believes if you find the suffering you're okay with, you're going to make it! No one follows a dream thinking about the pain they'll have to endure, but managing your suffering is a key component to achieving anything worth having.

Some people are born with the neurological makeup to be gritty and resilient, while others have to learn it. Whether you're a natural or not, there are limits to suffering. Skipping meals, thinking about self-harm, and dealing with mistreatment is a bridge too far. The reason this type of suffering is so harmful is that eating with friends, practicing self-care, and having a supportive team around you are the very things that will help you be unusually persistent.

The Buddhists are the Jedi Masters of suffering. For me, the pain of working at an emotionally difficult job was buffered by commuting on a bike. Seven miles back and forth across Manhattan was my misery stabilizer. The September 11th terrorist attacks were the worst pain I had lived through at the time, but if you ask me, "What did it inspire?" The answer is my marriage and family.

Navy SEALs have their own formula for handling the toughest job in the world. It involves a healthy respect for sleep, something that's hard to come by after spending weeks in battle. SEALs have the heart of a lion, even if they're built like normal folk. Some of them survived the toughest training imaginable by making sure they have a meal with friends. The takeaway is that we all need a team around us who has our back armed with superior listening skills.

You have my permission to fail. Hopefully you give yourself that permission, too. When life gets to be too much, and it will, stop and take some mindful breaths. Even better, take time to interview loved ones who have endured tough times. Find out how they managed their suffering and made it okay. I'm sure they will appreciate your time, and when it's your turn to face adversity, you'll know others have done it before you.

CHAPTER 3

True Friends See Your Weaknesses But Recognize Your Strengths

"I told my psychiatrist I think everyone hates me.
He said I was being ridiculous because everyone hasn't met me yet."
~ Rodney Dangerfield

When we're young, it's funny how all-or-nothing our thinking can be about friends. It's either they love us or hate us. We either have friends or no one wants to play with us. In reality, there's a lot of gray area. When I was in elementary school, I had a friend who had a pool, a barn with horses, trees you could climb, a fully furnished basement, and a subscription to the new cable channel HBO. He could have been a domestic terrorist, and I probably would have still hung out with him. To protect his identity, let's call him Jimmy.

Jimmy and I used to have these great sleepovers in his basement. We'd watch movies and make noise until the wee hours of the morning. We'd stay up to that hour when everything seemed hilarious but we had no idea why. One time, he dropped a table on my toe so hard the nail eventually fell off a few weeks later. He thought it was the funniest thing he'd ever seen, me rolling around in pain on the floor, not sure if I broke my toe.

Jimmy might not have been the best influence. Once, we were at my house recording ourselves saying nonsense into a tape recorder. He made some off-color joke about baseball player Reggie Jackson committing an act of domestic violence. I was a Yankees fan who loved Reggie, but I remember laughing nervously because I thought I should. My mom overheard us and got pretty upset. She talked with me afterward about why the joke wasn't appropriate.

A few weeks later, we were hanging out at his place and climbing trees. It was a cold day, and I was wearing my light blue and white winter jacket at the time. At one point, Jimmy got down out of the

79

tree and, before I realized it, threw a piece of his dog's poo at me. So gross! It hit me in the chest, so it was a pretty accurate throw. It left a brown stain, too, as poo often does. Then I heard Jimmy laughing hysterically, and I felt an anger inside that was red hot.

I jumped down from the tree, got into his face, and yelled, "What are you doing? Why would you do that?" He just kept laughing, so I left. I walked back home and we never hung out again. No more sleep-overs, no more hangouts at his pool. Nothing. I'm sure I saw him in school a few times, but eventually, he moved away. And today, that kid is comedian Jim Gaffigan. I'm just playing. Jim Gaffigan probably would have thrown Hot Pockets at me.

If I had been older, I might have talked to Jimmy about what happened that day. If I had the training I have now, I would have asked, "What's really going on with you?" Instead, I just walked away. I'm thankful for the moment, though, because it showed me that friends can be disappointing sometimes, even after you've hung out for a while.

Jimmy saw weakness in me being nice to him and exploited it. A true friend would never have done that. A true friend would have recognized how cool it was to have someone who lived nearby to climb trees and have sleepovers with and would not want to mess it up. The next logical question is, so what did it inspire? A motto that I live by to this day. If a friend throws shit on you, walk away and never look back. It also inspired me to identify true friends and keep them in my life.

Brain Matters:
Social Rejection

In the past two decades, there has been a lot of social psychology research on the topic of social rejection. For example, one study found a significant decline in intelligence test scores after participants were told they were likely to end up alone in life.[1] Those same participants showed no decline after they were told they would likely have a major physical injury one day. Another study found that participants ate more chocolate chip cookies if they were told that no one wanted to work with them on a group project.[2]

A meta-analysis of 88 studies found that social rejection frustrates us and lowers our mood and self-esteem.[3] The study also found that our sense of belonging and control were significantly impacted negatively in response to rejection. Social rejection also impacts motivation and behavior. In a study of the effect of social rejection, researchers found that the more intense the social pain, the greater the motivation for social reconnection.[4] Interestingly, after being rejected, a significant effort was made to reconnect with the person who was the rejecter. The study also found three neural regions associated with social rejection pain, as demonstrated by activity in the anterior cingulate cortex and anterior insula. These findings support the overlap between social and physical pain.

Taken together, it suggests that social rejection hurts and causes ripple effects that impact our mood and behavior. The more intense the social pain, the more dramatic the effort to reconnect. It's as though our brain is hardwired to remain part of the tribe and we try very hard to get back into the group. There are limits to this behavior, and at some point, it becomes better for self-preservation to leave. This suggests that being mindful of the people we call friends is an important act of self-compassion to try and avoid pain down the road.

Show Me Your Friends, I'll Show You Your Future

The Framingham Heart Study, a long-term ongoing examination of cardiovascular health, began in 1948 in the town of Framingham, Massachusetts. The original group of about five thousand people agreed to receive two physicals a year, followed by a behavioral questionnaire. The researchers would ask the participant about a friend who was willing to participate in the study and the study organizers would go and collect data from that person, too. The study now has over fifteen thousand people in its data set.

When the scientists compared the health data and social connections among participants, they noticed that certain behaviors were contagious. It turns out that our friends play a huge role in our behavior. For example, if you identify a close friend as obese, you're over fifty percent more likely to become obese than someone who does not report having an obese friend. If two people identify each other as best friends, and one is obese, that percentage jumps to three hundred! This pattern held for alcohol abuse, smoking, and a host of other behaviors that were not healthy for the heart.

Interestingly, social contagion was found with regard to happiness, too. If you reported having friends who were happy, you generally were happy, too. The opposite also proved true in which unhappy people have unhappy friends. Recent research used Facebook posts to confirm that smiling photos and positive status updates tended to occur in social groups. It is possible to "catch" happiness if you're around the right group of friends.

Doug Bratton: Positively Contagious Friends

When I first started as a speaker slash comedian, not surprisingly, I was terrible. It takes years to hone a skill like public speaking, let alone comedy. Thankfully, I had a supportive and positive group of friends who encouraged me to keep going at every turn. We met in high school at a leadership and prevention conference called Teen Institute of the Garden State (TIGS) which is now called the Lindsey Meyer Teen Institute (LMTI).

I went to the camp the first time the summer before tenth grade because my mom made me go. She was a teacher at my high school at the time, so I had to go. I used to ask students, "Who had a parent work at their school growing up?" One time at a conference, a kid raised his hand and said, "Both."

I was stunned. "Both your parents worked at your high school?"

He responded, "I'm homeschooled."

I was miserable the first few days of the conference because my mind was in the present. I kept thinking about leaving, which is a recipe for unhappiness, as we've discussed in the previous chapter. On the third day of the camp, everything changed. I started meeting people, and there was a dance where no one cared what you looked like on the dance floor. I loved it! By the last day, I didn't want to leave. I cried as we departed. So much for my gut instinct that it would be terrible. TIGS changed my life.

In future summers, I returned to the camp as a youth counselor and then a college counselor. The speaking thing happened partly because I founded a student prevention group on my college campus and because the director of TIGS had asked me to speak about it. If I hadn't had the social connection to camp, there is no way I would have gotten the opportunity to speak. More importantly, that social bond got me invited back. I've been speaking there since 1995, but those early talks were not good. I sat on a stool because I was so scared; I needed something to ground me.

That camp gave me much-needed experience, exposure to veteran professional speakers, and a bevy of friends who were willing to help guide me. I was passionate about getting up and speaking, but I had no idea what I was doing. It was the opportunity of a lifetime. It was like Bill Gates growing up near one of the only two supercomputers in the world, and his parents just happening to have the keys to it.

One of my best friends from TIGS is Doug Bratton. We met in high school as youth counselors, but it was when we started speaking on stage together that things really changed. We booked gigs at local schools and got to hang out eating at the best pizza places in New Jersey, which is saying something, and talk for hours about speaking. If you were listening to us over Poppa Tony's in Cedar Grove back in 1995, you'd probably think, "Who are those cockeyed optimists, and where can I get some of that amazing-smelling pizza?"

I would describe Doug as an unconditionally supportive friend who seems happiest when something good happens for one of his friends. It is so difficult to find family, let alone a friend, like that. As a result, he's the perfect friend to approach with an idea for a new project. When I started doing stand-up comedy, he said to me, "Matt, when you become a famous comedian ..." I don't remember anything after that because my head exploded. Every comedian knows that we just need one person to believe in us, and then we'll never quit, even if we should. That moment meant the world to me.

Doug went on to be the director of the LMTI program and is now the executive director of the agency that oversees it, along with a host of other programs. He's successful in prevention but also a very talented cartoonist. It's likely not an accident that the two of us have these hybrid careers since we've been there for each other since the early days. If we did a Framingham Study on Doug Bratton, I suspect we'd see numerous people who have similar things to say about Doug. If positivity is contagious, Doug would be a virus infecting people with smiles.

Brain Matters:
Adolescent Friendships

Adolescent friendships that last decades are a rarity. Adolescent friendships are fleeting, and most end after one to two years. In a study looking at 410 adolescents who reported 573 reciprocated friendships over the course of six years, they found adolescents are most likely to remain close with those who share similar traits.[1] For context, these were friendships that originated in middle school among students living in suburban middle-class neighborhoods in the northeastern part of the United States. The researchers collected data annually and followed the friendships until they were in twelfth grade.

Friendships that started in seventh grade had a 76 percent chance of "dissolution" by eighth grade. Each year afterward reduced the risk of the friendship ending, but the chances a friendship could start in seventh and make it until the end of high school was around one percent. The main reasons given for the breakup of friendships included differences in sex, peer acceptance, physical aggression, and school competence.

It turns out that dissimilarity is bad for long-term friendships, especially when it causes conflict and leads to negative feelings. According to the authors, when there is a dissimilarity among friends, it can create a sense that not everyone shares in the benefits of the friendship equally. In addition, partners who are "better accepted" or popular may take on reputational costs from associating with someone who is "less-accepted," especially if the friend lacks social skills.

The takeaway here is long-term relationships are exceptionally rare and need to be treated with respect. The ending of friendships is more common than we think, especially during adolescence, which can be incredibly disappointing. There's always hope of a reconnection down the road if you find yourself sharing values again.

Rob Torres: Master Clown

There are friends we click with right away, and then there are friends who are more of an acquired taste. Rob Torres was the latter for me, but not because he was difficult to like. He had a world-class personality and likability. We also met as

Rob Torres performing for
the Big Apple Circus

©2021 JIM R MOORE/VAUDEVISUALS

counselors in the TIGS program, and I got to watch his career take off. Whether he was performing in front of a crowd or connecting with people one on one, he had a skillset that made me a little envious.

After high school, Rob went on to clown college (yes, there is such a thing) and then studied street performing. By the late 1990s, Rob and I were both up-and-coming speakers at TIGS. He had created a tremendously engaging program for students that showcased his sense of humor, physical comedy, and audience interaction. I sat on a stool and struggled to hold the audience's attention, unless it looked like I was about to fall off, then they were riveted.

One of Rob's routines back then involved taking four chairs and arranging them in such a way that the participants could sit down and lean back into the lap of the person behind them. Once in place, the chairs could be pulled out one-by-one until the group supported its own weight. It was quite dramatic, and he executed it to maximize the audience's excitement. One day, Rob took me aside and showed me how it was done. He explained that it was an old Boy Scout demonstration that he had perfected during his time as a performer at Disney World.

A year later, Rob's career had blown up, and he was traveling the world with the Clyde Beatty-Cole Brothers Circus. Eventually, he would go on to work with Ringling Brothers and was the lead clown for the Big Apple Circus. He climbed the circus ladder, and it wasn't one of those free-standing ones that would just fall over. He had created a tremendous career that was going to sustain him for decades.

As a result of his international travel, he couldn't get back to camp to present anymore. In fact, he only came to the United States once or twice a year. I wondered if he would be okay with me using that chair demonstration in my presentation at TIGS. In my program, I talked about surrounding yourself with positive people and the chair thing would be a perfect fit.

I called Rob to ask him if I could use it. Most mortals would probably have said no, getting territorial about the routine. Not Rob. He selflessly agreed to let me do it with one caveat, "Make it your own." He had made it his own with the creative way he built audience anticipation during the activity. He wanted me to do something different. It's fine if you're going to do it, but if you want a career on stage, you always need to make things unique to you.

I tried my best to honor his guidance by turning the demonstration into a competition. I took two groups of four volunteers each and built drama in my youth audiences to see who would win. From the first time I did it, audiences responded. More importantly, it gave me the perfect lead in to make my point about social support and mental health. In fact, that opening segment went so well, I realized the rest of my program needed to get better. It's like telling a funny joke and then watching the audience get bummed out because your next five jokes are not nearly as good.

Twenty years went by, and Rob never returned to the TIGS Conference. His career had him working almost every week in faraway places. Thanks to our mutual friend Doug, whenever Rob was back in New York City, we got together for a meal. It was during those gatherings that I realized how much I genuinely liked Rob and how petty it was to be envious of his talent. I was put off by his popularity and the lasting effect he seemed to have on people's lives. He always treated me with open arms and gave me an optimistic perspective on the work I was doing. I'm so fortunate to have had a second chance to get to know him.

Rob Torres tragically passed away in 2018 from a heart attack at the age of forty-five. He was on a flight from Houston to Boston when it happened. Rob's girlfriend, who happened to be a medical doctor, was with him, but there was nothing that could be done. He went to the bathroom and never returned. The world lost a talented, charismatic performer far too soon. He was such a force of nature that his friends in the clowning community wrote a tribute book about him called *A Clown in Our Town*.

In the days and weeks after his passing, I was in shock. Young, healthy people aren't supposed to die suddenly and without any warning signs. It's profoundly disappointing to lose a peer, especially one who supported you. I found myself on YouTube at night looking at Rob's old clips. There's one titled "Applause Box" that's my favorite. He walks out in front of a crowd and captures their applause in a small wooden box. He then works the box and controls their applause to great effect. He did all this without saying a word because he had performed in countries where he didn't even speak the language.

While watching Rob on video, I realized that the box and the chair demonstration were both messages of support. We all need to have people to lean on and people who applaud us, even on our worst day. Rob did that for me, and in my disappointment over losing him, it inspired me to spread his name and message. At my next talk, I memorialized Rob by doing both demonstrations and talking about his legacy. There hasn't been a program since where I haven't talked about him. If he's looking down from above watching me, I hope he can say with a smile, "He made it his own."

Me doing the chair demonstration at a Rhode Island
middle school in 2014.

Brain Matters:
Future Liking

Computers analyze data and do a decent job of predicting the weather, disease, and even elections. Why not friendships? In a study of the neural response to other people, researchers at Columbia University examined what happens inside the brain when we meet someone for the first time.[2] They collected data from social networks and brain images to examine how new acquaintances impact brain activity and if that activity can be used to predict future friendships.

Prior to brain imaging, participants were all seated in a circle and were asked to go around the room and share why they had decided to participate in the study. From that conversation, they were instructed to pick out people in the group they could see themselves befriending. Then they were brought into the fMRI machine and shown pictures of themselves and everybody in the group. The goal was to assess the brain response participants were having to each person in the group. The researchers were specifically looking at the reaction of the reward center of the brain, where pleasurable responses cause an increase in activation, like finding a twenty-dollar bill on the ground.

Researchers followed up with the participants a few months later to find out how they felt about the people they had met. Interestingly, they found that increased brain activity during the initial meeting was significantly more predictive of who participants liked months later than subjective ratings. It was almost as if the subjective feelings about someone in the moment were not a true representation of how the person really felt. Over time, it was the brain response to another person that had greater predictive value over who a person likes down the road.

The takeaway for me is to not assume that our thoughts are always correct. It's okay to be wrong in your first impression. There are a lot of emotions flying around when we first meet someone, and it is easy to not be aware of what's going on under the surface. The beautiful part about being human is admitting when we have made a mistake. There is power in reflecting and reconsidering our feelings.

–·–

Gyne-Lotri Phobia

Rob Torres probably would have hated it if I only wrote about him in serious terms. He was a clown for goodness' sake. Back in the day, Rob was also a legendary prankster. Long before shows like *Impractical Jokers*, Rob was working at Disney World, running a remote-controlled garbage can called "Trash." People would throw refuse "in him" and he would talk back to them. I can imagine him on a hot day in Orlando, chasing down a poor kid who tried to throw out an eleven-dollar melted ice cream cone. "Hey, kid, where you going? That cone cost more than a year of college!"

For fun, Rob used to go into the Disney Store at the local mall with a walkie-talkie tucked inside a stuffed animal. He'd put it on a shelf and start talking through it when unsuspecting customers walked by. They thought the Aladdin plush toy was complaining about never being picked up, and it was just Rob around the corner having fun. He did so many more, too. He'd torture mall-goers by doing risky things with a stroller, growling like a dog, or making fake teeth out of lemon peels that would fly out of his mouth at the wrong time.

Rob's most memorable prank came at my expense. During my first few years of speaking at TIGS, I had a hacky joke from my act about being afraid of feminine products. I called it "Gyne-Lotri Phobia," named after an old commercial for a product called Gyne-Lotrimin. I know, so brilliant it's hard to believe SNL wasn't knocking down my door. It got a laugh, so I found a way to crowbar it into my presentations, which meant all my friends knew about it.

While hanging with camp friends one hot summer night, someone stuck a maxi pad on my hairy leg. It was funny. To play along, I grabbed a stick and began to peel it off. That got a big laugh, so I remarked, "Wow, these things must hurt like hell when you take them off!" The room roared with laughter at my ignorance. A female friend said, "No, they go on the other way!" I responded, "Sure, like no one ever screwed that up before!"

Rob must have been taking mental notes that night because a year or two later after I had made a joke at his expense, he decided to get back at me with an epic prank. He went out and purchased over a hundred tampons! That's dedication. I don't even know how many stores you have to visit to buy in that much bulk. He waited until I was speaking on stage, had someone grab the keys to my Honda Accord, and proceeded to hide the tampons in every crevice of my car. When I was leaving to go home, I got to my car and noticed friends spitting with laughter and taking pictures. It was truly a piece of comedic art he had created. I made sure to play up the moment, looking miserable while trying to get in the car. I announced to everyone, "I'm not really uncomfortable," but they clearly knew I was just trying to convince myself.

The prank didn't end there. Rob had hidden so many of those things that I couldn't find them all. Over the next several months, they would pop out at the most inopportune times. There was one that fell onto the head of a girlfriend as she pulled down the sun visor. Another popped out of a notebook while I was in a meeting with my graduate school mentor. Luckily, my professor turned his head at the exact moment it rolled out, so I was able to snatch it up and avoid an awkward explanation. The most memorable one, though, was the tampon that seemed to leap out of the spare tire well while I was trying to sell the car. My high school friend's dad was thinking of buying the car for his daughter when he asked me to look at the spare. He left looking very confused, but at least he bought the car.

I've often been asked, "Did you retaliate against Rob?" The answer is no, you never prank a clown. They have way too much free on their hands. Below is a picture my Honda Accord that day. Yes, that is my ugly shirt hanging.

Brain Matters:
Public Speaking and Social Support

My speaking career never would have happened without the support of my friends. Public speaking creates a lot of stress for most people, especially when you're inexperienced. As a result, the brain responds by enacting the fight-or-flight response even though the consequences are not life-threatening. The adrenal glands are triggered to release adrenaline and noradrenaline, heart rate and blood pressure go up, blood vessels tighten, and digestion slows down. Social support can modulate the stress of public speaking.

In a study looking at public speaking performance, participants with high levels of social support showed smaller increases in heart rate, blood pressure, and cortisol levels compared with those with low levels of social support.[3] Social connectedness, in general, is associated with positive outcomes for teenagers, including those in a minority group.[4] Taken together, this might explain why teenagers, who perceive stress more intensely than adults, tend to be so social. Perhaps they are instinctually looking for ways to reduce stress and anxiety, including while public speaking.

When it comes to public speaking or any performance, if a person is inexperienced, they might lack awareness of how many mistakes they made. It's called the Dunning Kruger effect, named after Cornell psychologist David Dunning and his then grad student Justin Kruger.[5] They published a paper that examined tests of humor, grammar, and logic, finding that performers in the lowest percentile also grossly overestimated their performance. Even if their actual score put them in the bottom quarter of their peers, , they estimated they were above the 62nd percentile.

We've all exhibited the Dunning Kruger effect at some point in our lives, but social support can play an important role in reducing the impact. Constructive feedback can help increase awareness without crushing dreams if it's delivered in the feedback sandwich. This is when two complimentary statements, one in the beginning and one at the end, are surrounded by the critique. The key is to sandwich between the positive statements, which softens the blow.

—·—

Fort in the Woods Friends

I'm so grateful for having good wholesome friends during my middle school years. There was a lot going on at home with my grandfather dying of pancreatic cancer and my brother getting into trouble with his friends.   crew back then was smart, funny, and really competitive about sports, but in a friendly way. They also seemed to have confidence in me that I didn't have in myself. I was never a big risk-taker, except if you count the time Marc, Jude, and I entered a school lip sync contest in eighth grade. We performed Run DMC's "You Be Illin'" while wearing Adidas tracksuits and baseball caps. If we did it today, our picture would be on the cover of *Cultural Appropriation* magazine.

We won first place in the contest, beating out a group of girls doing "Iko Iko" by Belle Stars. It was an upset that rocked our class of 63 kids. The girls were heavily favored with their outfits, choreographed dance moves, and good hygiene. It was also controversial because the judges took a while to confirm whether or not we weren't throwing up gang signs until they realized we were doing the surfing sign for "hang loose" for some reason.

We did have some raging "no girls allowed" parties back then. One was a sleepover at my house that turned into an eighth-grade legend. The party revolved around playing table top football and watching *The Texas Chainsaw Massacre*. There was nothing illicit going on, but we did have all the pizza and tin foil "footballs" you could want. It sounds corny now, but I created an NCAA-style bracket so we could determine a champion. Okay, it was corny then, too, but a lot of fun.

In the weeks leading up to the party, my friends and I just happened to have built a fort in the woods about a mile from my house. The fort was about twenty-foot long and eight-foot wide. It was a lean-to structure that used an old fence on one side to hold up the large branches. The roof was made of plastic bags, and the big luxury item was an old carpet from my parents' old living room that we used as a floor.

I think I came up with the radical idea that we should sneak out to the fort on the night of the party. I had never left my house at night without my parents' permission, but something about my friends being there gave me the confidence to suggest it. Every day at lunch that week, we planned our escape like we were breaking out of Shawshank. We would sleep in shifts until 3 am, then we would all get up and head out. We would bring sleeping bags, hot dogs to roast, and candy for dessert. As we talked tough, I doubted we would go through with it.

The night of the party was a brisk and clear November evening. The air smelled crisp and clean with a hint that winter was around the corner. After our table top football tournament ended, we watched the movie and tried to sleep, but who could sleep after watching Leatherface take down some teenagers?

Eventually, we all drifted off, but despite our planning, no one set an alarm. It would have been our fatal flaw, except around 3 am I woke up. I've always had this ninja-like ability to open my eyes at the exact time I want to wake up. It was either that or Leatherface was making me a light sleeper. I popped up and started waking the rest of the crew. They were reluctant, to say the least. My friend Tim voiced his final concerns, but he was overruled by seven to one. This was it. We were doing it!

We packed up our sleeping bags and made our way quietly outside the backdoor of my house. The moon was nearly full and looked huge on the cool fall night. I could almost hear the theme from the 1986 movie *Stand by Me* playing in my ears as we walked on the old abandoned railroad tracks behind my parents' house. It was one of those moments I knew I'd never forget as long as I lived. We were breaking the rules and facing uncertainty, but because we were together, it felt like everything would be fine.

The moonlight was so strong that night we didn't even need our flashlights. We arrived at the outskirts of the woods, and as we walked the last hundred yards, we could see our fort's ugly yellow carpet in the distance. I felt exuberant. We finally arrived after weeks of planning, and it felt like the coolest thing ever. One of the guys decided to build a fire so we could warm up and roast hot dogs. I can't imagine a more disgusting snack in the middle of the night—sooty hotdogs, but it didn't matter. We made it!

An hour or so after we arrived, we started getting groggy and laid down. Just then, out of the darkness of the trees, someone spotted two people walking through the woods in our direction. It was terrifying. As they got closer, we could see it was two police officers. Our friend John, for reasons we still can't understand, yelled, "It's the cops! Run!"

Thankfully, cooler heads prevailed and we all stayed put. We hadn't done anything wrong, had we? The cops looked very serious as they approached. I don't recall their guns being drawn, but I'm sure at some point in my retelling of the story, they were. The officers asked,

"What are you guys doing out here?" In our anxious state, we rattled off something about table top football party and Leatherface, and I'm sure they were completely confused. As they went through our bags, probably looking for booze and weed, they almost seemed disappointed. Old wrestling magazines and Nerds candy boxes fell onto the yellow carpet as the cops looked at each other as if to say, "These nerds actually brought Nerds!"

We were polite and answered every question they had. When they were done, much to our surprise, they told us we could stay until sunrise and then we needed to walk home. They made sure we put out the fire, but then they left. We never got in trouble. Not a summons or a court appearance, nothing. Looking back, we were quite privileged to have gotten out of there without a consequence.

We packed up our things in the early morning light and made our way back to my house. When we got home, it must have been six or seven, and the house was still quiet. We opened up our smoky-smelling sleeping bags, crawled in, and fell asleep. Three hours later, we woke up, ate breakfast, and everyone went home. No adult ever found out, until now. I hope our eighty-year-old parents don't ground us for it!

The night was special because we were able to take a risk in a relatively safe environment and it went fine. I never would have done it without my friends. It was almost as if my brain was different because they were there. I'm so fortunate that none of them was into weapons, alcohol, or other drugs. If even one guy decides to take that type of negative risk, the night ends much differently. I built confidence that night. In the vast disappointment that is being a teenager, that night was a victory, and I'll never forget it.

––·––·––·––·––·––·––·––·––·––·––·––·––·––·––·––·––

Brain Matters:
Teenage Brain and Friends

In a series of studies, Lawrence Steinberg's lab at Temple University was able to demonstrate that the presence of same-aged peers increases risk-taking for teens.[6,7] It's not true for young adults or older adults, just adolescents. In all the studies, they used a simulated driving machine to measure how many risks a person would take in an effort to get somewhere quickly. When alone in the machine, adolescent risk-taking was quite similar to young adults and adults. However, once peers were introduced, either in person or over a camera, teenage risk-taking significantly increased. The age when teens tend to take the greater number of risks is during their early teen years, between 13 and 15.

In a subsequent study, they examined blood flow in regions associated with risk-taking. The ventral striatum (VS) and orbital frontal cortex (OFC), both regions associated with decision-making and rewards, showed greater activation for teens than young adults and older adults, but only when their friends (live or perceived through a camera) were present. When teenagers were alone, their brain activation was quite similar to an adult.

Taken together, it is clear that adolescent risk-taking is a given. However, the type of risks they take, either positive or negative, depends on the support in their environment. Teenagers tend to be more anxious than adults, so it makes sense that they would need friends present to motivate them to overcome it. We can't stop teens from taking risks. That would be like asking a toddler not to whine. We can give our attention and support to positive risk-taking and try to deprive the negative risks of oxygen. We also can't socially isolate teens; it's just not beneficial for their mental health. We can focus on teaching them how to surround themselves with friends who support meaningful risks.

TRY THIS: Go Camping, Even in the Backyard

We live in different times today, so I'm not recommending middle school kids sneak out of the house without their parents' permission for any reason, especially not to build a fire and meet the cops. However, I do think camping is a positive risk that not enough people do these days. Sure, it's uncomfortable and a little scary, but it builds self-reliance and delivers a natural high, provided it's not raining.

It could be backyard camping, which I've done with my kids and a flat screen television, or at a campsite out in the woods. It could be a kayaking trip in Yellowstone National Park where you bring your tent, food, and bags to haul out your poop. It could be a day hike where you find a cool rock that looks like a sofa and sit for a while chatting with friends. Whether you're young or old, experienced or a novice, you will feel more alive when out in the wild.

On a Zoom call with hundreds of college students during their orientation, one young man told me he went hiking in Ricketts Glen State Park in Pennsylvania and had a "near-death experience." While his friends were inside their tent at night "getting high," he went out to look at the stars and came within six feet of a bear. That's not socially distant enough for me, but he started making loud noises, and the bear ran off. He continued to say that his senses were "so heightened," and he "felt so alive" that he didn't want to hang out with his friends who were altering their state of consciousness. In fact, he wanted less to do with them after the trip, realizing that all they wanted to do was numb out. He was done being desensitized. He wanted to choose activities that heightened his awareness and put him in touch more with being human.

Great Listeners

One of the most powerful moments of social support for me as a teenager came as a fifteen-year-old participant at TIGS camp, sitting in a small group on the dusty floor of a cabin. Each group had an adult leader, usually a student assistant counselor. Our leader was facilitating a conversation about negative people in our lives and asked, "Matt, how do you feel?" Just like the famous Maya Angelou quote, I don't remember what I said, but I do remember how it made me feel. Having an adult listen to me, really hear me, was like eating a warm brownie.

I knew that no matter what my career would look like, I was going to be that kind of person who truly listened to others. Growing up in a busy household filled with Type-A personalities, everyone was so busy. As the youngest, whenever I spoke, I always felt like I was losing the crowd. It did inspire me to tell better stories!

Psychologist Carl Rogers said, "When someone really hears you, without passing judgment on you, without trying to mold you, it feels damn good!" Being a good listener helps build deeper positive relationships and conveys to the world a higher level of intelligence. But it turns out there is more to listening than just nodding and laughing. If a true friend recognizes strengths, it starts with listening well and paying attention to those strengths.

TRY THIS: **Become A Better Listener**

Here are some tips that will help you perform better as a listener. I find these are a good refresher for me when my phone starts creeping onto the dinner table. Avoid simple phrases like "Okay" and "That's great," which may make you seem engaged, but don't actually make the listener feel understood.[8] Listening to someone and connecting with them is a much more active process. It starts with a decision to stop being so passive in conversation and expend more time and energy to listen more closely. Here are some common things you can do to be a more engaged and productive listener:

1) Make eye contact with the person you're listening to. Put away your screen or at least silence it.

2) Instead of interrupting someone to interject your next thought, give them time to complete their thought.

3) Try your best to be non-judgmental. When you're actively listening, it's not about you and your opinion, it's about the person talking and you understanding their position.

4) Listen without some agenda in mind, like you're waiting to get something from this person. Rather, listen just because you like being there in that moment.

5) Finally, ask questions. Whether you think you understand what someone is saying or not, asking questions lets them know you're interested in the conversation.

Meditation

I wish I would have listened to all the people who encouraged me to meditate over the years. From the age of seventeen until it stuck at the age of forty-two, I was a very occasional meditator. If I think way back, I was exposed to meditation in middle school. Prior to building nerd forts with my friends, I remember learning about visualization at basketball practice.

We had a guest speaker one day who talked about a study on using visualization to make better free throws. He said if you close your eyes, sit in a quiet room, and visualize yourself being successful, you would make more baskets in real life. When I got home, I closed myself in the closet and did the visualization. I'll admit, I just wanted an excuse to hide in the closet, but it definitely worked. I started doing it an hour before games, and I felt calmer on the court. In fact, in eighth grade, I scored 72 points in a game! And we won! It's too bad every league I played after that wasn't made up of short guys like me.

My first exposure to guided meditation was at TIGS camp over the weekend training to become a youth counselor. Dave Johnston, our coordinator, used a progressive relaxation exercise in the guys' cabin at night to help us calm down before lights out. He was hoping we would learn it and then share it with our own cabin during the week of camp. I probably would have, except that the progressive relaxation did not go well for me.

During my early years of doing stand-up comedy, I did the visualization technique before shows. I figured if it worked for free throws, it could also improve the percentage of my jokes that would hit. There are no closets in the green rooms, so I had to settle for sitting in the back of the room with my eyes closed. It definitely helped me reduce performance anxiety, especially for the big shows. I know comedians who drink on stage to relax themselves, sometimes to their detriment. The natural way is more empowering to me. Visualizing myself succeeding at something before I do it has created a sense of déjà vu. I had been there before, and everything was going to be fine.

Brain Matters:
Visualization and Mental Rehearsal

Visualization, a mental rehearsal technique, can help sharpen focus and increase confidence. It was first used after the 1984 Olympics when researchers found that Olympians who used visualization experienced positive psychological and performance benefits.[9] Since then, the technique has been used extensively in the United States by sports psychologists to improve outcomes.

In one study, a seventeen-year-old gymnast with high levels of pre-competition anxiety was treated with a progressive muscle relaxation exercise.[10] The gymnast described her symptoms as including heart racing, sweating, shaking, and preoccupation with what her "over-involved" mother would think. The therapy had her tighten and then relax one group of muscles at a time until she had covered her entire body. Then while in a muscle-relaxed state, the gymnast imagined all the triggering images of a competitive meet, such as the uniforms and sounds of the fans. She was encouraged to imagine a feeling of calm and focus while "seeing" all the triggering stimuli from the competition. The visualization was completed during numerous sessions, and she was also encouraged to practice at home. Three months later, she had improved her scores in competition, but more importantly, felt more relaxed, focused, and reported having more fun.

In New Zealand, researchers used a novel video game to help participants learn three skills on a virtual trampoline over a six-week period.[11] These novice jumpers were split into three groups: those who had five minutes of visualization practice after learning each jump, those who had two and a half minutes of visualization practice, and the control group who did math problems after learning each task.

The results demonstrated that doing any amount of visualization (five minutes or two and a half minutes) improved performance on the actual trampoline, compared to doing unrelated tasks like math. Within the mental practice group, the volunteers who did five minutes of visualization performed significantly better than those who did two and a half minutes. You may not need to crawl into a closet, but practicing visual imagery following learning a task will likely help you perform at a higher level.

———————————————————————————————————

TM (Transcendental Meditation): The Technique

An older counselor I met through the TIGS program, John Grund, was the most outspoken proponent of meditation in my life. He's super into mindfulness, often name-dropping legends in the field like MIT molecular biologist Jon Kabat-Zinn, who created a research-based stress reduction program called Mindfulness-Based Stress Reduction (MBSR). It's a long name for a technique that involves sitting in a chair and breathing. Of course, it's a lot harder than it looks. I tried it a bunch of times, and it felt like I was being waterboarded. My brain just couldn't appreciate sitting with my eyes closed on a perfectly good day.

John persisted, though, asking me if I had gotten into it yet and telling me I needed to talk to my audiences about it. My lucky break came when we moved to Princeton, New Jersey, and I met a guy in the neighborhood who had just opened a yoga and meditation studio. He told me he had been doing a form of meditation called Transcendental Meditation (TM) for over forty years. Much like mindfulness meditation, TM is a fancy word for describing sitting in a chair with your eyes closed. I was skeptical, but what sold me was watching a YouTube clip of Jerry Seinfeld talking about the benefits of practicing TM.

"I'm a regular guy. I'm not one of these people who has endless, boundless energy. But that (writing the hit show Seinfeld*) was not a normal situation to be in. So what I would do is every day when everybody would have lunch, I would do TM. And then I would go back to work, and I would eat while I was working. But that is how I survived the nine years (working on the show)."*

The television show *Seinfeld* inspired me to get on stage and try stand-up comedy, so to hear that Jerry used it was all the endorsement I needed. My TM teacher and I connected with our mutual love for *Seinfeld*. He was a sixty-something guy with lots of salt and pepper hair who dressed like a hamper. You would never confuse him for a Buddhist monk, but you might think he was ten years younger than his stated age. It turns out that's a common experience when you meet people who meditate. They often look younger.

My coach trained with Maharishi Mahesh Yogi, the guru who left India on a mission to teach the world TM back in the 1970s. The Maharishi was the inspiration for the *Star Wars* character Yoda, who even looks a little like him. Jedi mind control also seems loosely inspired by TM. My course in TM didn't involve lightsabers or levitation. It was pretty informal. We mostly just talked about life and TM. It started with an odd ceremony that included me bringing a bandana and fruit. I guess meditation brings you enlightenment, but not a snack.

At the ceremony, I also received a mantra, which is a nonsense word. It doesn't mean anything. I can't tell you mine, because then it would take on a meaning other than being my mantra. I don't say it out loud or write it down. I only say it to myself and only when I need it. The better I got at TM, the less I needed the word. When I first started, I was using the word constantly, now hardly at all. Of course, in the beginning, meditating for twenty minutes twice a day felt like torture, but now I look forward to it and need to be reminded when it's over.

At first, you cannot believe how difficult it is to sit and think about nothing. The brain is constantly active, even at rest, producing thoughts and feelings. It's one of the reasons it's so hard to have a good conversation with some people. They're not listening as much as waiting for a pause to give you their running monologue. We can't just turn off our cortex, but TM trains us to pay less attention to those thoughts. Soon, they disappear into the background. I do TM everywhere, even in the car, not while driving. I pull over into sketchy rest stops and random hotel parking lots, like a meditation vagabond.

It took my brain ten days to figure out that TM was all about rest. Twenty minutes, twice a day for ten days. That's seven hours of sitting awake with my eyes closed, wondering where I had gone wrong in my life. At some point, my subconscious realized, "Oh, this is about *not* exerting effort." My TM teacher reminded me often that my goal is effortlessness. For self-proclaimed lazy people, like comedian Jim Gaffigan, that's not hard. He once said, "I struggle with my laziness. I'm like, 'Should I sit down and do nothing or lie down and do nothing?'" For me, I'd always been driven by a motor, and it was hard to turn it off.

Once TM helped me power my brain down during the day, I started to go into sleep mode. My head would droop, and from the outside, it looked like I was taking a nap. I told my teacher they should call it TN for "two naps." Scientists who study TM believe the brain goes into a sleep mode, more similar to Stage 3 non-REM sleep, the kind we get early in the morning. The most restful phase of sleep. All I know is that when the timer on my phone goes off, I feel refreshed like I just got up from a good night's sleep.

The Impact of TM

The impact from TM was so positive in my life, I was convinced it must be the placebo effect. I had more energy, especially at night. I was more patient with my family. I was also waking up earlier in the morning feeling more rested than I had in years. In the past, if I did a long day of speaking followed by a long drive at night, I arrived home so grumpy and negative. I was like Oscar the Grouch, if his garbage can had wheels.

After I learned TM, I instead pulled over during long rides, did the twenty minutes and emerged with a smile on my face. Ten minutes later, I would be singing along with the radio. That's like the best version of myself. However, the ultimate proof, though, is how quickly

I fall asleep at night. I used to have such a tough time turning off my mind. It was like I was trying to solve the world's problems from my pillow. Now my wife complains that I'm snoring before her, when for years it was the other way around! Now I win the fastest to snore competition.

Overall, the quality of my life improved. It did not come from a pill or a drink. It was from sitting in a chair for twenty minutes twice a day! My cousin, who takes several pills a day to deal with his anxiety, anger, and attention, asked me about TM. After my mini-presentation on it, he said, "That's a big commitment." I pointed out, "More than arranging those tiny pills in a box every day?" I'm not saying TM is some panacea that's going to get you off your meds and happy all the time. It's just worth trying to see if it can help.

I'm so grateful that multiple people, including good friends, recognized that I could benefit from meditation. They saw my weaknesses but chose to recognize my strengths. They could tell that meditation would help me be a more peaceful and happier person. At least one of them saw me as someone who could spread the word about meditation with audiences. For years, all I could see was my inability to get into meditation beyond simple visualization techniques. It took friends and ultimately a teacher to show me the way.

TRY THIS: Start Your Own TM Practice

Here's the meditation schedule that I kept when learning TM. As the saying goes, if I can do it, so can you! First, I downloaded a free app called Meditation Timer. It has a brown icon with a person sitting in the lotus position, but if it's not available, I'm sure you could find nine others like it. It asks you to set up a preparation time (e.g., get comfortable in the chair), which I did for 30 seconds, followed by the meditation time of twenty minutes and a two-minute rest period afterward. Meditation precedes action, so pick a time of day that comes before your busiest, but also the most tired time of day. For me, that's 4:00 to 4:20. Yes, I get the irony of that. I don't need weed; I just sit and breathe and feel calmer. The first three months, I meditated twice a day for twenty minutes almost every day. If you miss a day, have some compassion for yourself. Life is disappointing. You'll get back on track.

If you've never meditated, give it a serious try for two weeks. If you do it every day for fourteen days and don't see any impact, then stop and do something else with your life. There's no need to force it. This is not another to-do list item that you avoid. If you feel the positive impact, you'll look forward to the twenty minutes. It will be like a gift to yourself, and you won't need a reminder.

Here's a student response after a presentation I did at his high school about meditation. It still makes me laugh.

"I thought your presentation at Salmon River today was awesome. Usually when we have presentations, they are always boring and stupid. I learned a lot today from yours and had some good laughs. I work on a dairy farm, and sometimes those cows get pretty frustrating. When I went to work today after school, and the cows were starting to get on my nerves, I did that breathing thing you talked about, and it actually worked really well. I will start using it more often."

Brain Matters:
How Meditation Affects Our Brain

There were several benefits of meditation mentioned, but here is some of the research. Meditation increases cortical thickness and makes your brains more vital as you age.[12] Not that you're going to age, but everyone else will. Meditation helps with sleep. Specifically, it helps older people exhibit a sleep brain wave structure similar to that of a younger person.[13]

When you're sleep-deprived (less than five hours per night), studies show that your mood is significantly more anxious, angry, and confused.[14] Over the past decade, anxiety has overtaken depression as the primary reason college students seek psychological services.[15] In addition, during that time, there has been a doubling of suicidal teenagers.[16] Given that teenagers often experience inadequate sleep on school nights, we shouldn't be surprised by the impact on their mood. Meditation can help to balance the mood after a poor night's sleep.

When you're sleep-deprived, your brain tells your kidney to release the stress hormone cortisol. This isn't a big deal if you're being chased by a tiger, but if it happens every day because you're sleep-deprived, it's not healthy. Cortisol has some devastating effects on your cardiovascular system over the long term, but it fuels angry and anxious feelings in the short term. The brilliance of meditation has been shown to reduce blood cortisol levels in beginner meditators after just three weeks. A study of two groups of meditators, those who stuck to their practice every day and those who were less consistent, found that after three weeks, both groups showed significant reductions in blood cortisol levels.[17] After six weeks, the group that stuck to it and continued meditating every day showed declines in blood cortisol levels. The meditators who completely stopped by six weeks no longer showed the effect.

The question often arises, "Is power napping the same as meditating?" There is research that suggests nappers have significant reductions in self-reported impulsivity and increased tolerance for frustration after a nap compared to non-nappers.[18] It is important to limit a power nap if it takes place in the afternoon to ten or fifteen minutes, to avoid a reset of melatonin levels and your ability to fall asleep at night. Naps are also tougher because it's challenging to find a place to lie down sometimes. Try it at work, and you just might be mistaken for a dead person.

TM Saved My Life – On the Road

I really believe TM saved my life. That's not an exaggeration. One time, I was introduced at a camp by a student who said, "This guy's a legend here. He's basically God." That was an exaggeration. The only funny part was thirty seconds later, someone in the front row sneezed. I responded, "Bless you, my child."

My life had just gotten too busy for me to make it through the day without rest. I was juggling a busying work schedule, including flying, driving, staying in hotels, and speaking that could get intense for months at a time. In addition, high client expectations were always on my mind. My buddy Ty Sells, a speaker friend with a perfect name for hawking merchandise, once said it's the expectations of the people who hire us that I won't miss when I retire. I could do a great job on Monday with three presentations to a tough crowd, but then Tuesday comes, and there's a new client who wants the same magic act all over again.

At home, I was juggling my marriage, two young kids, everyone's busy schedules, relatives, in-laws, and everything else on inadequate amounts of sleep. At home, I usually got six and a half to seven hours of sleep a night. On the road, I got eight or more, but even with adequate sleep, the constant mental and physical grind sapped me.

There were so many speaking trips when I did two presentations during the day and one at night, followed by a long drive home. Minutes before the evening program, I would feel like I could sleep. By the time I was driving home, usually in the rain for some reason, my mind would go to such negative places. I avoided speaking on the phone because I was in such a bad mood, even if things went well. After several years of this, my hair had aged like a United States President in the second term. On my 40th birthday, I made a joke about looking older than my age, looking for sympathy, and my buddy Dave said, "Well, you do travel a ton."

Adding one twenty-minute meditation before my evening presentation and trip home changed everything. I would find a quiet place, pull over, shut off the car, silence my phone, and start my Meditation Timer app. On my busiest days, my brain would go into sleep mode in a matter of seconds. The app made a dinging noise at twenty minutes, but it felt like it had been two or three minutes. When I was done, I felt mentally sharp, my mood was up, and I had plenty of energy to drive home and interact with my family when I got home.

TM Saved My Life – In the Air

On flights, when they conduct the safety announcement, I do TM. That's the perfect time. Who needs all the safety reminders? What am I, Sully? If we're going down, I won't know how to use the emergency door, but at least I'll be calm. TM also prepares me for any non-life-threatening stress I'm about to endure on the remainder of the flight.

One time I was eating my dinner on that sad little seat back tray table when a passenger sitting next to me started trimming her toenails. She was arm's length from my food! As an Italian American, there is a little Tony Soprano that lives right inside my chest. Prior to TM, he might have reached out like a mini-Hulk, grabbed that person by the neck, and asked, "Do you want to taste your clippings? Well, neither do I!" After TM, I calmly put my food away, turned my back, and read a book until she was done. I probably should have gone for a walk, but squeezing through those thin aisles might have exposed me to other people's actual toes.

I'm not saying TM is a panacea that works every time. I still get upset, but I just respond better. I can remember being stuck in the window seat on a cross country flight, right next to a person who smelled like he hadn't bathed—ever. It was an olfactory nightmare in my seat. I asked to be moved, but there was no room. It was one of those worst-case smell scenarios. I couldn't control it and it was relentless. I thought the smell would calm down once we were in the air and the plane got colder. Nope. Even after meditating, I found myself still agitated. I made it most of the flight without freaking out, but eventually, I broke down. I took my smelly gym socks out of my backpack, draped them on my seat back pocket, and hoped that my stink would overpower his stink. It didn't work, but at least it gave me a good laugh and some funny pictures to share.

My favorite TM story on a plane came the day I got bumped up to first class, which you assume is going to be amazing. After my meditation, I noticed the stewardess coming down the aisle taking our dinner order, and she said, "Dr. Bellace, will you be joining us for dinner this evening?" How formal. What am I going to say, "I'm sorry, I have reservations in the lavatory"?

She read the menu to me, "We have the stuffed chicken or the breaded shrimp. What would you like?" I told her that I'd like the chicken. She looked at the guy next to me, who had consumed a few tiny bottles of booze already, and said, "I'm sorry, sir, but it appears we only have the shrimp left."

That's not a big deal to most people, but I guess this guy had a shrimp allergy or something because he started yelling. "I can't believe you don't have enough chicken! All the money I pay for this seat. I want the chicken!"

The stewardess was flustered and said, "I'm sorry sir, I gave the last one to someone."

Then he explodes, pointing his disgusting finger in my face, "I know, you gave it to him!" It was the worst flight I've ever been on, but it had the best chicken. I was eating slowly and licking my fingers.

I didn't get mad at the guy demanding chicken. Before TM, I might have said something. Instead, I went on my laptop and wrote a complaint letter to United Airlines. To my surprise, they awarded me a few hundred dollars to be used on a future flight. That was definitely the better move, right? I never got angry, which is good for my cardiovascular system. I stayed calm, which allowed me to focus my emotions in a productive way on the complaint letter.

The best part of the story was that I got rewarded for my actions, which means the next time I'll likely behave in a similar fashion. I don't know if my friends, the ones who encouraged me to get into meditation, knew that it would help me cope in such specific situations. I do know that I've since thanked them for their support in making me a better human being. They have seen the little Tony Soprano living in my chest and thought meditation would be the perfect antidote, and they were right. They saw my weakness (anger) but recognized my strength (ability to practice meditation regularly).

TM Saved My Life – On Stage

Meditation has helped on stage in many ways but never has it been more evident than on a show in Buffalo, New York. I was the keynote speaker at the state Future Business Leaders of America Conference on a Saturday night in the Downtown Hyatt Regency. It was a nice setting for a show. Of course, any gig is better than walking into a school gym and hearing, "You don't need a mic, do you?"

There were five hundred people in the ballroom, all in dress clothes. I was required by contract to wear a suit and tie. It's a good thing they mandated it because otherwise, I was going to show up in bare feet and boxers like it was a Zoom call. Prior to going down to the event, I did my twenty-minute meditation. It had been a long cold week of driving around Upstate New York and doing programs at schools. I was tired, but the meditation put me in a more positive frame of mind.

Twenty minutes later, I sat in the front row about to be introduced. The lights went down, and I could feel the excitement in the room. The emcee had some opening remarks as people slowly got seated. I casually looked down and noticed my fly was wide open. I thought, "That's odd, I thought I zipped it up already." I discreetly pulled up on the zipper tab, and it broke off in my fingers! My jaw dropped.

This was panic time. I got up and raced backstage. I blurted out, "Does anyone have a safety pin?" They looked at me like it was 1950 and I had just asked for a smartphone.

I could hear my introduction being read from the stage, which wasn't as loud as the sound of my heart beating out of my chest. I looked around the room and spotted a roll of duct tape on a table. That was good news, but it was white duct tape. Who buys white duct tape? That's the most attention-seeking adhesive ever, after Penguin Tape and Flex Seal.

I was desperate, so I pulled off two pieces and slapped them on the inside of my pants. It worked! The pants held together provided I didn't make any sudden movement, like walking. Just then, the audience started applauding, so I waddled out to the center stage. I knew it was going to be the longest hour of my career.

I immediately noticed that my brain was working against me, producing thoughts that were not helpful. "Maybe you should just tell them what happened. It'll be funny." That was the first bad idea. What am I going to say? "I don't want to alarm anyone, but at any point during the performance, my fly could spontaneously burst open, and something floppy and white could fall out." Telling the audience would just have them staring at my crotch for the next hour, waiting for a different kind of show. This is where my meditation practice kicked in because I acknowledged the terrible thought and just let it pass. I didn't have to own it or act upon it just because my brain produced it.

I was able to calm my breathing and carry on with my presentation until the next stupid idea surfaced. "Maybe you should tap on it real quick like a baseball cup check." I did that once. The world only gives you one chance to do that, per interaction. Any more than that and they start wondering if something is wrong with you. I was able to let that thought go and continued speaking for a few more minutes.

Flop sweat started to form on my forehead and neck. My breathing became rapid and shallow like I was about to hyperventilate. My mind was racing with ideas for how I could flee the situation if it got really bad. Then meditation kicked in again and took over. It calmed my breathing down and restored order. I resigned myself to ducking behind the podium every few minutes, looking down to make sure all was in place and then casually walking to center stage. The crazy part is the audience seemed to be having a good time. They didn't appear uptight or distracted by my impending doom. Mercifully, I got to the end of the program and said good night. I had survived the presentation! I later told the guy who hired me, and he said, "I can't believe that happened. I didn't even notice, though it does explain why you kept ducking behind the podium!"

My plan after the program was to have dessert, go to bed, and then drive home the next day. Much to my surprise, I was filled with so much energy after the presentation that I got in my car and drove all the way home! I arrived around 3 in the morning but was rewarded with a full day home with my whiny kids. I mean, my lovely family.

I can't think of a better story for how meditation saved the day. Upon reflection, it didn't have to be quite so hard. I would have benefitted from having more self-compassion. If I had explained to my client what had happened, taken a few extra minutes to go back to my room, and changed into jeans, I'm sure it would have been fine. Alternatively, if I had simply untucked my shirt as I do every time I speak now, it would have gone much better. My mindset for so many years was I had to succeed no matter what. If I stopped the show, it was somehow a reflection of my ability and not some circumstance outside of my control. I didn't need to be the hero that night. It's great that it worked out, but a dose of caring for myself would have been easier. They say the show must go on, but they don't say it can't be delayed by a few minutes.

Brain Matters:
Self-Compassion and Mindfulness

Self-compassion is about being aware of our emotional distress but understanding that suffering is a human experience, and we need to be kind to ourselves. It's mainly about extending yourself a helping hand in situations of pain, loss, and failure. Self-compassion is particularly important when you've suffered a trauma.

In a study involving the Department of Veterans Affairs Center of Excellence for Research on Returning War Veterans in Texas, more than a hundred trauma-exposed Iraq/Afghanistan war veterans were assessed for level of self-compassion and mindfulness.[19] All the veterans had experienced similar levels of Post-traumatic Stress Disorder (PTSD) in the past month and were administered self-report scales called the Mindfulness Attention Awareness Scale (MAAS) and Self-Compassion Scale (SCS).

The results found significantly less severe symptoms of PTSD in individuals who were high on the self-compassion scale. These veterans were more likely to endorse the following statements about themselves: "When I am down and out, I remind myself that there are a lot of people in the world feeling the way I am," or "I'm tolerant of my own flaws and inadequacies." Scores on the mindfulness scale were also correlated with milder symptoms of PTSD. After accounting for PTSD symptom severity, high scores in mindfulness and self-compassion were associated with lower levels of functional disability. These findings suggest that treatment intervention aimed at increasing self-compassion could improve social, emotional, and occupational functioning in returning veterans with PTSD symptoms.

It also suggests that increasing self-compassion could help non-veterans improve their functioning. Many of us create these unforgiving internal environments where we have to perform at unrealistically high levels all the time. If you're the type of person who only takes off when you're sick or going in for a surgery, you're probably a good candidate. There are treatments that can help increase self-compassion, including the one below.

TRY THIS: HEALS Technique for Self-Compassion

If you'd like to develop self-compassion, there is a great technique that you can practice that I've found helpful. It's called HEALS, and it's a method of transforming anger into compassion that has been used by therapists for nearly two decades. It's reported to help reduce baseline levels of anger and reduce the frequency and intensity of episodic anger.

HEALS was initially developed for use with violent inmates in the United States, but it's also been used effectively with clients who experience even mild resentment. Most anger comes from what Psychologist Steven Stosny, PhD, the creator of HEALS, calls "core hurts." The feeling that you're disregarded, blamed, devalued, rejected, ineffective, inadequate, or unlovable can trigger an anger response. We learn these responses early in life, but the feelings associated with them can come flooding back when we're upset. Stosny also believes we're born with "core values," which are our intrinsic worth and lovability. The Lindsey Meyer Teen Institute refers to this as IALAC (I Am Lovable and Capable), and educators from the 80s and 90s know it as self-esteem. Stosny believes that when we're aware of our core values, it's harder to become angry because we see ourselves being helpful and compassionate.

The technique, which has similarities to mindfulness meditation, starts by recalling an incident that makes you angry. This would be a moment when you felt the emotion to a fairly strong extent. Next, you talk or write about it until you can feel the physical sensation of the anger. Then visualize the word, "HEALS, HEALS, HEALS," flashing over the face of the person who made you angry. It sounds hokey, but this interferes with your typical anger response and generates a new response to the emotion. I found it to be surprisingly effective at carrying over into real interactions, where suddenly the term HEALS was popping up on the forehead of someone who was irritating me. It definitely gave me pause before reacting to them.

The next step is visualization to identify and experience the core hurt that generated your anger response. Often mine revolved around feeling ineffective or blamed. This part of the technique is beneficial in so many areas of life because it's empowering to use our words to describe how we feel instead of letting emotions control us.

Once you identify your core hurt, think next about a core value. Be mindful of what is deeply important to you in that situation. For example, if you're feeling anger towards a parent, you might remind yourself of your desire to renew a loving relationship with them. We have a tremendous capacity to aspire to improve the lives of people around us, help those in pain to heal, build friendships and loving relationships.

There is a small-time commitment involved. It requires four to six weeks of practice. I tried it once a day, but you certainly could do more. Find a quiet place to go through the steps. It takes five to ten minutes at most. The key is to be consistent and remember, this is not something you'll be doing forever. This could be a nice addition to your meditation practice. You can even do an experiment on your-self to see which technique is better at reducing anger and increasing self-compassion.

RECAP

True friends know who you really are but support you anyway. They see your weaknesses but choose to talk about your strengths. The key is to surround yourself with those positive people and reach out to them when you need help. When we're young, our peers help us overcome anxiety and take risks that we wouldn't have taken on our own. The question is, what risks are you taking?

Choose excellent listeners to surround yourself with, and you'll genuinely feel happier. If you're lucky, they'll persist in getting you to do things that are good for you—like trying meditation. The busiest people among us need to rests our brain. Even if it starts out feeling like a waste of time, your brain will eventually get that it's about effort-lessness. Once you discover the superpower of a calmer mind and better decision-making, you'll have better frustration tolerance and be more resilient during tough times. Meditation is great, but it's not a panacea. You'll also need to have self-compassion and be your own best friend.

CHAPTER 4

You're Lucky to Live Sad Moments

"Do you ever leave the house without headphones? Wow!
Thoughts are not good. This whole time I thought I loved music.
Turns out I just hate my brain."
~ Mark Normand

The saddest point in my childhood came late in middle school. I'm privileged to say I made it that far before I really felt pain. My grandfather, a beloved man and former mayor of a popular beach town in New Jersey, was dying of cancer. My brother was in the party phase of his life, and it was causing all kinds of tension at home. I was entering eighth grade with thick Sicilian Eugene Levy eyebrows.

One day, someone poked fun at my bushy brows and I decided I was going to shave them down a little bit. There was no consultation with a professional. I didn't even mention it to my father, who is genetically responsible for giving me a near monobrow. I just picked up my razor, which I only used once a week, and did some manscaping. I thought the real problem was the length, so I started to trim the sides. That was a big mistake. Right away, I realized that to look perfect, they needed to be balanced on both sides. I just didn't have the skill to do that or to make them look natural.

When I woke up, it looked like I had two emotions on one face. I was half angry and half surprised. The worst part of the story was

that the next day was picture day. My freakish brows would now be saved for posterity forever in the yearbook! To make matters worse, I was the class president, so they blew up my picture twice the size of the rest of the class. The photographer asked me, "Do you want packet A (10 photos) or packet B (50 million photos, rich kids only)?" I said, "I never want to see this again." Oh well, then I heard, *click.*

Matthew J. Bellace
"Matt"

I don't recall anyone making fun of me after that, which probably meant they saw me and thought, "Oh no, look what we've done!" I'm so lucky social media didn't exist back then. I'm sure the comments would have been brutal. Someone would have pointed out that my eyebrows looked like they were drawn with black Sharpie. One of them appeared to be growing toward my hairline. I didn't know an eyebrow could do that.

I feel lucky to have lived this sad moment. It reminds me that when the haters come out, don't mutilate your eyebrows. Instead, pursue your passions. For me, taking my epic fails and turning them into comedy became an outlet that gave a different meaning to otherwise painful life events. If I could get a room full of people laughing, it suddenly didn't seem like a big deal anymore.

It gives me great joy to watch audiences laugh at my eighth-grade eyebrow photo. I've since learned lots of people have made unfortunate personal grooming decisions, especially in middle school. Besides, it takes the power away from the person who made fun of me in the first place and puts it back into my hands. The theme of this chapter is how we can be lucky to live sad moments in many facets of life, especially if we learn from the experience.

Suicide Risotto

On a speaking trip to North Central College in Naperville, Illinois, I learned a hard lesson about how disruptive technology can be for our emotions. My flight was delayed into Chicago, and by the time it landed, I was starving. Of course, I'm rarely so hungry that I won't still drive forty-five minutes to a great restaurant, and that's what I did. I picked a small but highly rated Italian place called Ricardo Trattoria in the city's Lincoln Park area.

When I got inside, I quickly ordered their signature dish, saffron risotto with tiny veal meatballs, and a bowl of bread. I impatiently scrolled through my phone while waiting for my meal to arrive. One bite in, and I was in heaven! That's what I love about great food—you just know right away. There I was, basking in the glory of creamy risotto deliciousness. It was so good that I took pictures of it to post on social media. Of course, it looked like a bowl of dog food like all my food pictures do, but it didn't quell my enthusiasm. I captioned it, "After eating this dish, all is right with the world ... until I check my news feed again. Lol."

My caption turned out to be prophetic. The next time I scrolled through my Facebook feed, someone who I didn't know, and I assume saw me at a presentation, posted a suicide note. It sounded authentic. Who would do that as a joke anyway? The person made it clear, he was going to end his life and there was nothing we could do to stop it. Within seconds, the concerned comments started pouring in. "Don't do it!" "I know you're going through a bad time, but life is worth living!" It was the modern-day equivalent of yelling to the guy on the roof.

It felt like every minute that passed was an hour waiting for someone, anyone, to provide information. I knew nothing about this young man. I didn't know what town he lived in or where he was going. Mercifully, an hour later, one of his friends wrote in saying he tried calling, but there was no answer, so he called the police in the young man's town. Two hours later, he was found unharmed in a park. It was such an emotional rollercoaster for me, one of his "friends," and I can't imagine what it was like for his loved ones.

A few weeks later, after a brief hospitalization, the young man posted on Facebook apologizing for scaring everyone and explaining what had happened. He was distraught over a breakup, especially after seeing his ex on social media enjoying a new relationship. He momentarily thought ending his life would take the pain away and make him feel better. I reached out to him to offer support and he seemed appreciative. Based on his occasional posts now, he seems to be doing well.

Reflecting on that evening, I realized how the smartphone and social media were both the villain and the hero. It's played the same role in my life, helping to make my day-to-day more convenient while also making life less emotionally stable. All I have to do is turn over my phone and make eye contact with it to open up Pandora's box. It could be a nice text message or a disturbing social media post. In the Chicago story, it was shocking to read but with a heartwarming ending about community support.

It would be short-sighted to have an entirely grim view of smartphones and social media. What if society is lucky to live those moments? What if it inspires people to be more empathic? What if the outcome is a savvier population when it comes to mental health crises? I'm grateful for being reminded sometimes of the fragility of mental health. I don't know if it needed to happen right after a tasty plate of risotto, but it wasn't all bad. We're all just a phone call or a text message away from being that person looking for a loved one or from being in distress ourselves.

It appears that smartphones are increasing the frequency with which we're aware that life is disappointing. In some cases, smartphones are amplifying the negative noise, like the constant blasting of images from natural disasters. Conversely, smartphones also provide instantaneous access to information that can make life better, such as learning how to meditate.

This chapter will examine the connection between the smartphone, social media, and disappointment. It will discuss how to control our digital lives by setting limits that work for us. In addition, it will look at a few things smartphones do to help improve our physical and mental health, like finding access to delicious and nutritious food or teaching us how to grow a garden. So basically, the chapter that started by discussing food and the phone will conclude by talking about the phone and food. It's like a palindrome of content.

Smartphones — A Misery Stabilizer

Smartphones are like Willy Wonka and the Chocolate Factory: swipe the screen and you're in a world of pure imagination. The only problem is it's a land of perpetual distraction. It's a slot machine that delivers intermittent rewards, some of which end up costing you money. This reinforcement schedule is what keeps us coming back for more. It can paralyze you with background noise and divide your attention, but lose your phone, and then real panic sets in. Smartphones might be the only thing that's truly there for us 24 hours a day. When I had COVID, my family kept me locked in my office, but thanks to my iPhone, they could still hear me complain.

Some people are so attached to their smartphones, they wear a version of it on their wrists. My wife is one of these people. When she gets a text message, her phone dings, her watch buzzes, and her iPad rings—and they're all within five feet of each other! This cacophony happens so that she can find out what the ninth person on a group chat thinks about a baby picture. I'm trying to have a conversation about refinancing our mortgage, and she's looking down saying, "Oh, Adorable!"

I'm not much better. I don't have the smartwatch or the iPad, but with my iPhone, anytime I reference an *SNL* sketch or a *Seinfeld* bit, my phone is out. I'm on a mission to show everyone around me what I was talking about as if I'm the only one on the planet with YouTube. Do we really need dinner interrupted by me showing a clip of Kramer playing the board game *Risk* with Newman?

According to psychotherapist Terry Real, smartphones are "misery stabilizers," similar to alcohol and other drugs and gambling. Smartphones briefly mask the pain of living for seconds at a time. They do a great job of delaying our feelings, that is until they don't. At some point, you have to put the device down and that's when you become aware of what's going on internally. It could be at night when you're trying to sleep or driving in the car, but the misery cannot be stabilized forever.

Smartphones – The Positives

Of course, the truth is smartphones have dramatically improved my life and the lives of millions of people around the world. I can see what my cousins in Sicily are cooking for Sunday dinner over Facebook and get inspired from half a world away while sitting in my car about to go grocery shopping for dinner. When it comes to driving, I hardly ever get lost anymore. Before GPS was in our pocket, I had so much stress about being late for work. One time, I flew to Pittsburgh for a speaking engagement, stayed overnight in a hotel, got up the next day, and proceeded to get lost looking for the high school. It happened to be one of the largest public schools in the state, so I don't know how I missed it! By the time I walked in, it was so late that all the students had been seated already and I only had half my speaking time left. The school had no idea where I was because I wasn't about to get out of my car and waste time on a call! They were nice about it, but I imagine the principal wanted to lock me out of the building and watch me melt down on the security footage.

Experts call this the information age for a reason. There was a time when if I wanted to know something—really had to want to know it—I had to desire that knowledge so much that I kept it in mind until the next time I went to the library. That could be days or weeks! I could write it down in a notebook like Ray in *Rain Man*, but it still required a certain amount of initiation. I had to walk into the library, which always smelled like spilled printer ink, look up the information in a reference book and then copy it down by hand like a biblical scribe. Once I was done, I had to find a payphone and call for a ride. It took like half the day just to learn about ancient Mesopotamia.

Now I can do all of that research in a matter of seconds. I barely have to care about the subject since all I need is enough motivation to control my thumb. Sure, the smartphone isn't always a reliable source. The information you get on vaccines may have been from an anti-vaccine website, but at least you didn't have to go to the library.

Smartphones have definitely brought people closer together. Today, I can call my mother and see her face whenever I want. Actually, I can see her ear whenever I want because she never points the camera at her face. When I was a kid, the best you could do with a long-distance loved one was to hear their voice while worrying how much the call would cost. Today, there are so many ways to communicate over one device. Comedian Gary Gulman says, "The phone is now the least seldom used app on my phone."

Brain Changes

The downside to all this screen time is something psychologists are just starting to understand. There is evidence of an increase in attention problems, distracted driving, difficulty with problem solving, increased anxiety, feelings of loneliness, and even suicides. These issues are all connected to one common problem: sleep deprivation. Smartphones contribute to lack of sleep since the blue light emanating from the screen suppresses a hormone called melatonin and negatively impacts sleep onset.

The real problem is not the phone as much as how compelling the content is on the phone. If all smartphones could do was give us GPS and email, it would be in a drawer right after we got home from work. Instead, we can get text messages, phone calls, social media apps, weather, news, television, movies, music, games, and so much more right in our hands! How can we be expected to sleep when there are seven seasons of our new favorite show on Netflix to binge? In the future, I imagine smartphones will come with warning labels like a pack of cigarettes. Instead of a skull and crossbones, it might read:

Warning:

This product may cause distraction, sleep deprivation, loneliness and binge watching. Do not attempt to operate heavy machinery while using, especially when your favorite show is on. You may also experience a fear that you're missing out on a better life, which you are...yours!

To be fair, much of the content we view on the smartphone is engineered to hold our attention. Coders have designed algorithms that favor material that gets the most eyeballs for the longest duration. The content triggers our negativity bias, drawing us in to look at what's wrong or missing. You can see the same phenomena in local 11 pm news with stories of who got robbed, shot, or burned near you. It's there because collectively, our minds go to the lowest common denominator. The problem is the more we hang out in that headspace, the more it drains our battery.

In her 2014 book *Facehooked*, clinical psychologist Suzana Flores examined the implications of Facebook and other social media on our psychological and social well-being. She concluded that there is healthy social media use, and it can have a positive impact on our lives, but there are also consequences of risky social media use. The book details the lives of her patients and how they've struggled with social media dependence, but how they grew and became more resilient through psychotherapy.

One of the ideas that seemed helpful was that we can "check in" with ourselves when something goes wrong rather than panicking, deleting accounts, or avoiding the phone for a while. This is kind of like the "sitting on your board" analogy presented earlier. Avoidance is like a misery stabilizer: it gives you relief in the short term but sets the stage for a stronger anxiety response the next time.

The book also mentions the idea that when our real-life emotions are affected by the number of "likes" we get, it's a red flag warning sign. It's an indication that too much of our identity is defined by that app, and it's time to focus on real world activities that deliver more lasting benefits. She suggests spending time helping other people or animals in need. I love the idea that when the phone bites you, the best way to bite back is to put it down and think about others. It's the quickest way to get out of your own head.

— · —

Brain Matters:
Effects of Social Media

Neuroscience research on social media is still in its infancy, but there have been a few studies looking at the impact it's having on our cognitive functioning. More than two thousand high school students from Los Angeles, California, were followed during a two-year period to assess the impact of digital media.[1] These were young people without symptoms of Attention Deficit and Hyperactivity Disorder (ADHD) at the beginning of the study. During the two-year period, the group with the highest frequency of screen use, which consisted of mostly checking social media, had significantly higher odds of having symptoms of ADHD (9.5 percent) compared with those who reported no high-frequency screen use (4.6 percent). The authors concluded that more research is needed to determine if this is a causal relationship.

A study on smartphones and addiction also showed a link between visiting social networking sites and risk for social phobia.[2] Specifically, 367 college students were administered the Smartphone Addiction Scale (SAS), the Brief Social Phobia Scale (BSPS), and UCLA Loneliness Scale (UCLA-LS). The results showed that young people who use their smartphones for social media had a significantly higher risk for smartphone addiction than those who used them for surfing the internet or making calls. There were also significant positive correlations between the SAS and the BSPS and UCLA-LS scores, meaning that there is a link between smartphone addiction and social phobia, as well as smartphone addiction and loneliness.

In another study, 143 college students undertook a three-week experiment to see if reducing social media use would improve their mental health.[3] The students were asked to limit their use of all social media apps, including Instagram, Snapchat, and Facebook, to thirty minutes or less per day. All the participants used the iPhone's Screen Time App to provide an objective measure of whether they were able to stay under the limit. To assess mental health, the students were given the UCLA Loneliness Scale and the Beck Depression Inventory (BDI-II) prior to and immediately following the three weeks.

The results showed that college students who were asked to reduce their use of screen time to thirty minutes or less experienced a clinically significant decrease in scores on the loneliness and depression scales. Not surprisingly, the students who reported the highest symptoms of depression before the study showed the greatest reduction in symptoms afterward. However, regardless of severity, students experienced a reduction in symptoms. Predictably, the students who were not asked to reduce their screen time did not experience a reduction in symptoms.

The authors of the study also suggested that the type of engagement you have with social media matters. If you're passively scrolling through other people's feeds, it's different than posting your own content and commenting on others. It may be the case that writing and expressing yourself, within reason, is more empowering and less depressing than just observing other people posting. The so-called "doomscrolling" effect of consuming large quantities of content can be detrimental to your mental well-being.

TRY THIS: Boundaries for Screen Time

People raising kids today are the pioneers of the Screen Time Generation. There are more and more studies coming out, but it feels like research on the topic is in its infancy. My wife and I have followed the American Academy of Pediatrics on media use for kids. As a result, we limit our school-aged kids to 90 minutes maximum of all non-school media per day in at least two sessions.

When I speak to parent groups, I try to listen and take notes about how they set boundaries. I notice I learn as much from them as they could from me on the issue. Their successes and failures will help the rest of us set boundaries on screen behavior. Here are some tips from parents around the country. Do you use any of these yourself? Have you tried them on your kids? If so, have you noticed a positive impact?

· Turn off all notifications.
· Check notifications on your time, not when the phone dings.
· No screens at the dinner table.
· No screens less than five feet from your face one hour before bed.

- No screens in the bedroom (buy an alarm clock, read a magazine).
- Daily time limits for social media (e.g., 30 minutes).
- Take a screen holiday for an evening, an entire day, or a weekend.
- If you're raising kids, set limits on when screens are off at night.
- Charge screens in the kitchen.
- If you're raising kids, get an app like Bark, which barks anytime someone accesses inappropriate material on your device. I asked a parent, "Did you ever hear it?" He said, "Only once."

Driving Meditation

In college, I had a love-hate relationship with my nearly three-hour drive to school, which I did several times a year. As I left home, the first hour was fine because I could still get my favorite New York radio stations. I could listen to Mike and Mad Dog arguing over how bad the Jets looked or Z100 blasting "The Sign," by Ace of Base for the nine hundredth time. Once I crossed the Delaware Water Gap into Pennsylvania, everything changed. There were slim pickings on the radio: country music, religious sermons, or high school sports talk, which was like a religion to them, too.

Eventually, I gave up and sat in silence. After a few minutes, my mind would wander. Thankfully there was no smartphone to grab, no podcast to listen to, or even audiobooks to play. It got painfully boring. Then a different part of my brain would kick in and I'd start reflecting on my life. I would envision myself at the beginning of an inspiring story that would lead to a happy and prosperous life.

That time in the car was like a meditation. I thought through relationship problems, working them in my mind like a Rubik's Cube. I thought about classes I was struggling with in school, envisioning myself buckling down and pulling out good grades. Mostly, I just daydreamed about my life after college. I often imagined myself on stage inspiring an audience with laughter and tears (mostly mine). I saw myself doing something thrilling, like writing a book. Wow, I really overestimated how that would feel.

Those car rides were some boring hours, but I was so lucky to have lived them. If rural Pennsylvania radio was better or if podcasts were a thing, I don't think I'd be doing this work now. "That's a bold statement," says the voice in my head. My career began on those rides. I spent an inordinate amount of time rehearsing stories and jokes in my head to an imaginary audience that I was sure would one day hear from me. It seems prophetic now, but I had a need inside of me to get the attention and love of strangers so I could share my truth.

In the silence of that car, my mind was in shuffle mode, mining through the stories of my life, looking for something to work on, something to perfect. I was searching for my identity during those car rides. I was trying to figure out what my niche would be in the world. Those mundane rides gave me valuable time to process things. Time that is hard to come by these days when digital distraction is just a swipe away.

Monkey Time

One summer during graduate school, I worked as an intern at the National Institute of Mental Health. In my laboratory, we were researching memory in Rhesus monkeys. It was an exciting time of life, as I was learning from such brilliant minds about the inner workings of the brain. It was a sad and lonely place for the monkeys and for the researchers since we were both stuck working in monkey cages all day. For me, it was the suffering that I was okay with, but it turned out to be a creative time for me.

Part of my job involved moving the monkeys from their home cage down the hall to the computer room for memory testing. These were not trained monkeys that would hold your hand, so I had to move them into a transfer cage and wheel them down the hall. For the most part, they were compliant, except for one that scratched me on the neck. I don't blame him. He was having a bad day. Of course, I had to spend the afternoon in the infirmary getting tested for a lethal strain of herpes called herpes B. No, this is not my way of telling you I have herpes. I tested negative.

On a normal day, I wheeled five or six monkeys into the computer room, one at a time, and had them sit in front of a computer screen for 20 minutes. They played a memory game and get Craisins if they guessed correctly. It turns out monkeys work pretty hard for delicious dried cranberries. While the monkeys were working, I had downtime. It was over two hours a day with no cell phone reception and no internet access. In my boredom, I started writing out material for upcoming presentations. That monkey time became so valuable to my future career!

The presentation I rehearsed the most that summer was for my high school alma mater's graduation. It was just a fifteen-minute talk, but it meant so much to me! I grew up there, so I wasn't about to bomb in the same amphitheater where I had graduated.

The trickiest part of the speech I prepared was the section talking about commitments. I decided to deliver a T.S. Eliot quote from memory. I feel more present when I'm speaking if I'm not reading something. Kind of a mistake. I rehearsed the line every day in that monkey lab, some days out loud. The monkeys would give me this look that said, "Why are you making so much noise? Go get me a banana." I wrote and rehearsed that speech until I was hearing it in my sleep. Reflecting on it now, I don't know why I didn't just talk about doing research with monkeys the entire speech. They were a lot more interesting than me at that point. I don't even know why I didn't bring a notecard with the quote on it.

The night of graduation, the weather was beautiful. Blue skies and 70 degrees. You could not have ordered a better night for an outdoor event. The graduates were dressed in their caps and gowns and their families were in their Sunday best. That actually intimidated me. I saw a man in a three-piece suit—a white three-piece suit! I thought, "Why would a distinguished man, so confident he would wear that, want to listen to anything I have to say?" My brain was working against me.

When I got introduced, it was like an out-of-body experience. I could see myself walking slowly to the podium, but it felt like I was sitting in the crowd. As I started speaking, everything seemed to be going well. I was telling stories, making jokes, and the audience seemed to be into it. Then came the big moment when I recited the quote: "And T.S. Eliot said ..." Long pause. Nothing. Silence. I looked out at the thousand-plus people in front of me and said, "And I forgot!" They erupted in laughter. My mind went from blank to sitting in that monkey lab. I saw the face of one of those monkeys and smiled. My anxiety dropped and the quote came rushing back into memory. I nailed the line and finished the speech!

That was one of the highlights of my career. A few weeks later, I was at Whole Foods in Montclair and the young person ringing me recognized me. "I saw your speech at graduation. You did a great job!" I tried to play it off like it was no big deal, "Oh that's nice of you! Was there anything in particular you liked?" She replied, "Oh I don't remember anything you said, except the part where you forgot the T.S. Elliott quote. That was funny."

To the average twenty-something, working alone for hours in a monkey lab would not be high on their list of summer jobs. Scooping ice cream at the beach, now that's a summer job. There's no risk of herpes B working in the dessert place. To some, that was a sad summer, but I was so lucky to have lived it. In fact, I returned the following summer to hang out with more monkeys.

Brain Matters:
Locus of Control

In psychological terms, locus of control is a reference to how strongly someone believes that they have control over the events that impact their lives. If you find yourself in a tough situation, like a long commute or a lonely job, you're more apt to deal with it well if you feel you're in control. The question is, do you think your behavior and abilities matter? Do you believe you can make a change in your life if you need to? If so, that's called having an internal locus of control. Conversely, if you feel the events of your life are controlled by an outside force, like fate, luck, or powerful individuals, that's called having an external locus of control. We likely feel both in the course of our lives.

Research suggests that there is a relationship between locus of control and mood, particularly depression.[4] In one of the first studies on the subject, people with an internal locus of control were more likely to report higher levels of depression. The study concluded that people who have a tendency to internalize and blame themselves for their pain and failure tend to have less stable moods.[5] Subsequent research did not support this finding, instead showing that having a strong external locus of control, not internal, was associated with depression.[6,7] These findings have been replicated throughout the world over the past three decades, suggesting that a strong internal locus of control is actually better for staving off depression. A person's beliefs that they have little or no control over the events in their lives play a significant role in the development of depression.

There is also a relationship between external locus of control and anxiety. Dozens of studies dating back to the 1960s showed a positive association between external locus of control and anxiety, such as stage fright and being a generally anxious person.[8] This is not to imply external locus of control causes anxiety, but there is a correlation. Taken together, it appears believing external forces have more control over your life than internal forces is connected with anxiety and depression.

This begs the question, what about religious beliefs (e.g., that a higher power is in control of your fate) and locus of control? If someone believes in a divine being, does that mean they exhibit an external locus of control, and are they more likely to be anxious and depressed? A meta-analysis of 444 studies found over 60 percent of the studies found religious people less likely to be depressed, while only 6 percent found them more likely to be depressed.[9] In a separate meta-analysis of 32 studies on religion and anxiety, almost every study found faith, prayer, connection to a religious community, and religious training were all associated with reduced anxiety.[10] This was observed in both a population of otherwise healthy people and various patient populations.

To answer the first question about religion and locus of control, previous studies showed mixed results. In a study using a large representative population, they found that individuals with an internal locus of control were more likely to believe in a higher power.[11] In addition, they were more likely to report that a divine power helped them in the past and would likely ask a divine power for help in the future. Those with an internal locus of control attended places of worship more often than those with an external locus of control, but they also were significantly more likely to maintain their religious beliefs and behaviors over time compared to those with an external orientation. This dispels the idea that the people who believe in a higher power are more likely to have an external locus of control and higher rates of depression and anxiety.

TRY THIS: **Cultivate an Internal Locus of Control**

Research showing the impact of external locus of control on mood suggests it could be beneficial to cultivate an internal locus of control. While we can't control every aspect of our lives, we can control our effort, attitude, and willingness to make a change. Cognitive behavioral therapists often ask clients to journal specific thoughts, as well as the feelings and behaviors that follow. The idea is to get an accounting of your internal thoughts to help challenge those thoughts that might be problematic for your mood and daily functioning. The thinking is if you can gain a sense of control over which thoughts to endorse and which thoughts to ignore, you'll improve your well-being. Research found that people exhibiting more internal locus of control tend to be more socially well-adjusted and less likely to experience emotional turmoil and better deal with stress.[12]

Below is a simple Cognitive Behavioral Therapy worksheet that can help you with identifying thoughts and behaviors and then come up with challenges to those thoughts. In a therapy session, a CBT-trained therapist would go through a few of these events with you, but there is still value in trying it on your own.

Event	Thought	Behavior	Challenge Thought	Predicted Behavior

Instructions: In a table like the one above, list some past events that led to some distress (e.g., an argument that led to anger or a situation that led to feeling more anxious), then list your thoughts and behaviors that followed. In the next column, write down a challenge to your thoughts, with a more positive or contrary perspective that challenges your initial thought. In the final column, list the new behavior that you predict will happen as a result of the new thought. Next time you face a similar distressing event, notice if this exercise helps you have a more well-adjusted reaction.

You're Lucky to Have FOMO

The fear of missing out or FOMO is a real phenomenon, and it's nothing new. The first mention of it was a paper written by a marketing strategist named Dan Herman in 2000, but the concept has now permeated into the culture. It's not just an affliction for young people; in fact, survey research has shown that seventy percent of adults have a suspicious feeling that they, too, are missing out on something better going on.

Social scientists have now expanded the concept to include the fear of being left out or FOBLO. This occurs when we discover we've been left out of an event and we feel it was intentional. In some ways, it's more painful than simply missing out. FOBLO should not be confused with FLOWBEE, the self-vacuuming hair cutting system that probably sold very well during the pandemic.

My worst memory of having FOMO still haunts me. It was my college graduation day, and my entire family was driving out to watch me walk across the stage, including my 85-year-old-grandmother. She was attending her fourth and final graduation at the school since my dad went there, as did my uncle and cousin. I can't imagine how proud she must have been to see two sons and two grandsons walk across the same stage.

The post-graduation plan was to have lunch afterward and then see them off. I was remaining on campus to start my graduate program the following week. Little did my family know, I had a baseball game for my summer team that afternoon, and there was no way I was going to make it. It was killing me. I played in every game on that team, and we were having a great season. I did not want to miss out. I kept playing the scenario over and over in my head, hoping that something would end early and I could make it. In fact, I had my baseball uniform in the car. I'm surprised I didn't wear it underneath my gown.

Once we got to lunch, my mind was entirely on making that game. I don't remember anything about our lunch. I was not present in the moment at all because I kept checking the time. If I could have gone to the kitchen myself and made everyone a sandwich to rush things a lot faster, I would have. I can still see myself getting up from the table, probably ahead of everyone else, and making our way to the cars. It was such a relief. I was finally free of them! I rushed to my car, got dressed, and drove as quickly as I could to the field.

When I arrived at the game, it was the bottom of the last inning, and there was no way I was getting in. One of my teammates was surprised to see me, but with that, "Why would you be here?" look on his face. When the game ended, I realized I had done something I would regret. I don't even remember who won. All I know is that my grandmother has been gone for more than fifteen years, and I would give anything to have that lunch back. I was so focused on leaving the entire time that I was never really there. I was mentally checked out thanks to my fear of missing out. Social media wasn't even a thing back then.

Today, thanks to social media, missing out is amplified and so much more intense. Now you get to see the fun everyone had without you. In addition, the pictures are curated with filters to make it look like people are enjoying themselves more than they probably did. You have receipts of the thing you missed out on. That's like digital torture. All of these pictures, videos, and comments could trigger feelings of envy, disappointment, and difficulty with emotional regulation. I don't envy young people for the minefield of navigating this stuff.

Despite all of this, I still feel you are lucky to live FOMO moments. I am grateful to have lived mine, even though it haunts me any time I think about it. Every moment you're torn over what to do is an opportunity if you choose to take it. It's a chance to learn how to resist momentary urges. It's a moment to reflect on what matters in life. What has more meaning? Writing it out now, there's no comparison between a once in a lifetime event with an aging grandmother and just another baseball game. There's no question today I would have just skipped the game. I'm not missing those three at bats!

TRY THIS: Techniques for Overcoming FOMO

FOMO is not going away anytime soon, but our reaction to it can lessen the impact. Here are a few things you can do to make yourself stronger:

1. **The F in FOMO is Fear.** Fear is a reaction to specific and observable danger, such as being carried away in a rip current or attacked by an animal. The fear component in FOMO is often about the imagined consequence of missing out. Challenge that fear by doing the CBT experiment explained above. What's the fearful thought? What's the behavior that followed? Now write out the challenge to your   original thought and the behavior that you predict will happen. If you start doing this regularly, I suspect you might be surprised at how much less FOMO impacts your life.

2. **Be okay with not having it all.** When we try to multitask,

cognitive psychology research has shown that we're less effective. Racing around looking for a better experience trains your mind to constantly look for the next thing. You can't be in two places at once, so after you decide where you're going to be, embrace it and don't look back.

3. Practice Mindfulness. Make a conscious effort to be truly present during an activity. Putting your screen down and drawing your attention to your surroundings will help you connect. Happiness is about being in the moment. When our mind is stuck in the future or the past, that's a recipe for being dissatisfied.

4. Remember the limitations of social media. Be a savvy consumer. The postings you see on social media are often curated images that a person wants to show you. It's rare for someone to truly be vulnerable and post something that puts them in a bad light. Therefore, social media posts provide little context for what happened immediately before and after the picture. All you can do is enjoy the moment you're living in anyway, so assessing how it compared to the moment someone else lived in a photo that day is not possible.

5. Gain control over your digital life. As suggested earlier, turn off all notifications. Check the phone on your time. You might find that you stress less and enjoy more when you don't have a screen buzzing at you like an annoying bug.

You're Lucky to Be Ghosted, At Least Once

When I was a teenager, if you liked someone and wanted to talk outside of school, you physically had to pick up the phone and call them. If that wasn't horrifying enough, most phones back then had cords, which meant I could only get about three feet outside the kitchen where my mom was hanging out. It was certainly not enough distance away from her to smooth talk anyone. My parents eventually got a phone in their bedroom, which I would use until my dad sometimes came in and blew his nose like it was a trumpet.

The humiliation didn't end there. If I was lucky enough to place a call in peace, it meant first talking to one of the girl's parents. It felt like running through a gauntlet of suspicion and judgment, making me sweat before an already anxiety-filled conversation. My heart raced so fast, I swore they could hear it through the phone. It's a wonder I didn't just hang up when I heard an adult's voice, not that I did that before Caller ID was invented.

Technology has solved the awkward phone call problem. Today, young people don't even make phone calls. Now you just take a picture of your junk, text it, and you're done! I have a friend who got one of "those pics," and it was from an unfamiliar number. After she dealt with the psychological trauma of feeling completely violated and grossed out, she told her husband. He called the number, and the guy picked up! His response was, "I texted the wrong number." I can't even imagine texting that to anyone, let alone someone whose number wasn't on my phone already!

Thanks in part to phones and other technology, relationships can get very intense in a short period of time. It used to be that you'd have to wait until college before you could spend day and night with a person. Now technology has allowed middle and high school students to have unsupervised social interactions at all hours. I guess it's not all bad. The teen pregnancy rate has dropped to record lows over the past several years, so I guess the phone is enough for them.

A big downside is the impersonal nature of it all, especially when things don't work out. The end of a relationship used to mean a face-to-face breakup or, at worst, a phone call. Sure there were plenty of times when things "fizzled out" with an unspoken parting of the ways, but today it can take on a much less personal feel. "Ghosting," which is essentially ignoring, defriending, or blocking someone you no longer want to speak with, has happened to a quarter of young adults according to a recent survey in the *Journal of Social and Personal Relationships*. Ghosting is more than just ignoring someone's phone calls. It denies them access to you and your digital life. You're sort of pretending that someone no longer exists. It's a great tool when someone mistreats you and you'd like to remove your attention, but it's cruel if used as a quick way to end a relationship.

Psychologist Steven Stosny would say that being ghosted touches upon our "core hurts," such as being ineffective and unloved. Many people have a fear of abandonment, either from being traumatized by a parent leaving or dying or simply being worried about losing someone they love. When someone chooses to leave you and gives no explanation, you're left with your own negativity bias, assuming it was something you did. If you find yourself compulsively checking to see if you've been unblocked, you may start to feel ineffective, like there is nothing you can do to change the situation. Here's an account from a college student named Mark who shared with me about a time he was ghosted by a longtime friend.

"I thought everything was going well with us. Trish and I had known each other since middle school and had an on-again, off-again friendship that had gotten romantic at times. I guess with history like that I never imagined she would ghost me.

One day we're texting with each other, and the next thing I know, I didn't hear back from her. It was out of character for Trish because she was always so quick to respond, but at first I didn't think too much of it. Then I noticed her Facebook page was gone, which was very strange. I got concerned, thinking she got hacked, so I texted her and asked if everything was cool. No response. Then I checked her Instagram account and noticed that she had posted something that day. All I did was hit "like" on the post, and minutes later, I was blocked! It dawned on me then that she was avoiding me. I felt like crap. I felt worthless. The worst part was I had no idea what I had done."

I suspect his experience was representative of many people who have faced the dilemma. As much as I wish I could take away his pain, here is why he was lucky to have been ghosted. My advice, which was similar to the advice of his friends, was to stop trying to reach out. Sit with the feelings of rejection and abandonment for a while and then use that energy to reach out to friends who treat your feelings with more respect. In essence, reward the people around you for their loyalty by giving them your support and attention. This is an opportunity, if you choose to take it, to truly value people who communicate with you and don't run when they get uncomfortable.

Here's what Mark told me when I ran into him two years later.

"My friends told me to never even try to contact her again. I followed their advice. It was tough at first, but now I realize it was the right thing to do. About a year and a half later, Trish emails me out of nowhere! I didn't even recognize the email address. I had to ask her questions to verify it was her, like 'Have you ever ghosted a friend from middle school?' Haha!

When I asked her what happened, she apologized and told me a long story about meeting another guy who was really controlling of her and demanded that she break ties with any male friend. I felt bad that she was being treated that way, but it didn't excuse the fact that she just disappeared on me. If Trish had told me before she left, I would have understood. It also would have saved me a lot of hurt feelings. I still hear from Trish sometimes, but it's not the same. I'm not into her at all. I know better now.

I call this the *Swinger's* effect, from the 1996 movie with Vince Vaughn and Jon Favreau. In the movie, the character Mike gets dumped by his longtime girlfriend. His best friend Trent advises him to stop calling her. He tells Mike to go out and have some fun because she'll probably come back one day. I don't want to spoil the movie, but just like Mark and Trish in the story above, Mike experiences significant personal growth thanks to the experience.

In Mark's situation, he acknowledged the negative feelings after his friend from childhood ghosted him. He didn't run from the feelings or be abusive to himself. His core hurts were brought to the forefront, and he reckoned with them. What I like about his response is he didn't seek revenge. He initially tried to track her down, but he backed off once he realized what was happening. In the end, Trish didn't think much about his feelings. His decision to focus his time and energy on people who weren't careless with his feelings was the right one.

This all reminds me of a joke by a comedian friend Joe DeRosa, "I'm adopted and people ask me all the time if I want to find my birth parents. I say, 'No, I took the hint.'" What I'm saying is, take the hint. When a person abandons you, it says more about their weakness than anything else. You cannot control what others say or do to you, but you have a choice in what action you're going to take afterward. If you go out and do a good deed for someone in your life who has been there for you, it will improve how you feel. Being selfless gets you out of your head and mood tends to go up. You are lucky to be ghosted if it leads to personal growth.

—·—

Brain Matters:
Think About Other People

A study in the *Journal of Clinical Psychology* examined 47 participants with clinical depression and/or anxiety to see if their life goals over a 10-day period correlated with the severity of their symptoms.[12] Specifically, they looked at whether the type of goals they had each day, either "self-image goals" (e.g., those focused on obtaining status or approval and avoiding vulnerability during social interactions") or "compassion" goals (e.g., striving to help others and making a positive difference in someone else's life) made a difference in their mood. They used structured interviews to chronicle goal setting and then a six-week follow-up to assess any changes.

The study found that a greater focus on self-image goals was connected to an increase in relationship conflict and worsening symptoms of depression. Conversely, a greater focus on compassion goals was associated with decreased levels of symptoms and less relationship conflict. It's almost as if the person who wakes up thinking about doing something positive for another person, especially a person in need, had more reasons to feel good about themselves throughout the day.

As a follow-up study, the researchers interviewed a significant other for each participant (e.g., spouse or close family member), asking them to rate that person's goals. They found that if a loved one rated them as having more "compassion goals," it correlated with higher ratings for the quality of the relationship than those with "self-image goals." Therefore, the impact of thinking about others has benefits beyond just ourselves, as our partners also benefit from a happier relationship.

—·—

You're Lucky to Eat Sad Meals

Entering my junior year in college, I had had enough of the cafeteria. The food was awful. The veggies were boiled into a lifeless mush. The pasta sat out dry until you topped it with the underwhelming red sauce. The chicken was cooked into a leathery consistency that was as dry as paper napkins. At some point during the year, you just noticed that everything tasted the same, probably because the cafeteria air had a cheap fried oil and grease scent to it. The only thing they did well was the ice cream, which was from an outside vendor called Bechtel's. At least they could order a tasty treat without messing it up. Overall, my mood around mealtime was down, and I couldn't take it anymore.

Before the start of the semester, my disappointment inspired a desperate plea to my mother, "Whatever you're paying the cafeteria for meals, give the money to me!" My plan was to cook meals in my room or order take out. Surprisingly, my mom was cool with it! I immediately felt empowered and was determined to make it work out for the best. It was also a tremendous way to learn how to cook.

In the first week, my dorm neighbors took notice. I heard things like, "Look at Bellace, eating like a dog." They said that because I ate most of my meals alone hunched over a tray. By the end of the first month, the comments changed to, "How do I get on Bellace's meal plan? It smells amazing in there!" Then they saw me with extra money to go out with friends to dinner, and they all wanted in.

I was so lucky to have lived those sad cafeteria food moments because I've never tolerated bad food again. However, it took experiencing the feeling of "ugh, this food sucks" for me to start connecting the relationship between nutrition and my mood. The key was to take the step from disappointment to action. Complaining about it feels good for a few seconds, but changing it felt good for the entire school year. I'm grateful that my mom allowed me to exert control over the situation. That made a big difference. I also got lucky because I could make food in my room and not get into trouble. I tried to be smart about it and not fry fish, but people still knew about it, and no one complained.

Amazing Childhood Meals

As a kid, I was a terrible eater. My idea of a good meal was anything with Easy Cheese. I ate peanut butter and jelly daily for lunch for the entirety of middle school. I'm surprised my nickname wasn't Skippy. I didn't even have a good reason. I was exposed to incredible meals growing up. My grandmothers were both fantastic in the kitchen. My Nana's holiday meals were legendary. People still talk about them decades later, and these are people who weren't even there. They heard about how great they were, and it left an impression.

My Nana's family emigrated from Northern Italy to the United States in 1910, and she was born a few years later. I was told her family was educated and weren't poverty-stricken, but they must have struggled enough to want a better life. I remember my Nana telling me she found it funny that peasant food, like pasta aglio olio (with garlic and oil), was considered fine cuisine in the United States. To me, that was evidence her family had struggled at some point, and their meals reflected that pain.

Like many Italian Americans of the time, her cooking wasn't a fusion of Italian and American but two cuisines on one table. There were traditional Italian dishes next to classic American ones. On Thanksgiving, she'd make turkey, gravy, stuffing, mashed potatoes, and cranberry, but we also had lasagna, meatballs, spinach torta (a savory cake made of eggs, spinach, and nutmeg), and several gut-busting desserts. I can still remember the feeling of being so full when I finished that I had trouble breathing. Watching football wasn't even about the game. We just needed an excuse to lay prone on an incline just to let the food work its way down.

My Sicilian grandmother was also born in the United States soon after her family immigrated. Her parents were poor. When I visited the old country, I could see why they would leave. It was rugged terrain and very hot. Her father was a laborer, and there wasn't much chance for a better life there. Their food reflected the simplicity of their lives, but with lots of flavor.

My grandmother was more of a specialist in the kitchen, perfecting certain dishes that she would make for important occasions. She never had to make a big spread because family gatherings were large, and everyone brought a dish.

Our Christmas Eve gatherings were like a scene out of a Martin Scorsese movie. My cousin Vic, one of three "Vic"s in attendance, hosted the party in his sprawling farmhouse in Cherry Hill, New Jersey. It was the best house for parties because there were many small rooms on the first floor. If you took a camera and filmed while walking room to room, you would see each generation pass before your eyes. The formal dining room had the old folks with their stories of the family. I wish I had written all of them down. My Uncle Ted was always standing up and making a speech about how women got it all wrong by wanting to work. As I walked through with my full plate of rigatoni and meatballs, I could hear raised voices and then huge laughter. Uncle Ted probably made a penis joke. They knew how to enjoy each other's company.

The next room was filled with the parents, who talked about politics, the economy, and their annoying teenagers. As I walked through this room, trying not to spill my meatballs, I heard more raised voices and huge laughs. Cousin Vic, Ted's son, probably made a penis joke. Then I'd finally get to the sunroom with the kids' table. It was filled with annoying teenagers, but always a few parents trying to feel young again. As the youngest in the entire house, I sat down and eat my pasta and soak in all the stories. I felt like I was getting classified information that wasn't intended for my ears. Before long, we erupted into laughter at how ridiculous our parents sounded telling penis jokes.

TRY THIS: A Special Dish from Your Past

The quickest way to brighten your mood tonight is to prepare a dish from your past that you know will make you feel good. Is it a family recipe that was passed down for generations? Perhaps there's a story that surrounds the dish that might even tell a story of how your family overcame hardships.

_ . _ . _ . _ . _ . _ . _ . _ . _ . _ . _ . _ . _ . _ . _ . _ . _ . _

Brain Matters:
Local Food

The most promising thing to happen to food in my lifetime is the local food movement. This is defined as consuming food mostly grown within a hundred-mile radius. It feels good to say we're supporting a local farmer, and it's assumed that local food is better for the environment, your wallet, and your health, but does science support this claim? The research on the issue is a mixed bag of costs and benefits.

The idea that local food is better for the environment makes sense. If food only travels ten miles from a farmer to you at the market, as opposed to three thousand miles, it's going to burn a lot fewer fossil fuel. It turns out that's not necessarily true. Research shows that the scale of the food delivered (e.g., how much) and the mode of transportation both play a role in determining environmental impact. Most of the emissions and energy used in the food system come from producing, processing, and distribution. That means that larger quantities will be more efficient than smaller quantities on all counts.[13,14] This means that one shipment by train, ship, or truck of mass grown avocados will produce fewer emissions than hundreds of small farmers delivering little shipments by pick-up truck.

The sales of local food reached nearly twenty billion by the end of 2019, up from five billion a decade ago, according to PackagedFacts.com. It certainly is the case that spending money on local products helps vendors by cutting out the middleman. Allowing the farmer to keep more of the profit can serve to uplift the economy. However, many consumers have the perception that local food is much more expensive than nonlocal food and will hurt their own bottom line. However, research on this issue suggests local fruits and vegetables that are sold directly at a Farmers' Market are less expensive than what is sold in grocery stores.[15,16] For home gardens, the National Gardening Association (NGA) reported that the average gardening household does pay for itself. Home vegetable gardens produce nearly seven hundred dollars' worth of fruits and vegetables, compared to the cost of just over two hundred dollars' worth of materials and supplies, like seeds and soil.

Finally, local food is believed to be more nutritious than nonlocal food because it sits around for less time after it's been picked. As a result of this perceived benefit, it is assumed that local food retains more vitamins and minerals. Just like research on environmental impact, the science on local food does not necessarily suggest it's healthier than nonlocal food. In other words, it's complicated.

A diet high in fruits and vegetables is associated with a reduced risk of heart disease and certain types of cancer.[17] Research has shown that people with access to food markets where consumers can buy directly from farmers have lower rates of diabetes and lower body mass index.[18] This does not suggest that eating locally causes these health outcomes, but there is a connection. It could be the case that communities that are already healthier have more demand to eat locally, so farm markets thrive there. In addition, there is research that shows people who buy local fruits and vegetables or grow them themselves tend to eat a more diverse selection of fruits and vegetables.[19]

The best argument for local food seems to be that it's healthier because of freshness. Transporting tomatoes across the United States takes significantly longer than the farmer who picks on a Friday and sells it to you the next day. There is research that shows the nutritional quality of fruits and vegetables peaks at harvest but quickly declines over time.[20] In fact, within a week, fresh produce can lose nearly half its nutrients.[21] Frozen or canned fruits or vegetables might contain more nutrients than a fresh product that's been sitting around too long or exposed to high heat or humidity.

The bottom line is science suggests that finding any excuse to consume more fruits and vegetables is better than not eating them at all. Whether they are locally sourced or not, getting nutrients from the source improves our health. If you don't have access to local food, growing your own is a nice life hack that may be good for your wallet and increase the nutrition of the food. If growing your own is too prohibitive, then fresh or frozen is still better than nothing.

Sad Food-Inspired Garden

When I was living in New York City, disillusioned with my local supermarket produce, I started visiting a local Farmers' Market. It was held on Saturday mornings in an abandoned school playground next to a hospital. It felt like a place you'd buy drugs, not cauliflower. The vegetables I bought from the Farmers' Market looked amazing and seemed to taste better. I got so into it that I went every week, even through the winter months. At that point, I don't think it was local produce anymore. Avocados aren't native to the Upper East Side in mid-January.

My trips to the drug playground for veggies inspired me to start planting herbs in a flower box on my window sill. Eating fresh pesto from the basil I grew felt very satisfying. It was like a science experiment that I could eat.

When we moved to New Jersey, we found a home with a big backyard and an overgrown garden. Almost overnight, I became a farmer. It was like I had a dormant Italian gene that kicked in and made me rip out weeds and chase away animals. My neighbors must have thought an unstable madman moved in next door if they saw me bolt across the backyard barefoot to chase away Thumper.

I was determined to clean up that garden and take it down to flat earth. In the process, I touched poisonous pokeweed plants, stinging bees (they don't all sting), and lots of poison ivy. It took a month and a few bottles of topical anti-itch cream to turn it into a functioning garden again. By the way, one of the most intensely enjoyable sensations on the planet is running your poison ivy blisters under increasingly hot water, as hot as you can tolerate. It feels amazing and the itch will subside for hours. It's not worth getting poison ivy, but if you've got it, you should give it a try.

During the pandemic, gardening gave me a socially distant activity, but it also gave me hope. No matter how bad things may be in the outside world, that short walk to the garden was like the Mister Rogers train to the Neighborhood of Make-Believe. Instead of King Friday, biology is the temperamental ruler of the land. My family rarely joins me out there, so it was like a second bathroom. It was therapeutic, too. No amount of time in the garden ever felt like enough. I could spend an entire day there just working and observing.

This is my garden in June. It's like a mini-farm. On the left, you can see strings. That's a pole for sugar snap peas. The blue cage in front with a stick in the middle is an heirloom tomato plant. To the right of that, you'll see a large zucchini plant. The red bag in the middle has potatoes growing in it. The kids love dumping them out and picking out the potatoes. Along the left side are all golden cherry tomato plants. They are my favorite. Sweet like candy!

SPOTLIGHT:
Dara Bellace, PhD, My Wife

*"My wife is also a psychologist, which means our kids
have no chance of being normal."*
~ Matt Bellace

*This chapter's focus on food, from garden to table, leads to the inevitable
discussion of food and weight. One of the more disappointing aspects of normal
aging is that adults gain about one to two pounds per year. That might not
seem like much, but it adds up. The rate of obesity picks up through ages 40 to
60 and impacts over 40 percent of adult Americans. In somewhat of a panic
response, we look for a quick fix to a problem that took years to develop. As a
result, fad diets are still fairly popular despite evidence that they don't work in
the long term. My wife, Dara Bellace, PhD, is a clinical psychologist with world-
class training in the treatment of eating disorders, so I went to the kitchen and
interviewed her for this segment.*

*First, let me say that I feel for my wife in that she has a tough job. She goes
to work and listens to patients talk about their struggles with food all day, then
she comes home to a foodie husband who talks about what's for dinner and a
Jewish mother who is convinced she's never eating enough. My wife can't catch
a break!*

*Dr. Dara agrees that diets are a disappointment, but you're lucky to live
through one if they inspire better choices. In fact, the problem of yo-yo dieting
or "weight cycling" is bad for your health, so hopefully one is enough. According
to her, the side effects include increased weight gain over time, increased blood
pressure, risk of diabetes and heart disease, and general frustration.*

*Fad diets are fascinating, though. I've never seen a product advertised so
much that works so poorly. Of course, it might work for a little while, which
probably saves the advertisers from lawsuits. Some of them sound, pardon the
pun, tough to swallow. Lemon juice and cayenne pepper? Where's the Pepto-
Bismol? Only eat once every three days? That sounds miserable most of the
week, but at least I'll have those unhealthy binges to look forward to! Kashi Go
Lean Crunch cereal for breakfast every morning? I tried it once, then threw
out the entire bowl and thought, "Maybe that's how you lose weight?"*

My wife's message is clear on the subject of fad diets, "It doesn't matter what new technology you use to track calories or deliver food to your front door, if you can't sustain the change over the long run, the weight will come back." In many cases, it's the weight returning and increasing, which serves to make people feel hopeless and fuels more extreme behavior. She told me, "We all have to eat, so then there's this shame associated with it that can give rise to further restriction, binging, and purging."

According to Dr. Dara, "When you go to extremes and reduce intake dra-matically, your body kicks into what is known as efficient metabolism. That means your metabolism is slowing down because your body is trying to make the most out of the food you gave it." Despite all your efforts, it's as though your body is working against you. You think you've been successful after quickly dropping some weight only to find out it has returned.

"The diet industry presses on with more and more bizarre diets despite the science," Dara stated. "What if I eat only clean food or all sugar-free or paleo? What if I fast every third day or only eat cauliflower? Well, knock yourself out, but if you can't sustain it for the rest of your life, don't bother." In fact, she encourages us to do away with the concept of dieting altogether and think about sustainable change.

TRY THIS: Moderation

Dr. Dara says to focus your attention on "small obtainable goals that include eating moderately and making incremental changes to your activity level." We all need to eat to survive. Unlike alcohol and other drugs, we can't avoid fueling our bodies. Rather than obsessing over eating behavior, such as through eliminating foods or frequent fasting, instead try a minor adjustment to your routine. For example, if you enjoy a sugary drink with every meal, try a less sugary drink like Honest Tea. In addition, try only having one a day instead of two. I've done this, and it's worked pretty well. I've replaced a sugary drink at dinner with flavored seltzer water. Don't laugh until you try Spindrift with lemon. I really should get paid to sponsor one of these products I keep mentioning.

Not noticing might be the point to making successful change. If you're hardly aware that a change took place, you're more likely to sustain it. In addition, your metabolism won't be in survival mode if the changes are small and sustainable. In a perfect world, you should make one small change and measure the difference over time. Then you can add a few more changes, like less dessert during the week or no snacking after 9 pm, and see what happens. Treat it like an experiment and see how you respond.

Another suggestion is portion control. Continue eating everything you like, especially the most nutritious foods, but limit the number of portions or the size of portions. When you do that, it doesn't feel like a shock to the system. When I did this, I noticed that I felt physically more comfortable moving around after a meal. Unintended consequences were that I started playing sports more in the backyard with my son and daughter or going for a walk in the neighborhood. The positive reinforcement of being active made me want to continue the behavior.

There's also an interesting new app called Noom that uses psychological techniques and coaching to help you create better habits and live a healthier life. I don't have any investment in the company, but I should since it sounds like a good idea. Any supportive program that focuses on small and sustainable goals is the way to go. From what I've read, it's not a weight loss program but rather a plan for dealing with the thoughts and emotions that tend to be barriers to weight loss. The thinking is if you can lower those barriers, you can make progress toward health and wellness goals.

Brain Matters:
Obesity and Homeostasis

Health problems associated with obesity are a leading cause of mortality worldwide. In the United States, over a third of the population is considered obese and another third is considered overweight. It is a major health issue that appears to be getting worse. A review of the literature on diets and weight loss found that up to two-thirds of dieters regain more weight than they lost on their diets.[22] Research on dieting generally draws two conclusions: diets do lead to short-term weight loss, but these losses are not maintained. As noted in one review, "It is only the rate of weight regain, not the fact of weight regain that appears open to debate."[23]

Exercise appears to be a confounding variable in many of the studies on diet and weight loss. That means it is influencing weight in ways not associated with the diet. For example, if two people try the same diet, but one is much more active than the other, their weight outcomes will be much different. It might seem like a basic thing to control in research studies, but it turns out humans vary widely in their level of activity. When the amount of exercise is controlled, the impact of the diet on weight is greatly diminished.

A more recent idea in dieting is "intermittent fasting," or time-restricted eating. It's the concept that eating in smaller windows of time, separated by periods of fasting (>12 hours), will aid in weight loss. The technique has received attention in recent years partly because it's easier to follow than complicated diets. There was also some preliminary evidence that it was effective in mice and humans. However, a 12-week randomized clinical trial on overweight and obese people did not replicate those early studies.[24] They found a modest decrease in weight loss for those in the time-restricted eating group, but it was not significantly different than the control group, who were told to eat three meals a day (with snacking permitted).

The larger point is that homeostasis is playing a role in weight control that is outside of our control. The word derives from the Greek words "homeo," meaning similar, and "stasis," meaning to stand still. In the field of weight control, homeostasis is an important part of understanding the problem because the body may be working against the dieter to maintain a certain set point.[25]

Using a scientific approach to weight loss means starting small, changing one behavior at a time, and measuring the change. Incremental changes in activity level and portion size, not major changes, like fasting every other day or training for your first marathon, will create the longest-lasting change. In addition, with so many high-calorie food choices in our society, cues like feeling hungry and full are the best guides to eating. Listen to yourself and respond when you sense it's time to stop.

RECAP

You're lucky to live sad moments even if you don't feel so lucky when they happen. They're an opportunity to be inspired. They're a chance to change things up. The sad moments can come in many forms. It could be someone making fun of you or ghosting you altogether. It could be the fear of missing out or the pain of eating terrible food. It seems our smartphones deliver sad moments at the swipe of a finger, even while you're having a great day. Sad moments are unavoidable in life sometimes.

The good news is you have a choice in how you're going to respond to these moments. Smartphones command your attention and the constant pull to respond immediately is there, but it doesn't have to be that way. When you're emotionally activated by the phone, choose to put it down, turn off the notifications, and help someone else. Better yet, you could tend to a garden and watch things that you planted grow up. You'll feel better and the world will be a brighter place. If you're plagued by negative thoughts and constantly assuming the worst, that's sad. If you take those thoughts and challenge them, neutralizing their impact, and gaining some control over them, that's a win.

Sad moments give rise to beautiful responses. If you lose weight on a diet and then gain it all back, that's a sad moment. However, if it gives rise to you never dieting again and choosing moderation, that's a positive. Employing an internal locus of control improves your well-being. If you're stuck in a lonely place in your life for long stretches, that can be sad. If you take that lonely feeling and explore activities, like writing, that are very difficult to do when you're around people, you may feel much differently about those moments. And if that writing gives rise to the next great play, song, or television show, you will definitely feel lucky to have lived that sad moment. You might even look forward to the next one. Life is disappointing, but there are moments when that's a wonderful thing.

CHAPTER 5

This Too Shall Pass

"This too shall pass. It may pass like a kidney stone, but it will pass."
~ Ruth Buzzi

It seems like every grandmother has a favorite saying. My Nana used to love to sing, "The old gray mare, she ain't what she used to be," in reference to herself. It's a line from an old-timey song about an aging horse. My Nana struggled with Alzheimer's dementia, and when she said those words, it was like her way of acknowledging it.

My wife's grandmother, affectionately known as GG, was fond of saying, "This too shall pass." It's a Persian adage that reflects on the temporary nature of life. I always took it to mean that whatever is bothering you at the moment will soon be gone. She was right, of course. Time passes, and our emotions change, leading to a sense that things weren't as bad as we thought. It's called hindsight bias in which we tend to perceive events that occurred as more predictable than they were when we lived them.

In the final months of GG's life, she dealt with a lot of nerve pain and breathing problems related to years of smoking. You could even see it on her face in photographs. She had a strained look that belied her usually energetic and upbeat personality. During one of our final visits, when she was struggling to stand up and move around, she said, "This too shall pass." That was the first time I didn't take it to mean her pain, but rather her life.

My wife loved GG more than anything, and when she passed away, I knew I wanted to do something to commemorate her life. I took my own advice and sat with the emotions for a bit, knowing I would probably get inspired at some point. When it was time to sell GG's home, my mother-in-law gave us two swivel chairs from her living room. The chairs used to sit in GG's sunroom, which was the place we often congregated and talked while we visited. Our kids liked to spin around in them until someone fell off laughing. It was the day I brought the chairs into our house that the inspiration hit me.

I realized that I needed to create a calm space in our home, similar to what we had enjoyed at GG's, and the swivel chairs were the perfect impetus to start it. The room would be the place to sit, read, talk, meditate, or just spin.

Our house has a sprawling first floor with six separate rooms, including the kitchen, which is next to a small room with a fireplace. My wife never liked the idea of the wood burning smell inside our house, so we never lit a fire in it. There was a desk and shelf for books, but no one ever sat in the room. We stored some things in there, but it never had much of a purpose. As I rolled GG's swivel chairs into the room, I realized a renovation would be the perfect gift!

The first move was to convert the wood burning fireplace to gas, so we could turn it on with the click of a button. I did not realize how involved this decision would be. There were permits and inspections for electric, gas, and fire. It turns out, you can't just make a homemade gas fireplace like it's a treehouse. I got the room painted, and it took months, but every time I got frustrated, I would repeat, "This too will pass." Soon enough, the day arrived when all I had to do was press a button, and voila! The room warmed up like an electric blanket. It's a small space, and with the heat, it became a toasty room.

When my wife saw the room for the first time, it was like one of those reveals on a home improvement show. Her face lit up as if I had turned her ranch into a three-story colonial. It meant so much. I always knew GG was like a second mother to her, but there was something about her passing away that inspired me. Today, there's a prominently displayed photograph of GG, my wife, her mother, and our daughter in a picture frame that reads, "Four Generations." Above the fireplace, I found the perfect sign, which reads "This Too Shall Pass."

TRY THIS: Memorial Project

It's never too late to commemorate someone you've lost. It could be a family member, a friend, or a coach. Think of a person who made a big impact on your life and changed you for the better. Is there a project dedicated to their memory that you could take part in? My

Uncle Vic (we had like nine Vics in my family) hit the first home run in the first season of the Collingswood, New Jersey Little League. His son dedicated a plaque in his honor at the ballfield. It required permission and a little money, but it was a wonderful ceremony honoring his dad's life. It doesn't have to be for the deceased either. Perhaps there's a teacher who inspired you, and you want the world to know. In college, a fellow student and I offered to make dinner for our favorite professor. I made gnocchi al pesto, and he loved it. We'd never seen him so happy before. You might not have an extra room lying around to spruce up, but perhaps there's a shelf or a wall that would be a perfect spot. Having something you look at every day can add emotional value to your home.

Brain Matters:
Older People and Coping

In the story above, an older person delivered the advice "this too shall pass" to younger people. It begs the question, "Are older people better at coping?" It's difficult to examine the question because scientists for years lacked a situation that was sufficiently stressful and common across the population. The pandemic provided an unprecedented opportunity to measure extreme stress and whether older people were better at dealing with it.

In a study performed during the early months of the pandemic, 945 Americans aged 18 to 76, were surveyed to assess the frequency and intensity of a range of emotions, from positive to negative.[1] It was the case that older people were at a much higher risk of getting sick and dying of COVID-19 compared to younger people, so presumably, their emotions would be worse. However, the results showed that age was associated with relatively greater emotional well-being, even when variables like personality, health, and demographics were controlled. Older people indicated experiencing more "positive states," like being relaxed, amused, happy, and peaceful, and fewer "negative states," such as frustrated, irritated, and sad. These results were confirmed by a similar study done in Canada on 800 adults.[2]

The fact that older people fared much better emotionally than young people during the early months of the pandemic does not rule out the day-to-day differences that could be responsible. Younger people are more likely to have young children around the house, suffer from unemployment, and have less money in savings. Older people may have also been more able to pay for delivery and stay comfortable at home. However, the results suggest that older people might be employing strategies that help them preserve well-being better than younger people. Perhaps sage advice that "this too shall pass," might be part of a broader way of perceiving pain, loss, and failure that allows older people to be more resilient.

Depression Versus Disappointment

"I had a privileged life. And I got lucky. And I'm unhappy."
~ Bo Burnham

In a book on disappointment, it's essential to examine depression because there is a big difference between the two. One involves negative moods, like sadness or anger, which can be temporarily debilitating. The other one is depression. Depression is a multi-headed beast that can hit anyone, regardless of gender, race, religion, education level, or wealth. It can leave you with little energy to do anything, even get out of bed. It took a speaker friend of mine with boundless energy on stage and reduced him to someone sleeping 16 hours a day. His major goal was to go outside for a walk, but he would end up convincing himself he would do it if he just got a good night's sleep. Disappointment, on the other hand, might bring you down for a bit, but then can give rise to inspired work. It could trigger depression in those susceptible to mental illness, but in an otherwise healthy person, it can produce tremendous energy.

This is not to say those suffering from depression can't produce inspired work. Just look at the paintings of Vincent Van Gough or the music of Ludwig van Beethoven to appreciate what those with depression can do. It's just important to distinguish between depression and disappointment because they can look quite similar at first. Generally, the depressed brain has a much tougher time thinking creatively, being flexible, or exerting effort. The disappointed brain tends to be distracted and emotional but soon quite focused.

Disappointment: Mine

The first eight weeks of the pandemic, and hopefully it's the only one I ever have to live through, was the darkest period of my adult life, as it was for many people. My suffering was multifaceted. I was the father worried about not being able to provide for his family, the man who lost his professional identity, and the husband who felt emasculated. My mood was so low that I had a hard time appreciating all the social support around me. I was in denial over being an economic victim of the virus and would become agitated at people who suggested quick fixes to my situation.

I was dealing with all of these feelings while being pulled in the direction of overseeing remote school for my kids. Their teachers were wonderful, but they had never taught distance learning, and it fell on me to get my 2nd and 4th graders to finish assignments. There was minimal remote teaching going on in the district, so it was often only me trying to teach math or language arts. My wife was working, and I wasn't initially, so it fell to me.

My thoughts would go like this all day, "How will we pay our bills? Did my son finish his self-portrait for art? Is this the end of my career? What should I do with them for gym class?" These thoughts would race through my head all day long. I found myself being "busily bored," trying to help the kids complete their work with half my brain on my business. As terrible as it was, I was privileged to not have to leave my house. I was neither an essential worker nor a first responder. I was fortunate. And I was miserable.

As the weeks went by, I applied for all economic disaster assistance available to me and waited. I knew that live performances, like the ones I was accustomed to doing, would not be allowed for a long time, probably not until a vaccine was available. I had prepared myself financially for a disruption in income. The off-and-on nature of speaking work and the unpredictable nature of our country's president at the time motivated me to take out a business loan in case of emergency. I was prepared, but it sure didn't feel like it. My mind started to produce the thought, "My family would be better off with me dying of coronavirus and them collecting the life insurance policy." Like I said, it was a dark time.

As March slowly became April and then May, I felt more and more cynical about my life and our country. I had people telling me it would be fine, but the negative voice in my head didn't believe them. My friends reached out to offer their support and even try to get me speaking work. I was flattered by their efforts, but my mood was still down. I was so bummed that my accountant said to me, "We've got to keep you happy, Matt. You're a motivational speaker. If we can't keep you upbeat, we're f'ed."

In the eighth week, everything changed. One day, I noticed my bank account had increased. I had to refresh the screen because I thought it was a mistake. A deposit from the Economic Injury Disaster Loans (EIDL) program had arrived and I hadn't been notified. I had applied the first week of the shutdown but hadn't heard an update since. I was so excited because it was money I didn't have to pay back. A few hours later, an email came in from my bank letting me know that my PPP (Paycheck Protection Program) money was approved. Again, this is money that I didn't have to pay back. Most importantly, that same week, I booked a few virtual presentations. Suddenly there were signs of life in my business. The cavalry had arrived! Overnight, my relentless fear of losing everything had abated. My mood picked up. I had more energy and a more positive outlook. GG was right: this, too, had passed.

What I just described was an example of my intense disappointment, which lasted for eight weeks. When my situation changed, my mood changed. That's not being depressed. I had a depressed mood but not a clinical condition. I was adjusting to some negative life events, which was completely understandable. My life wasn't suddenly perfect. The pandemic was still raging, but at least I was more productive and less agitated. Depression is a different story.

Depression: Drew's Story

An actor and comedian I met named Drew suffered from debilitating depression. I'm told he was a fun-loving guy in high school, playing sports and cracking jokes, but during college, he gained a lot of weight and seemed to lose interest in many of the things he used to enjoy. After college, he had a hard time holding down a job or making enough money to get his own apartment. He tried psychotherapy and medication, but they only helped for a little while.

In the late 2000s, he began doing stand-up comedy in New York City. One night we were on the same show at Stand-Up New York on the Upper West Side. Drew and I were hanging out before the show with another comic. When he got introduced and made his way on stage, the other comedian said to me, "I've got to get away from that guy. His negative energy just brings me down." I felt terrible for Drew because, at that moment, he seemed the most upbeat I'd ever seen him.

A year or two later, his treatment was going better, and it seemed his depression was improving. His affect wasn't as flat as it had been, and he was getting on stage more frequently. He had even produced a one-man show about his condition called "Clinical Depression (The Funny Kind)." I went to see it on the night it debuted, and it was great. Watching a room full of people laughing and enjoying material about his depression was a moving experience. It was as if the depression had been holding down his creativity.

I imagined how he could market the show for college students as a humorous and educational program on mental health awareness. "Drew could tour the country and make a huge impact," I exclaimed. I shared my thoughts with him and even offered to help him get into the speaking circuit. He seemed genuinely interested and excited at the idea. A few weeks passed by, and nothing ever came of it. I called. He never called me back. I asked a mutual friend why Drew hadn't followed up with me, and he gave me that shrug of not knowing. Drew was doing menial jobs that he didn't like. I suspect he wanted very badly to see his show help others. As the saying goes, opportunity knocks, but it won't kick the door down. How did he not follow up? It didn't make sense.

One of the hallmarks of depression is an unexplained lack of motivation. When a person desperately wants to make a change but cannot find the will to do it, that's an indication that larger forces are at work. Sadly, Drew took his own life in 2018. It was shocking but not surprising all at the same time. He had tried many treatments, but the condition persisted. I suspect Drew suffered many disappointments along the way. Even if his one-man show was a huge success, I suspect it would not have changed his outcome. Disappointment is situational, depression is global and long term. I was disappointed by the pandemic, but Drew had depression. It's not to say that depression cannot be treated. It's not to say you can't be creative while going through the ups and downs of depression, but it's just different.

Depressive Disorders

"Depression is the greatest acting teacher in the world. I can smile through anything. I just want the ground to open up and swallow me whole."
~ Anonymous

Depression is feeling hopeless, but even more, it's feeling that you're helpless. Depression is the inability to enjoy the things you used to enjoy. Depression involves feelings of worthlessness. It results in the inability to think or concentrate. It can result in you thinking about taking your own life. It can lead to you actually taking your own life. Depression is also so much more. If you experience any of these symptoms, it's not a level of suffering that you should be okay with.

The manual that psychologists and psychiatrists refer to when diagnosing is called the DSM-V (Diagnostic and Statistical Manual of Mental Disorders, Fifth Edition) and defines depression as a common and serious mood disorder. Diagnosis is more involved than you might think because you could have one of several possible conditions. There are thirty pages worth of depressive disorders in DSM-V, a book with more pages than the Bible but thicker paper.

Let's look at one condition called Major Depressive Disorder. The diagnostic criteria requires that you have five or more of the following symptoms present during a two-week period. It has to represent a change from your previous functioning, and one of the symptoms has to be a depressed mood or loss of interest in things you used to enjoy. To put it another way, the person can't be walking around with depression, saying, "I'm totally depressed, but my mood is good and I can't wait to play hockey later!"

Criterion 1: Depressed mood (e.g., feeling hopeless or empty) most of the day, nearly every day. This one can be reported by either the subject or by others close to the subject. Note, in children or teens, it could present as irritability instead of sadness and tears. I know that sounds like all teens, but if it's happening nearly every day, it's a problem. The next time a teenager responds to you in an unusually angry way, it could be the depression talking. This might explain a lot of angry posts on social media, which doesn't excuse the behavior but makes me feel some compassion for them.

Criterion 2: Diminished interest or pleasure in all, or almost all, activities most of the day, nearly every day. The clinical term for this is anhedonia, which sounds like a country in Northern Europe. It's not, that's Estonia. Knowing and pronouncing that word (an-he-doe-nee-a) correctly will either make you sound smart or like a know-it-all. It's a fine line. What's also a fine line is diagnosing anhedonia because sometimes it can look like someone changing their mind.

I do life coaching with some local high school students. One young man, let's call him Dom, was brought in by his mother complaining that he doesn't want to do any of the activities he used to do. Dom is a talented two-sport athlete, but in his senior year said, "I just don't care about sports anymore." He has friends who want to hang out with him, but he blows them off a lot. When asked about it, he says, "I guess it's just as good to play video games remotely with them, but lately, I don't even want to do that."

Dom's overly involved mother has been known to go to great lengths to get him involved in activities anyway. She has signed him up for sports camps without asking him and even invited his friends over once, but telling him at the last second so he couldn't cancel. It was the opposite of what my brother used to do as a teenager. He liked to ask my mom if he could go out with friends, and of course, she would say no because he had just gotten into trouble, and he responded, "Well, it's too late. They're in the driveway!" It even worked a few times.

What separates Dom from a kid expressing a preference for one activity over another is that he hasn't replaced the old activities with anything new. When he told me that he no longer enjoys video games, it screamed "anhedonia." This is a kid who reported loving video games a year or so earlier, even wanting to be a professional gamer at one point. He played them more than he played sports. For him to tell me, with a very flat affect, "Lately video games just don't do for me anymore," I knew it was time for him to seek treatment beyond life coaching. I spoke to his pediatrician, and he suggested treatment for mild to moderate depression.

Criterion 3: Significant weight loss (when not dieting) or weight gain. If you're looking for a number, it would be losing or gaining five percent of body weight in a month. That's almost ten pounds for an average man. You also need a decrease (or increase) in appetite nearly every day.

Criterion 4: Insomnia (too few zzzs) or hypersomnia (too many zzzs) nearly every day. The lack of sleep could take the form of waking up in the middle of the night, ruminating about your life, and not being able to fall back asleep. It's hard to imagine getting too much sleep, but if you're regularly in bed for more than ten or eleven hours a night, and you're not a toddler, you should be concerned.

The speaker friend of mine mentioned above is a good example. He noticed it as a change in his normal functioning but couldn't "snap out of it." Some friends and family love to impart trite suggestions like that, especially when they've never been depressed. A comedian friend of mine's mother found out he was taking antidepressants, and she said, "You don't need medication, just take a long walk and eat a meatball sandwich." He said, "Mom, I can't walk off depression."

Criteria 5-9: For the sake of time and to keep you from catching zzzs right now, I've consolidated the following five criteria: physical agitation, lack of energy, feelings of worthlessness or guilt, reduced ability to think, and recurring thoughts of death. That last one isn't just a fear of death but rather recurrent thoughts of suicide, a specific plan, or an attempt. Depression does not always have to do with suicide, and suicide can occur in people who show no signs of depression. That's what makes it such a challenge to prevent.

There are some caveats, including you must be experiencing significant distress. That means if you have a depressed mood and meet the criteria for at least four others, but it's not bothering that much or interfering with functioning at work or school, then you don't have a major depressive disorder. You might one day in the future when another stressor comes along, like a pandemic, and pushes you over the edge.

What's important to know is that diagnosis is not an exact science. I often question the value of the diagnosis and label put on a person. Mental health professionals don't have a blood test for depression-like influenza, so there are inaccurate diagnoses. It's especially tough when you're trying to diagnose a child or teenager. What looks like one thing at age 12 could end up being something else by age 18. The point is if you're concerned about yourself, a loved one, or a friend, encourage them to seek the help of a qualified mental health professional who takes the time to listen to you.

Here's a summary of the symptoms of depression versus the experience of disappointment. It's important to note that since disappointment is not a recognized condition, there aren't an empirically based set of symptoms. In my research for this book, I have found some common reactions to disappointing events that appear to impact most people I've interviewed.

The Difference Between Depression and Disappointment

Symptom	Depression	Disappointment
Mood	Depressed mood for more than 2 weeks; Irritable for children and teens	Less than 2 weeks
Sleep	Too much/not enough	Disturbed, less than 2 weeks
Concentration	Difficulty concentrating	Difficulty concentrating
Self-esteem	Feelings of worthlessness	Feelings of worthlessness
Change in appetite	Eating too much or loss of appetite	Eating too much/not enough
Interest	Lack of interest in activities	Lack of interest in activities
Suicidality	Thoughts or attempts, possible	Thoughts possible, but attempts rare
Activity Level	Restlessness/slowness	Restlessness, less than 2 weeks

---

Brain Matters:
Treatment for Depression

Depressive disorders are a major concern for public health in the United States. According to the National Institute of Mental Health, 17.3 million adults in the United States had at least one major depressive episode in the past year, which represents about 7 percent of the population (8.7 percent for females over age 18 and 5.3 percent of males). About one-third of cases are considered to be treatment-resistant. As a result, the need for evidence-based fast-acting treatments for depression has never been greater.

A systematic review to determine the efficacy of brief psychotherapy (i.e., ≤ 8 sessions) for depression found that therapy, consisting of either cognitive behavioral therapy (CBT), problem-solving therapy, or mindfulness-based cognitive therapy, was effective in the case of any of the three.[3] There was a small but significant effect in as few as six sessions in the case of CBT. Ideally, therapy would last as long as it takes, but when resources are limited, it is helpful to know that even a brief course of treatment can make an impact on the acute phase of the disorder.

The most effective approach appears to be the combination of psychotherapy and medication. A systematic review of 32 studies on the combination of psychotherapy plus medication, found sufficient evidence that combined treatment is superior for major depression.[4] They also found that the effects remained up to two years after treatment. The authors concluded that treatment with medication alone might not be the most optimal care for depression.

No discussion about depression is complete without mentioning suicide. There is a commonly held perception that talking about suicide or asking questions can increase suicidal tendencies, especially among teenagers. One study examined this myth by reviewing published literature on whether talking about suicide brings on suicidal ideation in adults and adolescents. They found no statistically significant increase in suicidal ideation among participants when asked about suicidal thoughts.[5] In fact, they concluded the opposite. Talking about suicide may reduce rather than increase suicidal thoughts and may lead to a greater likelihood of seeking treatment.

If you feel that you may be depressed, please seek help. You don't have to go it alone. Talk therapy is effective for the treatment of depression and it's non-invasive! That's the best part. It only requires that you be as open and honest as possible with your therapist. I'm partial to clinical psychologists who were trained in CBT and use a research-based approach. You can find a CBT therapist near you at the Association for Behavioral and Cognitive Therapies website, www.findcbt.org. If you can't find one near you, make sure you seek out a licensed and qualified therapist who treats depression, listens well, and shows empathy and compassion for you. Online therapy has also become an increasingly popular option and emerged during the pandemic. The most well-known at this point is TalkSpace.com, which offers to connect you with a licensed therapist anywhere, anytime.

–·–

TRY THIS: **Six Ways to Cope with Negative Moods**

Whether you're experiencing a short-term bout of disappointment or facing treatment for a Major Depressive Disorder, there are things you can try that have been shown to improve your mood. This list is not a panacea, but I would treat them like mini experiments. Try each one out, rating your mood before and after to see what impact they have.

1) Exercise

At the risk of giving advice like, "Take a walk and eat a meatball sandwich," there is something to exercise and mood. In fact, any therapist worth their degree is going to recommend that you start moving your body. Treating a depressed mood requires action, but when you're feeling down, this can seem impossible. Exercise seems similar to tasting nasty medicine when you don't want to do it. It's counterintuitive, but when you're exhausted, exercise increases your energy level and improves your mood.

There is considerable evidence that exercise can be used as a behavioral treatment to improve symptoms of depression. One study looked at 30 moderately depressed men and women and randomly assigned them to an exercise group, a social support group, or a wait-list control group. In the exercise group, participants walked 20 to 40 minutes, three times per week for six weeks, and showed significant alleviation of symptoms of depression.[6]

A longer-term study looked at the impact of a 12-week aerobic fitness program on psychological well-being a year later.[7] They found psychological improvements over the initial 12 weeks of the fitness program compared to a control group. At the one-year follow-up, psychological benefits remained from where they were at the beginning. Interestingly, the exercise group did not increase the amount of weekly exercise they performed over the yearlong follow-up period. Therefore, maintaining a regular fitness program can have long-term psychological benefits.

A meta-analysis of 37 studies on exercise and psychological well-being examined many different hypotheses as to why exercise seems beneficial.[8] They ranged from how exercise is a positive distraction to exercise endorphin release and what is known as the monoamine hypothesis. That last one states that exercise leads to an increase in the availability of monoamines, which are brain neurotransmitters such as serotonin, dopamine, glutamate, and others. These neurotransmitters are all known to diminish during bouts of depression. A number of studies found evidence for an increase of these neurotransmitters in plasma and urine following exercise, which was linked to improvements in symptoms of depression.

2) Maximize Your Light Intake

In the winter months, when there are fewer hours of sun, you need to find a way to increase your light exposure. Sunlight increases the production of serotonin in our brains, which is known to boost your mood and help you feel calm.

In December 2017, I took my wife on a trip to Spokane, Washington, in early December. It was her birthday, and what woman doesn't want to go to Spokane for her birthday? The worst part wasn't that I was working half the time, it was the fact that the sun set at 3:58 pm! Only 8 hours and 33 minutes of sunlight in the day! My serotonin levels were bumming after a few days, but there was a silver lining. It was holiday time, and Spokane is one of the best places to see holiday lights, especially in nearby Coeur d'Alene, Idaho. I'll bet those two things are probably related.

If you cannot move to Yuma, Arizona, one of the sunniest places in the United States, there are some things you can do. Try to go to bed earlier and wake up at sunrise. Even thirty minutes can make a big difference. In addition, walk a dog, hike with friends or do some gardening during the day. Few things are happening outside in the winter, so you've got to create opportunities. Runners, thanks to the body-heat-generating nature of the sport, seem to gather in all weather. In fact, there is probably a run club or a 5K race near you. If you do start a new habit of being more active outside every day, pay attention to your mood. One way I know my mood has been improved by something is when I start looking forward to doing it again the next day.

You can also try increasing the amount of natural light in your room and workplace by opening blinds and sitting near a window when you work. If all else fails, try buying a natural spectrum energy lamp (aka a light box). Bed Bath and Beyond sells one for under $40. Just fifteen minutes each morning in front of the light has been shown to improve mood for hours.

3) Increase Incidental Social Contact

The power of positive social support is impressive, but did you know even a little bit can make a big difference? The random social interactions of daily living, which are easy to take for granted, can improve your mood. The ten-second conversation you have with the cashier or checking in with your neighbor might not seem like much, but remove it, and you will feel it.

Incidental social interaction is one of the reasons that I loved living in New York City. On the surface, it feels like such an impersonal place, but in my neighborhood, I was constantly seeing the same people. It's not unusual to stop by the neighborhood grocery store or ice cream place every day because you're walking around already. Before long, I developed friendships with one or two people at each place. They knew me, and they knew my family. It's hard to imagine unless you live in a small town, but it was such a boost to my mood. Also, the people-watching was fascinating.

As comedian David Cross put it, "In New York, you are constantly faced with this very urgent, quick decision that you have to make about every 20 minutes. And it doesn't matter where you are—indoors, outdoors, in a park, in a museum, in a restaurant ... about every 20 minutes, immediately, you have to go, [gasp] 'Oh my God. Do I look at the most beautiful woman in the world or the craziest guy in the world? Look at her, she's beautiful! But look at him, he's wearing orange footie pajamas, and he's got tinfoil on his head, and he's playing a Casio!'"

There are two reasons that this incidental social contact can improve mood. The first is the conversations that happen are a welcome distraction from the thoughts in my head. If I'm having a bad day and I'm suddenly talking to someone about their life, I get a break from mine. The other reason is novelty. In a big city, you're exposed to lots of stimulation that engages the senses. One time I saw a man riding an elliptical bike. It was a standing bike, for lack of a better description. He was so high off the ground, it made me laugh out loud. I was afraid he might hit his head on a bridge. I also noticed how I completely forgot what else was going on in my mind before I saw that guy.

4) Pet an Animal

Petting an animal releases the hormone oxytocin in the brain, which increases feelings of connectedness. It could be a dog, a willing cat, or even a guinea pig. Oxytocin is a neuropeptide produced in the hypothalamus, deep inside the brain. It's known to stimulate milk ejection during breastfeeding and uterine contractions during labor, but it's also released when petting a dog.[9,10] In fact, dog owners who gaze into the eyes of their pet for 30 minutes had a 300 percent increase in oxytocin compared to non-dog owners.[11] They even found the dogs experienced a 130 percent increase in oxytocin levels!

During the pandemic, I was desperate for ideas for my daughter's 8th birthday. So many had been canceled or were over Zoom, but I wanted to find another way. It was one of those parenting moments where I thought, "What are we going to do? She loves puppies, but she's not ready for a dog yet. I wonder if I can hire puppies for the party?" It turns out you can! A local woman brought her Cocker Spaniels, who were therapy dogs for anxious kids. We invited my daughter's closest friends (in masks and socially distant), and they each took turns petting and playing with all the puppies. It was a huge success. She hugged me after and called me the best dad ever! Of course, three hours later, when it was time to get off a screen and go to bed, I was back to being "the meanest." Life is disappointing after all.

5) Appreciating Art

Inspiring works of art can change how we feel. A beautiful painting can transport us to another place and time. A meaningful song can conjure up emotions from the past. A great movie can motivate you to take action in the present. How many people started running after watching *Rocky*? Notice I said running because if there's one thing Rocky Balboa didn't do in that movie was teach you how to fight. His idea of blocking a punch was throwing his face at it.

As an adult, stand-up comedy is my favorite art form. It's been called the poor man's theater. Laughter is the ultimate way to elevate my mood. Few things compare to telling a joke and getting a laugh. Eddie Murphy, one of the biggest comedians on the planet when I was a kid, grew up with an alcoholic father. He witnessed the power of comedy when talking about his family problems on stage.

When you grow up in an environment with alcohol or other drugs, either you learn how to make it funny to survive or you start using yourself. In a recent interview, he said, "I never drank. I don't drink. Some people wind up drinking. I went the other way. Not for me."

One of his most memorable stand-up bits was called "Drunk Father," where he mocks his inebriated dad from the stage. Murphy said, "Whenever I would do him on stage, nobody would be laughing harder than my mother, because it was true. My dad had a drinking problem. There could be ten thousand people, and my mother would be screaming the loudest. Because of that, my dad stopped drinking." That's a powerful statement for how art can be motivating.

6) Better Nutrition

A Mediterranean diet is associated with better heart health but also improved mental health. The theory being that a diet rich in mono- and polyunsaturated fats—as opposed to saturated and trans fats—which can lead to clogged arteries and heart disease, reduces inflammation. Specifically, the diet includes fruits, vegetables, extra virgin olive oil, fish, yogurt, small amounts of nuts, legumes, and grass-fed meats. I just learned what a legume is (peas and beans), and I think my mood went up a little!

An Australian study looked at the impact of dietary change on 150 adults with depression.[12] The study enlisted two females to every male, which reflected the proportion of depression in the general population. Participants were put into two groups, the diet change group or a control group. The diet change group was given cooking workshops over the course of three months and received nightly food baskets providing them with ingredients such as extra virgin olive oil, fruit, nuts, tomatoes, legumes, and tuna. In addition, they were provided with Omega-3 fatty acid supplements in the form of fish oil.

Three months after the study, assessments of mental health, quality of life, and diet were done. The diet change group was eating more fruit, nuts, and other items from a Mediterranean diet than the control group. Also, there was evidence of significant improvement in mental health and quality of life compared to the control group. In the six-month follow-up, they found that these mood improvements were maintained, along with less intake of fast food and snacks of limited nutritional value. The authors concluded that learning basic cooking skills paired with nutrition training was empowering, which in itself was a mood boost.

Challenge Cognitive Distortions

Now that you've had some exposure to the idea of documenting thoughts and feelings in the previous chapter, it's time to take it to the next level. Whether you're experiencing depression or disappointment, it can cast a negative light on everything. Your facial expressions can flatten, your tone of voice can sound agitated, and word choice can become more negative. In psychology, the term *cognitive distortion* is used to define thoughts that are negatively biased, and more importantly, inaccurate. One of the ways to address it is by raising your awareness of it so that you can self-monitor it in the future.

Imagine you're at a social gathering, and a person exclaims, "What beautiful weather we're having today!" The depressed brain shoots back, "It's about time. Last week's rain storm was a disaster." It may have been the case that the storm was pretty bad, but matching an upbeat comment with a negative might not be the most socially appropriate response. A buddy of mine, Comedian Ted Alexandro, refers to these people as "downgraders" in conversation. Some people upgrade in conversation. "How are you?" You respond, "Pretty good." They respond, "Great!" That's the upgrade. The downgrade goes, "How are you?" You respond, "Great!" They respond, "Okay, okay." It's as if they're saying, "Take it down a notch, buddy."

If you think you might be a "downgrader," there is something important to remember. The thoughts produced by your brain are often not meant to be believed or shared with the world. It could be your cognitive distortion talking. It's likely part of a pattern that has become automatic and may have even served you well sometimes, but you want to be a more positive person. The key exercise for you is to identify the negative thoughts and replace them with more balanced thoughts. Here are some examples of distortions and their counters:

Cognitive Distortion	Negative Thought	Counter Thought
Overgeneralizing	"Nothing ever works out for me!"	"I didn't work this time, but it might the next time."
	"I can't do anything right!"	"If I keep trying, I'm sure I can get it right."
All-or-Nothing	"If I don't succeed, I'm a total failure."	"I'm sure there are plenty of paths to success."
	"If I don't get this, I'll never be happy."	"There are lots of things in the world that can make me happy."
Catastrophizing	"This is the worst thing ever!"	"This feels bad now, but I can handle it."
	"What a nightmare!"	"This too shall pass."

Anxiety

During the first few months of the COVID-19 pandemic, one of the most common mental health complaints was increased anxiety. A 2020 article in *Psychiatric Quarterly*, which I'm sure you read every quarter, found that emergency room visits for psychiatric conditions increased by 52 percent. Gee, I can't imagine why. They only asked people not to leave home, except to go food shopping, wear a mask, and wipe down the mail with antibacterial wipes that could be found nowhere. If that wasn't bad enough, we were told that diarrhea could be a symptom of coronavirus. As the economy was collapsing, who didn't have a bit of diarrhea?

In the greater New York City area, we're used to mass hysteria. Every winter, when the forecast includes snowstorms predicted to dump three or four inches of snow, people respond by emptying out supermarkets. They act like twelve hours in the house is going to turn into the movie *Alive* with people resorting to cannibalism if they don't get milk and eggs.

It's all relative, though. People in Minnesota must laugh at three inches, while those in Georgia wonder whether their school might need to be closed for the week. I would say the response to COVID seemed similar. Rural states chuckled and initially thought it was a hoax to bring down the President. Other places, like Rhode Island, tried to ban New Yorkers from visiting their states. It was unsuccessful because it's illegal. If that was legal, I'm sure New Englanders would have been banning New Yorkers long ago.

The anxiety response was designed for real threats, including pandemics, tornados, and charging tigers. There is no question that anxiety feels bad with the pounding heart, sweaty palms, and chest tightness. However, humans evolved this response as an early warning system to sense that something is wrong. It's like the emotional equivalent to a horrendous smell. Your brain wants you to avoid eating it, so the smell is noxious.

Anxiety can be more of a friend than an enemy if it's used to help you get back on track. Anxiety becomes a problem when it defies logic. If your alarm bells are going off over something benign or in the middle of your sleep, you've got a problem. Experiencing anxiety before a big game is a lot different than being stuck in the locker room having a full-on panic attack.

It has been heartening for me that more young people talk and write about anxiety and their anxiety disorders in recent years because it finally feels like people are taking it seriously. During the pandemic, I felt like the mental health aspect of it was at least a consistent story. During the Spanish Flu pandemic of 1918, little was written about mental health in popular or scientific literature, according to Greg Eghigian's 2020 article in the *Psychiatric Times*. That's despite the fact that the suicide rate rose during that year.

The biggest myth concerning anxiety is that there is not much a person can do about it. It is the most highly treatable psychological condition. The best way to curb it is to learn how to control your breathing. That sounds like a simplistic approach to dealing with anxiety and panic, but it turns out breathing deeply and slowly helps the nervous system reset itself to pre-anxiety levels. This book has lots of different breathing exercises to practice. They are best done when you're calm, so they can be put to work effortlessly when you're not.

Brain Matters:
Panic Disorder

Panic disorder is one of the most common anxiety disorders with a lifetime prevalence rate between two to five percent. Nearly one-quarter of adolescents aged 13 to 17 report some form of anxiety.[13] In the DSM-V, panic disorder is defined as having chronic unexpected panic attacks and persistent worry and concern for at least a month. The hallmark of this condition, like so many, is that there is a change in a person's functioning and quality of life.[14]

The physical symptoms of a panic attack include rapid heartbeat, chest or stomach pain, difficulty breathing, weakness or dizziness, sweating, feeling hot or a cold chill, and tingly or numb hands. These can happen anytime, anywhere, and can happen without warning. They can even wake someone from a deep sleep. They are more common in women than men and typically begin in young adulthood.

Anxiety disorders, including panic, are passed down through genes. In an interesting study on the genetic risk of panic disorder, researchers examined patients and their families for sensitivity to carbon dioxide. A panic attack can be induced by increasing the amount of carbon dioxide in the air to 35 percent. The study noted that most people who suffer from panic disorder will experience an attack when they inhale these high levels of carbon dioxide, though healthy volunteers without a history of panic will not. In addition, relatives of panic disorder patients were shown to experience panic while breathing in high carbon dioxide, even if they have never suffered from an anxiety disorder.[15] This reaction suggests a physiological mechanism for how panic is genetically passed on.

—·—

The Combo: Anxiety and Depression

It seems to me that anxiety is easier for people to talk about these days, especially young people. It's almost like stress is a badge of honor for being busy. I don't see this as much with other mental health disorders, like depression, even though they co-occur so often. In fact, nearly 60 percent of the people diagnosed with anxiety will go on to have symptoms of depression. These illnesses are considered "comorbid," which sounds like two people dying together, but it's not. That would be co-mortal.

You might think it sounds like the exception to have two conditions occurring at the same time, but it's more of the rule. According to the National Alliance on Mental Health, up to 93 percent of the patients using Medicare to pay for treatment have four or more comorbid conditions. Here's a comparison of the symptoms of both major depression and generalized anxiety disorder, a condition with similar symptoms of panic disorder.

Symptom	Major Depression	Generalized Anxiety Disorder
Mood	Depressed mood for more than 2 weeks; Irritable for children and teens	Irritability
Sleep	Too much/not enough	Hyperactive at times
Concentration	Difficulty concentrating	Difficulty concentrating
Self-esteem	Feelings of worthlessness	Feelings of insecurity
Change in appetite	Eating too much or loss of appetite	Loss of appetite
Interest	Lack of interest in activities	Excessive worrying
Suicidality	Thoughts or attempts possible	Thoughts and attempts possible
Activity Level	Restlessness or slowness	Restlessness or slowness due to muscle tension

On the surface, anxiety and depression can seem so different from each other, but the symptoms have more overlap than you think. Take facial expressions. An anxious person might appear hypervigilant with eyes wide open, but others wear a flat expression on their face. Those who struggle with depression also have a flat expression on their face. Another example of overlap is what I like to call someone's internal motor. An anxious person may have racing thoughts, and their speech is so rapid it seems pressured. Try listening to a person talking with pressured speech. It's like taking a drink from a fire hose. It's impossible to keep up! You don't often see that with people struggling from depression, but a depressed young person who is irritable might seem to be forcing words into a conversation and with a similar feel. In the end, it comes down to taking a thorough history and getting a complete picture of what's going on for someone.

- -

Brain Matters:
The Depressed and Anxious Brain

Prior to the accessibility of brain imaging techniques like functional MRI, it was assumed that the depressed brain lacked activation and the anxious brain had too much. It turns out both the depressed and the anxious brain display increased and sustained reactivity to emotional information. The theory is that a person with a brain that reacts strongly to emotional information is more likely to have problems with anxiety or depression.

The amygdala is a brain region known to process emotional information from the outside world (e.g., angry faces) and shares with neighboring brain regions that help integrate this data with other brain regions processing different emotional information (e.g., angry words). In studies examining the amygdala, there is evidence of increased activation in those struggling with depression and anxiety.[16,17,18] The conclusion is that these findings are consistent with the experience of there being some overlap in symptoms in anxiety and depression.

The concept of "this too shall pass" suggests if you do nothing, psychological distress will magically go away. Unfortunately, that's not the case, and you'll just be prolonging unnecessary suffering.

In a study that examined the amount of time it took for those with untreated mood and anxiety disorders to receive treatment, 729 outpatients with diagnoses ranging from major depressive disorder to generalized anxiety disorder were surveyed. Patients with major depressive disorder showed the shortest average duration before treatment at 39.08 months, while those with panic disorder went longer, an average of 44.35 months. That is surprising considering how acutely uncomfortable the symptoms of panic attacks can be, including chest tightness, increased heart rate, and sweating. Those with obsessive-compulsive disorder waited even longer at 90.57 months.[19]

Major depressive disorder can be highly recurrent, and the length of episodes can vary. The symptoms can worsen if left untreated and lead to significant impairment, self-harm, or suicide. People dealing with this disorder can experience partial or full remission. The risk factors for developing a recurrence include a history of other psychiatric conditions, family history of depression, personality, stressful life events, trauma, and lack of social support.[20] As a result, it is difficult to predict when a bout of depression will pass. Suffice it to say that seeking treatment is the best way to reduce the duration from onset of symptoms to partial or full remission.

Medication is effective in the treatment of depression, but research suggests those with severe depression show the greatest improvement.[21] That was the conclusion of a meta-analysis, which looked at hundreds of peer-reviewed research studies on the topic. To put it another way, the benefit of antidepressant medication increases with the severity of depression symptoms.

Going back to the concept of a psychological immune system, it's as if minor to moderate depression is more treatment resistant. It's like giving fever-reducing medicine to someone with a one-hundred-degree temperature and seeing no change, but that same medicine in someone with a one-hundred-and-four-degree temperature drops it to normal. If you're on the fence about treatment or unsure if you have a bad enough case, please consult your doctor. Don't assume any case is too minor to seek treatment. There are benefits of therapy that extend far beyond just symptom reduction.

—·—

Fame Too Shall Pass

In my career, I had the opportunity to perform in comedy clubs regularly for seven years. I began as an open mic comedian and worked my way up to a paid emcee and then a featured act, who performs about thirty minutes of material before the headliner. That spot is also called the middle, which is where the term "middling" in life comes from. It's not the spot you want to be stuck in your entire career, but some comics never move up.

My career in speaking and my growing family took me out of the scene before I got a chance to see if I could ascend to the headliner role. I'm fortunate that I get to do comedy for a living, albeit as a keynote speaker, but the skill set is similar. I do miss the rush of performing at comedy clubs. There was something seductive about a Saturday night show, packed house, and feeling great energy in the room. When you know people have been waiting all week to laugh, and now they've paid to have you deliver the laughs, it heightens your senses as a performer.

When I was starting out, it felt like a star could be born at any show. I could be at an open mic, and if a comedian did really well, I assumed they would be famous someday and wrote their name down. Of course, even when someone killed it, their life didn't immediately change. I did encounter a few comics who went on to become well known, but fame has so many levels that I'm not sure they would call themselves famous.

I never got into stand-up to become famous. Fame just never seemed that appealing to me. In public, celebrities look like caged animals being photographed at the zoo. It might start out exciting, but maintaining a high level of popularity in the fickle world of entertainment seems exhausting. It always struck me that the white-hot spotlight that gives attention could easily burn you or worse, turn off. The "this too shall pass" idea applies to those highest of high moments in life. They don't last forever, so it's important to be grateful for them when they arrive.

In my career, I've been recognized a few times, though I'm not sure if anyone remembers my name. I'm like a character actor from a film you kind of remember. One time, on a vacation in Aruba, I got recognized at the airport. We had just landed and a student from one of my programs came over with her mom and said, "I totally remember you from my school!" She got my autograph and left. Two minutes later, my wife returned from the bathroom, and I said, "You'll never believe what happened! I got recognized by a fan." She never believed me—to this day.

My favorite story of being recognized came in New York City in the late 2000s. I was in the tail end of my physical therapy following knee surgery when it happened. I was getting stretched out by the therapist on a row of tables when a woman getting stretched out next to me turned over and said, "You're Matt Bellace!" My therapist gave me a look that meant, "Are you someone I should know?" I looked back at her with that cool "I'm kind of a big deal" face and said, "It's okay, this happens all the time." It doesn't.

It turned out to be a mother of a high school student who attended one of my presentations and won a CD. That's how long ago it was— CDs were still a thing. I used to give out an audio recording of my live program as a thank you to those who volunteered to help me on stage. Her son got one and apparently listened to my CD so much in the car that she memorized the sound of my voice! I was blown away.

The whole thing might have gone to my head, except what happened next. I had biked to physical therapy that day and locked up my bike on a street sign near the entrance. As the mom and I walked out together, I'm sure she was looking around for my limousine when I unlocked my Trek, put on my helmet, and started pedaling. Nothing says "big star" more than rolling up your pant leg and biking against traffic on Third Avenue.

Brain Matters:
Pursuit of Fame and Mental Health

What does aspiration to be famous do to your mental health? In the 1990s, researchers at the University of Rochester conducted in-depth surveys of 100 adults, asking about their guiding principles, values, and aspirations in life. They compared those findings with measures of well-being, including vitality, anxiety, and depression.[22] Participants in the study who valued approval from other people, similar to being famous, reported significantly higher levels of distress than those who valued self-acceptance and friendship. When internal goals include self-acceptance, affiliation, community feeling, and physical health, there are higher levels of well-being.

SPOTLIGHT:
Paul Gilmartin, Comedian

When I was in graduate school, there was a show on the cable network TBS called Dinner and a Movie. It was made for people like me who lived alone and ate meals watching television. The co-hosts of the show were comedian Paul Gilmartin, who has the soothing voice of an NPR host, and actress Annabelle Gurwitch. Along with watching Seinfeld and cooking shows, it was one of the few guilty pleasures I afforded myself in an otherwise monk-like existence at the time.

In 2015, I got an opportunity to meet Paul in person as a guest on his podcast, The Mental Illness Happy Hour. He tapes the show in Los Angeles, so I visited during a speaking trip to the area. On my drive to meet him, I started thinking about how tough it must have been for him to achieve a certain level of fame and fortune, only to see it stop when the show finished. When I was performing in clubs, the ultimate goal for many of my peers was to have their own sitcom on network television. Today, the television landscape is completely different, with multiple streaming services and few viewers for each one. Even saying the word "sitcom" sounds like I'm talking about vaudeville or silent movies. At some point, if Paul has similar dreams to other comedians, he must have had a hard time coping with career disappointment.

It turns out the podcast was developed in response to Paul's desire to seek more connection than just doing stand-up or television. It's meant to be a part-humorous and part in-depth discussion of mental illness. As he says in the introduction, "It's not meant to be a substitute for professional mental counseling, it's more like a waiting room that doesn't suck." Paul is very open with his personal battles with addiction and depression.

During the podcast taping, I found him to be so honest and insightful about his own struggles, I had to reach out to him for this book. "People are quick to minimize those struggling with depression, despite never having experienced it themselves," Paul shared. It's true, depression gets dismissed for various reasons. Some assume they know what it is because they've experienced disappointment or they have been sad over a breakup, but it is simply not enough. "Thinking you understand clinical depression because you've experienced situational sadness is like thinking you know Italy because you've been to the Olive Garden," Paul joked.

"One of the things that often gets lost in discussions of depression," Paul explained, "is you know it's ridiculous while you're experiencing it." That statement reminded me of working with patients struggling with anxiety disorders, like obsessive compulsive disorder. They seemed acutely aware of how illogical their compulsions were, like touching a light switch ten times before leaving the room, but they still did it to avoid some imagined horrible consequence. The behavior reduced their anxiety, so it was rewarding to them, but it was so hard for them to stop doing it. Until I interviewed Paul, I hadn't heard anyone make that same statement about depression.

"For me, depression is a decline of my baseline mood—unrelated to what's going on around me." He continued, "I ask myself, am I still able to take pleasure in my normal hobbies, like guitar, seeing friends, or even smiling?" He's describing the experience of anhedonia, mentioned earlier, and is the inability to take pleasure in activities you used to enjoy. It's almost as if the feel-good chemical in the brain has run out. There's nothing left in the tank. "My favorite quote is, 'The opposite of depression is not happiness, it's vitality.'"

As someone in show business, Paul has seen his share of disappointments. His 16-year run on **Dinner and a Movie** was a hit for TBS. He was praised by a critic who called it "the first television show to combine well-worn theatrical movies, improvisational comedy, and culinary education. That, combined with his **Comedy Central Presents**, and you wouldn't blame him for thinking big things were about to happen. That might still happen, but they might not. That *feeling of uncertainty in the face of clear talent is challenging to accept.*

Paul maintains a positive outlook, "Almost every good thing I have in my life has come from something disappointing," he told me. He was speaking my language! "Disappointment forced me to learn, grow, and let go; let go of what my life could be like. It's an attitude thing," he said.

In speaking about what disappointment inspires, he said, "After my divorce, I built deeper friendships and opened up more." He explained that the gains he made weren't pain-free. "It brought up demons, like being forced to deal with being alone and dying alone. But I had lots of help. None of this was a genius insight in the first place." I disagree. I think Paul's genius was listening to others and being accepting of their help. He had a choice, and he decided to embrace the disappointment, learn from it, and propel himself to a better place.

Apropos to our discussion on anxiety and depression, here are some quotes from anonymous listeners to Paul's podcast Mental Illness Happy Hour *over the years:*

"Depression is anger without the enthusiasm."

"Depression means nothing matters, but I should be doing something important with my life."

"I want to bury myself in a pile of blankets and sleep forever."

"Anxiety is the feeling you get in your throat before you burst out in tears, but you can't cry."

"Anxiety is when your mind is an unreliable narrator."

"Having anxiety means gaslighting yourself."

RECAP

My wife's grandmother was right—the discomfort of a negative moment does not last forever. It's a comforting thought that disappointment gets better with time, but sadly some pain does not go away so easily. Anxiety and depression are longer-term struggles, but they don't have to be afflictions that only pass when you do. There are empirically-based effective treatments, such as cognitive behavioral therapy with medication, that can reduce symptoms and improve the quality of your life.

If we're fostering an internal locus of control, there are activities that we can do to boost our mood. Being active outdoors, increasing our exposure to light and incidental social contacts are reliably shown to improve mood. Petting animals, appreciating art, being mindful of our nutritional intake, and appreciating different forms of art are also mood boosters.

You are stronger than you think. You can challenge your cognitive distortions. Improve your thoughts, and your mood will follow. You don't have to accept a constant negative monologue telling you that life won't work out for you.

We live in a society that covets fame and fortune. Many people pursue both only to find out how fleeting and unhealthy they can be. As someone who attained a level of fame, comedian Paul Gilmartin said it best, "Almost every good thing I have in my life has come from something disappointing." Reaching for the stars is encouraged when we're young, but no one talks about the value of not getting there. It's assumed to be sad when you fail, something never to be discussed. You will fail sometimes, that is true. When it happens, sit down in that quiet place, perhaps an area you've dedicated to the memory of someone you love, and say to yourself, "This too shall pass."

CHAPTER 6

Disappointment Inspired

"We do survive every moment, after all, except the last one."
~ John Updike

My father was my muse when it came to writing jokes. Growing up I used to get upset at his abrasive comments and "winners versus losers" philosophy of life. He was a perfectionist and very successful in his career, so he thought it gave him permission to tell everyone how we should do things. I was really affected at time, ruminating on his words and actions for hours or days. At some point, my frustration inspired a different perspective. Instead of taking him seriously, I saw the absurdity in everything he did. For example, if he got bored with a conversation, he would get up and leave the room. That hurts when you're the only two people in the room.

Instead of getting mad at him and either talking back or brooding about it, I used my sense of humor to cope. I thought of the jokes as disappointment inspired. It opened up a whole new world of laughs as sometimes the punchlines would just write themselves. One time I asked him, "Dad you're married almost 50 years and you don't wear a wedding ring. Why not?" He just looked at me with a smirk and said, "I don't want to be prejudged." As what, faithful? Who has a problem with that?

My dad did not like to give hugs. If he had to hug me, he treated it like he was afraid our penises would touch. He assumed the A-frame position and quickly did lots of back tapping, hoping I'd end it. Memories like that used to bother me, but when I started writing comedy, they just became new bits. I can remember sitting at the dinner table as a teenager and my mom was yelling at him for not listening. She was almost screaming, "Joseph! Did you even hear what your son said?" Meanwhile, he was cutting an apple with the precision of a surgeon. He didn't flinch. He never got defensive or said a word.

He just stared at the slice and got wide-eyed as he popped it in his mouth. Whenever my wife accuses me of not listening, I remember that moment and laugh. I probably look a lot like my father with that apple.

That Call

On a late afternoon in November, I was finishing up work for the day when I saw my mother had left me a voicemail. It was brief and she sounded very upset, so I called her back immediately. "Your father had a terrible accident," she said while her voice trembled. "He fell in the garage and hit his head. He may have had a stroke. I don't know. We're at the hospital." At that point, my entire world stopped. This is the call we all dread. A loved one has experienced a life changing negative event. I was numb with shock and felt a weight on my chest. My parents were almost a thousand miles away, so my mind was racing through the options of what do and when.

My dad worked on Wall Street for over two decades, most of the time as a financial analyst for Merril Lynch researching companies in the telecommunications industry. He was there at the very beginning of the technology revolution, overseeing the rise and fall of companies like Lucent, Ericsson, Cisco and Scientific Atlanta. He got started right as AT&T was broken up by the government into many companies, so it was a hot sector of the industry. As an analyst, his job was to carefully examine the viability of each of the companies and determine whether or not their stock was worth buying or selling. My dad was highly decorated for his work, winning awards almost every year.

I tell you all this to say that he was an extremely cautious man. Whether he was evaluating a company or cutting fruit, he was as risk averse as you could be. In fact, he never invested his own money in stocks. Imagine that, a man who made a living suggesting stocks never bought any for himself! When the market crashed in 2008, I assumed he lost a ton of money. I called him and asked, "Dad, are you and mom okay? I saw the news about Wall Street collapsing." He responded, "I don't put my money in stocks. I've been telling them this would happen for years!" He almost seemed happy about it.

In retirement, he was even more cautious with his daily life. He worked out every day and read obsessively about health and fitness.

He cut out articles from such esteemed medical journals like Men's Health or GQ, taped them to a piece of paper and underlined the important points. He didn't smoke or drink and the only pills he took were the 87 vitamins he downed each meal. The man had the most expensive urine in the country. He was literally pissing my inheritance down the drain.

As he got older, he walked slowly. He shuffled his feet. He drove slowly. He only left the house after checking three times to see if the door was locked. When he golfed, he stood over the ball for an unbearably long amount of time before starting his swing. The wait was so long other golfers with him would get tired of holding up their own body weight. Everything he did included an extra measure of vigilance. So how the hell could someone like that fall and hit his head with such force it changed the course of his life?

Two hours into the ordeal, my father was uncommunicative, a sign the brain isn't getting enough oxygen. A brain scan found no evidence of a stroke, but the fall caused a fractured skull and internal bleeding known as a subdural hematoma. He was immediately flown to a trauma center in Savannah to have brain surgery, hoping to relieve the pressure inside his skull from the bleeding.

My dad was otherwise in good shape, so my mom requested that they do the surgery and remove the subdural hematoma. She told me the alternative was to do nothing and let him pass. What a brutal decision to make. One minute your husband is fine, then two hours later you're deciding whether or not you should save him.

I was in the midst of writing chapter seven of this book when I got the call. My reaction was a combination of shock and profound sadness. I knew from my training that at 84 years old, his outcome was unlikely to be a happy one. I felt a heavy sensation in my chest, like a weight vest was strapped to my upper body. There was also a sense of impending doom that was inescapable. My dad was alive, but for how long? I had a feeling that the worst was about to happen and there was nothing I could do to stop it.

Four hours in, I started having flashbacks to life before he fell. I thought about the last time we spoke. It was a few days after his birthday, a date he happens to share with my son who turned eleven. My kids sent him a funny birthday card, which of course he didn't under-

180 Matt Bellace, Ph.D.

stand, so we called him to explain it. That's always a waste of time. Once you explain it, the humor is lost. To salvage a laugh, I said to him, "Next year Dad, we'll get a card that's more on your level." He smiled and we said goodbye. Thinking about that card a few hours after his fall made me physically nauseous.

Six hours into the ordeal some hopeful news came in. His surgery was successful in removing most of the hematoma. He survived and was in the recovery room. At that point, I probably had made a dozen phone calls with family and friends to give them the grim news. For the first time on one of the calls, I had a laugh. I felt guilty about it, but I knew if I was going to get through this, I needed my sense of humor.

I booked the next direct flight to Savannah, Georgia, one-way tickets for my brother and myself, leaving the next day. My kids were very upset at the idea that I was leaving to get on a plane during the pandemic. It was the first time in nine months that I had flown and I think it was a reality check for them that this was really serious. I didn't sleep well that night, waking up at 4 am in disbelief. It did feel good to get some rest though. In retrospect, I should have started meditating immediately when I woke up.

When we landed in Savannah, I remember joking with my brother that if I was dad, the hospital would not be our first stop. My father was obsessed with working out and reading, so he probably would have ignored the emergency and announced, "I'll see you guys at the hospital in a few hours. I'm going to the gym and getting a paper." The joke was on us. When we got to the hospital, they would not let us inside due to COVID restrictions. It was heartbreaking.

We paced around outside the hospital entrance in the warm Savannah air. When we saw my mom, we put on our masks and hugged. The fact that we even needed to think about that moment demonstrates how difficult it was to function during the pandemic. The hospital allowed my mom to see him, but not us unless he was drawing his last breath. They never even gave her a COVID test, it was a pandemic rule. No exceptions. We saw him over FaceTime and he wasn't conscious.

During the pandemic, millions of families around the world were excluded from seeing loved ones at hospitals and nursing homes. It's like adding insult to the injury of having a loved one fighting for their life. There was no argument to be made. No protest was going to change it. My brother and I were stuck outside and all we could do was go over and over how it happened.

The Analysis

When we got to my mom's house, one of the first things we did was try to understand how my dad fell. We talked about the topic more than anything else. In excruciating detail, we broke down every aspect of the scene, like it was the Zapruder film of the Kennedy assassination. We did a frame-by-frame analysis in our minds of how such a careful man could end up with a fractured skull.

Based on the information we gathered, my mom was inside the house while dad was pulling in his car. He had a classic Mercedes convertible which he rarely drove, so on that day he had taken it out for a spin. When he returned, based on his previous routine, he would have parked the car outside the garage, opened the door and walked in to adjust the rug that went underneath the car to prevent it from dripping fluids on the garage floor. My mom saw him pull up, but went back inside the house to get a water bottle because she was on her way out to go golfing.

From there, we surmise he bent down to move the carpet and either tripped or got dizzy. He must have looked for a place to brace himself because we saw a swivel chair on the floor beside the carpet. The chair had been scheduled to be thrown out later that day. We think he tried to sit down quickly in the chair, but toppled over backwards, sending him down hard on the back of his head. When my mom returned, the chair was found on its side and my dad was crawling on the floor in the corner of the garage, throwing up. My mom asked him if he fell, and he repeatedly told her no. When she tried to help him up, he complained she was hurting him. My dad only admitted later to the EMT that he had fallen down.

I'm sharing this sad story with you partly because it fascinates me how compelled we were to figure it out what had happened. In fact, we spent more time talking about it in the ensuing days than any other topic. It turns out it's a human trait to try and explain the unexplained. We can devout tremendous resources to make sense of the senseless. No one will ever really know how my dad fell that day; there were no cameras. On some level it doesn't matter, either. What's done is done. However, there is something inside each one of us that wants answers in these situations.

Brain Matters:
Explaining the Unexplained

Psychologist Jerome Kagan believed that figuring out uncertainties was one of the most important aspects of human behavior. He felt that when we are faced with the absence of understanding, we exert a tremendous amount of energy to try and reach a clear explanation. Kagan felt that our drive to eliminate the unknown can also be found in our efforts to achieve wealth, fame, friends, and power. As we acquire these highly valued social rewards, we reduce the likelihood that our future will be filled with economic uncertainty, loneliness, and obscurity. Social psychologist Arie Kruglanski referred to humans striving to explain things as an "aversion to ambiguity." We don't like not having answers to important questions.

In a study on the need for understanding of terrorist attacks, researchers looked at a measure they called the "need for closure." One of the five experiments they performed involved Americans being shown a short video, either about the 9/11 terror attacks or a neutral video about work.[1] Then the participants completed a task which served to distract them from what they watched. Several minutes after the task, they were given a survey asking questions related to need for closure (i.e., I would describe myself as indecisive, I hate to change plans at the last minute).

The results suggested that the video reminders of the terrorist attacks significantly elevated the participants' scores on the need-for-closure survey compared to the control condition of watching a video about work. None of the participants had been involved in the 9/11 attacks, but just being reminded of what happened that day led to a heightened desire for resolution. The authors also felt that this need for closure helped to identify who was part of the group. Who had the shared experience and who hadn't. That makes sense, those willing to spend the time and effort to seek resolution must care deeply about the topic.

Ghost of Insecurities Past

My sleep was terrible the first two nights after my dad's accident. I woke up with visions of him lying in a hospital bed hooked up to tubes breathing for him. Every morning we took a poll in the house and the third night all three of us slept well. We were like babies hitting that sweet spot of finally sleeping through the night. It didn't shake the sense of impending doom, but it allowed everyone to function a little better throughout the long days.

My brother and I took turns driving my mom two hours roundtrip to the trauma center in Savannah. We would drop her off and then wait to FaceTime with dad. We all played the role of cheerleader, trying to get him to open his eyes or raise a thumb. At one point, my brother called in and spoke to my dad, saying "Dad, we're here. Wake up!" Immediately his monitor went off with a loud alarm. His blood pressure spiked. We all laughed because my brother used to stress my dad out all the time when we were young, so it's nice to know some reactions never fade.

I noticed that old feelings of inadequacy emerged for me during those days. I was thrust into the role of default medical advisor as my family was understandably looking for answers. My experience working in traumatic brain injury taught me that doctors tend not to answer your questions early on because they just don't know how things will play out. I have the ability to answer some questions, but I'm not a trauma doctor or neurosurgeon and there are limitations to my knowledge.

It was excruciating standing in front of the hospital on a cell phone, trying to listen to doctors talk about my dad during rounds. I could only hear every other word, but seconds later was being asked by my family to make sense of it. The whole thing brought me back to the pressure I had felt to pursue medical school when I was a student. At that moment, I wished I had gone. I was being visited by the ghost of insecurities past.

Fortunately, we have a cousin who is a retired heart surgeon who also helped out. He was a life saver when it came to making decisions, just as he had been an actual life saver in his career. Social support also arrived in the form of a friend who was trained as a neurologist and his friend who was a neurosurgeon. They both gave me permission to text or call anytime. You can't put a price on that type of assistance.

The ineffectiveness I felt inspired a strange new behavior in the days following my dad's accident. Every morning, I when I woke up I made my bed. I realize that's not that unusual, but I've been super consistent about making the bed. My wife either enlists me to help her or does it herself out of frustration that I can't make hospital corners with the sheets. I think the best explanation for why I started doing it was highlighted in a graduation speech given by Former Navy Admiral William McCraven to the graduates of the University of Texas at Austin:

"If you want to change the world, make your bed. If you make your bed every morning, you will have accomplished the first task of the day. It will give you a small sense of pride and it will encourage you to do another task."

In the hours and days after my dad's fall, I felt so helpless and my efforts so futile that making my bed seemed rewarding in comparison. It was something I could control. It was a small action that made me feel competent, even if only for that moment. It also made me look for other ways to be helpful throughout the day. In a time of chaos and confusion, we all need a win. Making the bed is a slam dunk.

Brain Matters:
Dopamine and Work

There's a theory that the neurotransmitter dopamine is a "teaching signal," like a coach who praises us when we've done well and scolds us when we've failed. Like everything else in neuroscience, there is more to the story. Current theories propose that fast changes in dopamine levels (second-to-second) support learning, while slower fluctuation changes (minute-to-minute) are involved in motivation to complete the work. In a coaching relationship, both short-term effort and long-term commitment is required.

In a study at the University of Michigan, researchers examined both fast and slow fluctuation of dopamine levels in an area of the rat brain associated with reward.[2] It's called the nucleus accumbens and each rat had a device implanted in their brain that allowed researchers to control the amount of dopamine added into the nucleus accumbens. They found that altering dopamine levels on a minute-by-minute scale caused the rats to show varying degrees of motivation in a task. The more dopamine increased over the long term, the more interest the animal showed in completing the task. Changing dopamine levels on a second-by-second basis altered their ability to learn how to maneuver through a maze for treats. The authors concluded that the fast fluctuations demonstrated the learning response, a more short-term reaction, rather than motivation, which is longer term.

Ultimately, it may feel like a tedious task to make your bed, but your brain will reward you with a little bit of dopamine for completing the task. It's probably not enough to even make you smile, but if accomplishing the task motivates you to tackle the next task in your day, then it will be worth it.

_ . _

Disappointment Inspired

Two days after my dad's accident, my mother put us to work. The pain and sadness of this entire experience was being sublimated (to use a psychology word) into something productive: cleaning things up! I applaud my mom's "can do" attitude because it made us all feel productive and perked up our moods. I guess it was the dopamine!

It was clear that my dad wasn't coming home any time soon and if he did, he would not be able to do the things he used to do. My brother was assigned to help my mom with the finances so she could pay bills. My job was to clean up my dad's office. That sounds like an easy task, but my father had become a bit of a pack rat in recent years. He wasn't ready for an episode of Hoarders, but he did have stacks of articles and newspapers strewn about the room and vitamins all over the house.

When he worked on Wall Street, my dad researched the companies he followed and the stock market. In retirement, he dedicated much of his time to researching health and fitness fads. If you had a newsletter or sold vitamins that promised better heart health or lower cancer risk, my dad probably sent you money. We had lots of laughs that day about the odd things he kept. There were files dedicated to yoga or Vitamin D: they were not scientific articles from The New England Journal of Medicine, however; they were more like Bob's homemade newsletter on Super Green Smoothies. He also had cut out articles about people who spent all their wealth before they died and didn't leave a penny to their kids. I think he was trying to tell us something.

The greatest disappointment for me while going through the reams of paper wat that my father always seemed too busy to talk. When I called, my mother would have to coax him to get on the phone. When we vacationed together once a year, he'd disappear for hours to read and "do work," not making himself available. He wasn't hurting anyone, so I never said anything. It was just the crushing realization that day, standing in the office, seeing what he was actually doing that bummed me out. We really never did anything as father and son. He never called me up and said, "I'd like to grab lunch or spend a weekend doing something." It turned out he was too busy cutting out silly articles to spend any quality time with me.

The disappointment of my dad's messy office inspired my mom to have me clean it. The disappointment of the lack of intimacy in my relationship with my father inspires me to have a closer relationship with my kids. It's easier said than done, but it starts with being present. Slowing down and not being so busy. Deciding that the to-do list can wait if there's a special conversation happening or a snow day coming.

I'm not sharing this because I think my dad was a bad guy. On the contrary, I'm privileged to say he was there if I really needed him. He was like the famous Iditarod dog Balto. In 1925, a potentially deadly diphtheria epidemic swept through Alaska and the only serum that could stop it was hundreds of miles away. The weather conditions were too cold to fly, so officials decided to move the medicine via dog sled. A Siberian Huskey named Balton led the team to complete the mission and became an instant celebrity. A statue of Balto was erected in New York City's Central Park ten months after he delivered the medicine. The inscription reads the following:

"Dedicated to the indomitable spirit of the sled dogs that relayed antitoxin six hundred miles over rough ice, across treacherous waters, through Artic blizzards from Nenana to the relief of stricken Nome in the winter of 1925."

Below that quote, there are three words inscribed, "Endurance, Fidelity, Intelligence." My father displayed all three of those qualities throughout his life. He endured a competitive career on Wall Street to provide for us. He was always faithful to my mom and never did anything to hurt her. Finally, he always tried to be intelligent and think things through, especially when there were big decisions to be made.

Cold Water Therapy

Three days into my dad's tragic ordeal, we finally had some good news. During our morning FaceTime, I yelled, "Dad, squeeze mom's hand!" Two seconds later he did it! Later in the day, the nurse asked him to give the thumbs up sign and he did that, too! We were elated. His brain was still working and we had hope.

I was so excited, I went into Savannah to walk around and call my wife to share the news. I walked by a store with a swimsuit sale and decided to go in. As I was buying a pair of cool gray and orange striped Billabong shorts, I joked with the cashier, "Now if only there were some waves around here, I'd go out in these!" I didn't think she could hear me since we both had masks on, which was required in Savannah by the mask mandate. As I was waiting for her response, this big dude standing right behind me with a bushy beard and no mask says in a Southern drawl, "Just go to Fern-an-dina Beach. They got waves there!"

I didn't know what was worse, that beard or him chiming in during pandemic with no mask. I just want to go for a swim, not catch COVID.

Our moods were up in the car ride back to my mom's, excited that finally there was a glimmer of hope. I could see how much she loved my dad. We joked about how the head injury might make dad mellow, interested more in listening to music than obsessing over money and cutting out health articles. We pictured this world where he starting enjoying time together and gave himself permission to eat a burger once in a while. My mom just wanted him to be happy and live out his remaining years without being so stressed out.

When we arrived home, there was still two hours of sun left in the day, so I headed to the beach. It was about 60 degrees with water temps in the low 60s, but I was going in the water. I had my new swimsuit on, which could've just given me coronavirus, so I was going to make the most of it! The waves at that beach were usually flat, but on that day there were these tiny one-to-two-foot waves. Given what I know about natural highs, I couldn't wait to get in.

The water was cold enough that I needed a few minutes to adjust, but as long as I got busy swimming or body surfing I'd be fine. I rode every wave I could for the next hour straight. Standing in chest high water, I would watch the waves roll in and jump towards the shore, paddling until I got it. The water was so shallow, I even ran aground a few times, scraping my chest and arms. I didn't care. The cold water felt therapeutic relative to what I was going through.

I went there again with my brother later in the week and we swam like we were kids again. It was like being on vacation in Ocean City, New Jersey back in the 80s. There's something primal about facing life and death issues that made returning to nature feel restorative. Our bodies had been through a psychological trauma, stuck on a plane, in a car, outside a hospital and at home. We worried about getting COVID. We feared my dad dying without saying goodbye. Physically we needed some kind of challenge to our system to feel better. It wasn't going to change the situation, but the cold water gave us an opportunity to get through it a little better.

The Major Challenge in the Game of Life

Towards the end of the first week after my dad's injury, the routine was starting to get to my mom: the two-hour round trip to the hospital, the sitting with my dad who was mostly unresponsive and then endless conversations about what their life might look like going forward. On one of our drives, she shared with me a saying her yoga instructor once told the class, "Breathe in courage and breathe our fear."

My mom told me that mantra was going through her mind a lot as she entered the hospital each day. She told me it gave her strength. When we parked, I walked her to the front of the hospital and gave her a hug. I held her arms and said while talking a deep breath, "Breathe in courage, breathe out fear." As we did it, a nurse was walking out of the hospital. You can only imagine what she had been through during the pandemic and as she overheard us, she immediately got choked up. "Oh, that's so sweet" she said.

Two days later my brother and I flew home. It was the day after Thanksgiving and we needed to tend to work and see our families. There were some promising signs with Dad and talk of moving him out of the ICU, so we thought we'd leave and come back in a week or two. He was spending several hours a day off the ventilator, even made it through the night once. He was opening his eyes occasionally, though he still wasn't talking or moving the left side of his body. It seemed like progress at the time.

On December 5th, 2020 I got the call from my mom that dad had passed away. Despite the positive signs in the first week, he never regained full consciousness and couldn't survive without a ventilator or a feeding tube. He never wanted to live like that for one day, let alone two weeks. I suspected it might happen, but you can't imagine the feelings until they're upon you. The heavy sadness and finality of it all.

Disappointment Inspired Obituary

Once again I found myself 750 miles from my parents and grieving. I was lucky to have my wife and kids by my side because during COVID no one else was going to hug me for comfort. My mom asked that I put together an obituary for my dad, which sounded like a big job until I sat down to do it. It felt good to be useful and interesting to learn details about my dad's life that I never knew. I must have done a good job, because I received kudos from my mom (a tough critic) and various literary members of my family. My dad's old assistant even paid to have it put in *The New York Times*. If you like reading obituaries, here it is:

> Joseph Bellace, Telecommunications Analyst at Merrill Lynch & Co, a longtime Little Falls, NJ resident and Hilton Head Island transplant, passed at 84
>
> Growing up in South Philadelphia, Almonesson and Collingswood, NJ, the son of first-generation parents from Sicily, Joe Bellace always valued education.
>
> His parents, Rose and John Bellace, never got a chance to attend high school, as they needed to work to help their families. Joe graduated Collingswood High School in 1954 and became the first in his family to go to college.
>
> After graduating from Bucknell University in 1960 with bachelor's degrees in economics and mechanical engineering, he accepted a position in RCA Corporation's defense communications division. Several years later he decided that he would rather pursue a career that allowed him to use his background in economics in a more creative and challenging environment.
>
> He enrolled in the Wharton School of the University of Pennsylvania, earned an MBA and then worked in data communications marketing at AT&T Corporation. Soon afterwards, he set out for Wall Street to cover the telecommunications industry from a different vantage point—that of the sell-side analyst. Bellace worked at several smaller firms before joining Merrill

Lynch, Pierce, Fenner & Smith in 1983. Two years later he debuted on the All-America Research Team as the second-place analyst in Telecommunications Equipment; from 1985 through 1998, the year before he left the firm (whose name by then had changed to Merrill Lynch), he appeared in the rankings 19 times, including 11 first-place finishes.

Telecommunications, like equity research, was undergoing its own transformation in those years. "When I started there was one sector and one analyst—me," he recalls. "When I finished there were three: Telecommunications Equipment, Wireless Equipment, and Data Networking," according to Bellace in a 2011 interview with Institutional Investor. By the end of time at Merrill Lynch, he was covering 27 companies and overseeing a staff of five—with whom he readily shares the credit for his success: "One person alone never could have accomplished this. It was, as my wife puts it, a terrific team," he says.

After he left Merrill, Bellace worked as an independent consultant covering the telecommunications equipment sector for Jefferies & Co. and served as an adviser to the equity research department of Oakland, California–based investment bank Internet Securities.

Joe retired to Hilton Head Island, SC with his wife of 54 years, Louise (nee Basso). He remained quite active in the Indigo Run community, working out every day at the gym, playing tennis and chatting with friends and strangers alike. Much of his day was spent researching market trends, health and fitness; but despite his years working with telecommunications companies, he never carried a cell phone. "Jersey Joe," as he was affectionately known, loved to listen to live music at the Jazz Corner and go to lunch with his buddies, the MOTOs.

Mr. Bellace died on Dec 5, 2020 at Memorial University Hospital in Savannah, shortly after a fall at his home in Hilton Head Island, SC.

In addition to his wife, he is survived by his sons, Michael and Matthew Bellace, their wives Antoinette and Dara, respectively, and three beloved grandchildren, Roy, Sidney, and Mateo. He was predeceased by his brother Victor.

Due to COVID health restrictions for the safety of all, no formal services will take place at this time. Donations given to your favorite charity or cause in his name would honor his memory.

A Major Challenge

My dad was always into reading motivational quotes at holiday meals. It was cheesy, but since he deprived himself of most of the food, we indulged him. Usually at the end of the meal, he would take out a piece of paper and announce that he was going to read some of his "life philosophies." I would roll my eyes and chuckle, but it became a tradition. We even started asking about it if he forgot to do it. When my mom asked me to clean my dad's office, I found some of his quotes. The very first one was dated July 20, 2016 and it read:

When you enter the 4th Quarter of the game of life — everyone will face a major challenge which will have to be addressed, —

My dad was an expert at predicting the success of companies and based on this quote, also an expert at predicting his own fate. When he passed, it didn't seem real. During the era of COVID, not being there to see him or having a service, made it almost feel like it didn't happen. We were robbed of the ability to say goodbye and to grieve in the way we had been accustomed our entire lives. This is the story that so many people shared during the pandemic. My heart goes out to anyone who faced this type of disappointment.

What I noticed in the days after my dad passed was the sudden flood of calls, texts, and emails. It was a distraction and a mood booster. I found myself retelling the entire story a dozen times a day to family and friends. After the fifth time it started to get easier. I imagine that's what Adele felt about her breakup after performing "Someone Like You" a dozen times in concert.

I am so thankful for everyone who reached out. There wasn't a Facebook post or text message too small that I wouldn't respond to it. There were a few people who didn't reach at all, people who I thought would, but never did. They proved themselves to be disappointing friends or family, but I chose not to focus my energy on them. I wanted this time in my life to be about what I had, not what I didn't have.

192 Matt Bellace, Ph.D.

Many local friends showed tremendous generosity. They knew there couldn't be a funeral service, so they organized a meal train. That meant they bought dinner for us each night from a restaurant of our choice. It was such a thoughtful gesture. I think food actually tastes better when someone else is paying for it!

The best parts of that period were the stories and memories of my dad that were shared. One gentleman said my father was, "one of the most positive people I've ever known." I laughed out loud at that one. Many said, "He was such a wonderful listener! He made me feel like I was the only person in the room." I wanted to hold up a picture of him and say, "Wait, we're talking about this guy, right?"

It was clear to me that the world experienced my father in a way that I had not. There were glimpses of it, but outsiders seemed to get the best version of him. That was disappointing, but also comforting to hear great things about him at such a terrible time. I would say I held it together emotionally pretty well for a day or two. Then one evening, while washing up the dishes, I made some sarcastic comment about how my dad won't be propping up the vitamin industry anymore with all his purchases, and the words just stayed in my head. As I began walking up the stairs, I realized that I couldn't talk to my dad ever again, even if I wanted to, and I just started to weep. Thankfully my wife was there to comfort me. Social support is the key to resilience.

I also noticed that we all grieved differently over the course of the following weeks. My brother reported feeling anger, which was interesting given his history of butting heads with my dad. My mom had good days and bad days, as would be expected. The support of friends in her community was a life saver. They gave her things to do and people to lean upon. I had a general feeling of sadness that was consistent through every day, but I was functional. I shopped for the holidays, put up decorations, got work done and helped around the house. Sadly, I had little to no enthusiasm for the holidays, which I compensated for by buying more gifts than normal. As a result, my son called it "The Greatest Christmas Ever!" I'm not sure where shopping falls on the Stages of Grief, but it should be on there.

Brain Matters:
Stages of Grief

The five stages of grief were first presented in the 1970 book, *On Grief and Grieving* by Elisabeth Kübler-Ross, a Swiss-American psychiatrist. She wrote it as an interdisciplinary study of our fear of death and inevitable acceptance of it. The stages include denial, anger, bargaining, depression, and acceptance. Despite the absence of empirical evidence or clarity how people go through the stages, they've stuck deeply in the minds of the public and healthcare professionals.

According to Kübler-Ross, the stages have been very misunderstood over the years. They were never meant to be a neat and tidy way to categorize the grieving process, but rather responses to loss that many people have. Criticism of the stages includes the fact that grieving is not orderly or predictable. Most people adjust to bereavement in their own time, not according to steps. We should never expect grieving people to react in a certain fashion. The added pressure is not helpful while coping with pain and loss. Finally, one review study cited that only 17 percent of the bereaved showed a trajectory that resembled "common" grief after a death.[3]

Considering the criticism, Kübler-Ross's writing made a tremendous impact on the care and treatment of dying patients. The simplicity of the stages may be one reason the concept has been so difficult to move beyond.

Denial is important because it helps us survive the loss. When we learn the news, the mundane details of our lives become less meaningful. Our routines make no sense and we are in a state of shock. We can initially become numb and act as though we're emotionally in denial of what happened. There may be a reckoning where we wonder how we can go on or if we should go on. This might be a biological way of not overwhelming ourselves more than we can handle. As you proceed, you'll feel stronger, but all the feelings you were denying begin to surface.

Anger is a necessary stage of the healing process if you're willing to feel it. The more you experience anger, the more it will begin to dissipate and let you heal. There are so many emotions you may be dealing with, but anger is familiar. Pain is really driving the anger, since it is natural to feel deserted and abandoned by a death. Grief at this stage is like being lost, adrift at sea with no connection to anything. Getting angry at someone in everyday life might be your reaction and it could feel better than feeling nothing at all. The anger is just another indication of the intensity of your love.

The stage of bargaining can be found in two parts. Prior to a loss, you'll be willing to part with anything if the person survives. After a loss, the bargaining may take the form of a cease fire, where you beg to do something to put things back to the way they were. There is a strong desire for our loved one to be restored to the way they were. It's like dreaming about going back in time when we know that's not possible. There is often a lot of guilt in this stage as we wonder what we could have done differently.

It's important to note that stages don't last for a discreet period of time. They are responses to feelings and can last for seconds, minutes, hours, or much longer. We don't enter and move on to another stage in a linear fashion. We might jump back and forth or seem like we're in two stages at once.

Depression comes after bargaining is over, as we move into the new reality of present day. Grief enters our lives in a deeper way and feels like it will last forever. This is not a sign of clinical depression; rather, it is mourning, and it's an appropriate response to grief. In fact, the DSM-5, the manual of diagnosing mental health disorders, takes grief into account when diagnosing clinical depression. This is the phase you may be told to "snap out of it" if you're surrounded by those who lack empathy. It's natural to feel depressed. It's not a state in need of fixing.

The final step is acceptance. It's not that you're "okay" with it all, but rather a feeling of a new normal. This stage is just about accepting the reality that our loved one is physically gone and not coming back. We can learn to live with it if even if we don't like it. We must learn to adapt to this new life situation to allow ourselves to grow and live with purpose. To find acceptance may be about having more good days than bad ones. We can invest in ourselves and in others, perhaps with new levels of enthusiasm.

There are alternative perspectives to the stages, though less well known. The trajectory of the grief model is fluid in nature, it includes three phases. First, it involves dealing with the event itself, which may or may not be traumatic in nature. The second is the active work of grieving, including going through belongings and keepsakes. The last phase is the long-term aspect of coping called "forever grief," which may never be complete. In addition, the Dual Process Model of Coping is an alternative that states the grieving individual confronts the pain at times, but at other times avoids the tasks of grieving. This model proposes that adaptive coping involves the need for "dosage of grieving," or taking a break from dealing with the stress.

Disappointment Inspired: Less Worrying About Money

In addition to obsessing over his health, my dad was compulsive about money. Both were driven by anxiety. His fear of death compelled him to spend countless hours cutting out and organizing articles about exercise, disease, and food. His rituals around eating were as exhausting to watch as his pre-swing routine in golf. When it came to money, he was convinced in retirement that he would be broke. This might seem logical until you realize that he and my mom were very responsible and quite comfortable. Unless he lived as long as Yoda, there was little chance of being in the poor house. His anxiety was so high about money, that when I once suggested he buy a patio heat lamp he barked at me, "No more assets!"

You could argue that his obsessions and compulsions were not hurting anyone other than annoying my mom. In fact, I had many laughs when we found his check registers documenting every penny he spent from 1972. He saved every one! He didn't just put in his expenses; he wrote little notes, too. If you made my father keep a diary that's exactly what it would look like: "I spent $15.32 on clothes. $10.32 for work clothes and $5 on the kids."

I learned that he paid $7 per week for daycare when I was a toddler. It went up to $8 a day when I turned two by the way. When I was 13 years old, he started paying me to mow the lawn by writing out a check. The only problem is I didn't have a checking account. When he handed it to me, I probably looked at him like, "What the hell am I supposed to do with this?" Who am I kidding, I'll bet he mailed it to me.

The real problem with his behavior is that it took up a tremendous amount of time. He was always too busy. He never had more than a few minutes to spare before his routine would be calling. He missed opportunities to spend time with friends and family in the service of his anxiety-reducing rituals. After he passed away and the full scope of his behavior was clear to me, it created a tremendous desire for me to stop my own focus on money.

I chose to be self-employed and I love it. In fact, my dad endorsed it. However, the biggest downside to working in the gig economy is financial insecurity. I'm lucky if I know how things look three months out, but after that is a bit of a mystery. After my dad passed, I realized how much time and energy I had devoted to reducing my anxiety that we were going to go broke. That might make sense in the first few years of working for myself, but I'm fifteen years full-time at being a professional speaker. I've got a reputation and thousands of presentations under my belt. Some years might be better than others, but if a global pandemic didn't send me to the poor house, nothing will.

Two months after my dad passed, I did something I would have never done before. I made a decision to do a major project on our house that we had put off for years. The tail end of a pandemic might not seem like the time to invest large sums of money in a new siding job. Or is it? The old me would have worried that it would bankrupt us and therefore, push it off yet again. The new me went the other direction. I hired the best siding guy we could find and moved forward with the job, giving myself permission to not worry about money.

I'll admit on the first day of construction, when an 18-wheeler backed a dumpster and a porta potty into my drive way, I felt some buyer's remorse. I wondered how many "extras" my guy would try to get me to do and how much it would cost. As the weeks went by, we were so impressed with his work that we agreed to everything he wanted. When he said, go with the big gutters, we did it. When he suggested a front porch would add curb appeal, we did it. When the bill came in and it was big, I just laughed and thought, we'll be fine.

What I did not expect was the mood boost provided by new siding on my house. I'm privileged to have had the means to see the project through, even if it meant taking on some debt. However, the conversations it started with neighbors and the pride it generated for our house were benefits I truly enjoyed. The job became a symbol of hope that the pandemic would soon be over and that we had the confidence to make improvements to our home in the face of it.

Interestingly, many of the friends I spoke with about home renovations told me similar stories. One friend went through a divorce (not his decision) and was left with the family home. He was feeling very down when his wife left, so he painted his house and transformed his landscaping. He told me it was therapeutic to meet his feelings of loss over the relationship with improvements he could see. This concept reminds me of the time we converted our study into a room memorializing my wife's grandmother. It provided some measure of closure to a sad moment.

Disappointment Inspired: Writing

The disappointment of losing my father was the final inspiration for completing and editing this book. I tapped into an almost endless reservoir of energy. I retreated into my office, opened the file and get lost in the writing. I'm not saying it turned me into Hemmingway, but I know the book improved as a result of my increased efforts.

I noticed that the simple step of getting started on any given day was easier. When I started writing the book a few years ago, I had the hardest time closing my email and thinking about the book. I had a million excuses for why I couldn't do it and the project languished. Days after my dad's fall, I found I could not put enough time into writing. Suddenly, I could write for two to three hours and still wished it was more. It became a little sad for me to stop. I would call it a mini-depression because I had a hard time going from deep thoughts about the book to driving my daughter to hip-hop class.

Writing was therapeutic for me on two levels. When I was writing about my dad, it felt like I was confronting my grieving. Talking about him in the past tense was not easy, but a necessary reminder that he wasn't going to be calling me or mailing articles ever again. The other level that felt good was being productive. He was such a disciplined man who valued work above all else. Although I made the decision to be more engaged in family life, I knew that completing the book would honor his memory. Short of taking vitamins and obsessing over my cholesterol levels, finishing the book would be what he wanted.

Pain into Progress

I had an electronic companion while writing this book, an Excel spreadsheet where I documented my progress. Each time I wrote, I'd jot down how far I got and what topic I was writing about. It was a lot like my dad's check registers, so I guess I'm not fully cured. I did find it to be helpful to see the data as time went on. When I looked back at it, I noticed an interesting yet not so surprising trend: major disappointments coincided with increases in pages written.

Prior to my friend Rob Torres's untimely passing in July of 2018, I had completed 93 pages of the first draft of the book in the first year of writing. I had actually taken two and half months off and wanted to give up on the book before I learned the news. It's hard to describe how shocking and helpless it feels to lose a friend. It was way too soon. This shouldn't have happened. I would bring him back in a heartbeat over finishing the book if I could, but I had no control over it. In the year following his passing, I more than doubled my output. I finished a first draft and started going back over the chapters. On my desk the entire time was a picture of Rob, reminding me to honor my friend and finish.

When the pandemic hit, I stopped writing for three months. The pain and frustration of being locked down, anxious and unexpectedly in charge of remote school left me with no energy. I had all but given up, again. My wife asked me one night, "How is the book coming?" I snapped back, "What book? At this rate, I'll never finish."

When summer arrived and there was no more school, but summer camps were allowed to operate, I found myself with time to write. The first day in four months I had at home with no kids was like a dream. I could not believe the energy I had. The book became my sole focus. I completed the entire second draft. My dad's passing propelled me to the finish line. I suppose I was inching towards it already, but it empowered me. I was disappointment inspired.

My Disappointment-Inspired Chart

Over the course of this book, I've used personal examples to illustrate points about how pain, loss and failure can inspire positive change. I've simplified them in chart form below. These include the initial event (the storm) and my age at the time, the type of disappointment, the maladaptive response, which can be either a feeling, thought or behavior and the adaptive response (beautiful wave).

"Storm of Life" Initial Event, Age	Type of Disappointment	Maladaptive Response	"The Beautiful Wave" Adaptive Response
Dumped by my girlfriend, 25	Pain, Loss	Ruminated and "beat myself up"	Bought a kayak, improved my mood, Still surfing and kayaking 20 years later
Losing my grandfather to cancer, 13	Loss	Thought, "God, take me instead," family dysfunction	Threw a ball (a lot), became a better athlete, 8 varsity letters, coaching my son 30 years later
Failing first biology test, 18	Failure	Felt like an inferior student, test taking anxiety	Gave up idea of "perfection," focused on love of learning, lead to a Ph.D. in clinical neuropsychology
My dad passing away after suffering a traumatic brain injury, 47	Loss	Beat myself up over not being able to answer everyone's brain-related questions	Inspired to complete this book

Natural High to Forget the End of the World

You can't take away a long-term pain with a quick pick-me-up. However, the little mood boosters were welcome additions to my day while I was in mourning. One of the favorites in my family is singing and dancing in the living room to music. I don't know why I said "to music." If you saw a family singing and dancing and there was no music, you'd probably get concerned for their well-being.

The tradition of dancing in the face of pain, loss, or failure started for me in college. The student group I founded in 1993, C.a.l.v.i.n. & H.o.b.b.e.s., was given a former fraternity house on campus in my senior year. One of my favorite memories of living in the house is the dance parties. It could be Halloween or the Spring Formal, we would move all the furniture in the living room and set up a DJ table.

One time, we had a black light party where we laid plastic on the floor and walls and gave people goggles and liquid soap to throw around. The black lights made everything glow and we all left smelling lemony fresh. We were a non-drinking group, so we had to get creative to have a good time!

The most memorable part of every dance for me was the last song. It became a tradition to dance to R.E.M.'s, "It's the End of the World as We Know It (And I Feel Fine)." I use the term dance lightly here because it was more of a jumping up and down motion, like in a mosh pit. We sang the lyrics out loud, as many as we could remember, which is nearly impossible given the pace of the song. When it ended, we all collapsed together on the floor in unison. After the black light party, we didn't even need detergent to wash our clothes. I remember lots of laughter, sweat, and an occasional black eye. It was also a natural high that often lasted for hours.

I guess we all related to the message of the song: even then you think the world is ending, you can still feel fine. I was a privileged kid at a private college, but back then it felt like our world was ending. There were intense days when your dream of becoming the valedictorian ended, you were cut from the team, or dumped by "the one." These disappointments can literally make you feel like you're falling apart if a lot of your identity was wrapped up in them. I found it therapeutic to be in a group singing those lyrics.

In the weeks after my dad passed, still mired in a global pandemic, dancing and singing felt great. If even for a few minutes, moving our bodies around, making up lyrics to songs and just being silly sent the message to our kids that everything was fine. It was fine. Parents get older and die. It's part of life. But when you're still alive and in good health, it's a reminder to get out and live.

Dueling Pianos

In the summer of 2019, while living in Princeton, New Jersey, we decided to go to a dueling pianos concert in town. If you've never seen one of these, there are two pianos and two musicians competing for tips. If you dislike the song being played by one, you can tip the other and they'll start playing another song. It was fun, but it was also a hot July evening and no one was dancing. As we neared the end of the event, I approached the piano to stop the other from playing "Mony, Mony" by Billy Idol.

My request (you probably guessed it) was R.E.M.'s "It's The End of the World As We Know It (But I Feel Fine)." One of the piano players looked at me and said, "I love it! That song has more lyrics than any song ever written." I sarcastically replied, "You're welcome." As I returned to my seat and waited for the song to begin, I realized that this was not going to be like a C&H dance. In fact, it was likely that no one would get up and dace. I couldn't let that happen.

As the song began to play, I sat there feeling ashamed that I didn't have the courage to dance. I had a flashback to a documentary I recently watched called *The Bill Murray Stories*. The entire movie was dedicated to reporting on sightings of actor Bill Murray at random places, like house parties, weddings, and baseball games. When he got invited to random parties by fans, but he sometimes actually showed up. According to the documentary, he didn't just sit down at the parties, he washed dishes, danced or performed with the band. I left that movie feeling like Bill Murray was trying to teach us how to live in the moment.

The movie had a tremendous impact on me. I realized that I could be living more in the moment. After I speak in front of large crowds, I rarely take advantage of my momentary celebrity and visit a class-room or an office. I could be more spontaneous, showing up in a psychology class or joining a music class to say hello. Usually my sched-ule is very tight, or I'm hungry, so I have a built-in excuse for playing it safe. Bill Murray would probably say to me, "Matt, have fun because we're only on this planet for a short period of time. Stop taking your-self so seriously. Enjoy the moment!"

Thinking about that movie inspired me. Before I knew it, I got up in front of the crowd at the dueling pianos concert and starting jumping like I was back in C&H House. My wife looked at me as if to say, "What the hell are you doing? We live here!" I tried not to make eye contact with her, out of fear I might lose my courage. I jumped alone for thirty seconds, which felt like an eternity. That's when the most amazing thing happened. Children, including my six-year-old daughter and her friends, starting jumping with me! A few seconds later, they started coming up to me and saying "uppie," which is the international word for "pick me up." So I did. Their parents were looking at me like, "Why are you touching my kid?" I was thinking, "Well, they asked me to."

No other adult was dancing except me, which prompted one of the piano guys to say, "If you're not dancing like him right now, you're doing it wrong." That just fueled me more to keep going. I made it the entire way through the song and nearly had a heart attack with all the uppies. As the song ended, one of the piano guys shouted, "Give it up for the guy with twelve kids!" And everyone cheered.

After the concert, while we were leaving, parents were coming up to me saying things like, "You're an inspiration!" All I did was jump for four minutes, but they felt they had witnessed something positive.. I took the time to notice how great I felt in the minutes and hours after that dance. I was sweaty for a while and my heart rate was up, but so was my mood. I was smiling and had significantly more energy than if I hadn't done it. That experience was a natural high, just like it had been in college. I think even Bill Murray would have been proud.

At Least He Didn't Get COVID

At this point, you may think, "What a terrible year he had! Well, at least he didn't get COVID." Well, sorry to break it to you, but I did. And I was so careful, too! Thankfully no one else in my house contracted it, despite me being in close contact with them for days. Can you believe that? My wife and kids did not get it! I think I'm a little disappointed in COVID. The most contagious disease in a century and it couldn't survive my wife's extraordinary cleaning skills.

Of course, since it is human nature to explain things, I spent much time trying to figure out how it happened. The best explanation I came up with is it happened while holiday shipping. It presented in such a confusing way, too. I went outside in the cold for a run one day and started coughing afterwards. For years that had always happened to me if I ran in the winter. I had forgotten about it since I almost never run. The next day, I was a little sore and still had an occasional cough, so I Googled "exercise-induced asthma." I thought, "I'm finally going to get to the bottom of this!"

Just to be safe, I decided to book a COVID test, but only to rule it out. Days passed and I felt better. I even went running again and ran a personal best! The day of the test came and I thought, "That was an exercise-induced cough, like the ones I used to have. I don't need the test." I had no fever, chills, nausea, fatigue, loss of taste or smell or other weird symptoms. However, I went for the test simply because it was on my list to do. A few days later, an email came in from CVS with the results. My daughter walked in and I announced, "Sidney, got my COVID test results and they're ... positive?" I was in shock.

My COVID test results.
I added the emoji.

I wore a mask everywhere, so I probably inhaled a small viral load, reducing the severity of the illness. It still lasted fifteen days and I felt miserable at times. I had trouble breathing, had a terrible rash, a weird hallucination, and a stomach problem. However, being isolated in my office with two children in the house was kind of sweet. Every parent needs a little quarantine sometimes.

More than half a million Americans lost their lives during the pandemic, millions worldwide. The collective disappointment of what we've been through will likely change our society for the better in years to come. Pandemics of the past have improved public health and personal hygiene. I'm sure there will be countless beautiful waves to follow in time. There will be untold numbers of careers inspired by COVID, including scientific research and medicine. Already, we've seen the innovations like telemedicine for doctors' appointments and improved ventilation systems in schools and office buildings. Towns could have been blocking off streets for walking and dining all this time! The pandemic has forced people to reimagine work and the value of long commutes. I wish it wouldn't have happened, but there are so many positive outcomes.

The beautiful wave from me having COVID is an increase in gratitude for my family and nature. I've taken more time to appreciate little moments throughout the day. For example, I bought a small chair to use for sitting outside in my garden. It sounds so simple, but that seat gives me permission to take a break and watch the world go around.

I love sitting out there during sunsets, listening to my kids play while studying the birds and the bees as they wrap up their work for the day. If I catch it at the right time, I can marvel at the colors of dusk, which are so soothing to my soul. The deep blue and orange only lasts a few moments and then they're gone, like a funny joke. The cool air feels nice on my skin, a departure from the harsh heat of the day. As I gaze over my vegetable garden and imagine the great produce I'll be eating soon, I smile at the accomplishment. "There is nothing more local that this," I think with pride. Life may be disappointing, but when it works out it's important to acknowledge it and be grateful.

*I'm so grateful you took the time to read my book.
If you're disappointed in it, I'm sorry, but I hope
it inspires some positive!*

Thank you!

ENDNOTES

Chapter 1: The Most Beautiful Waves Come From the Biggest Storms

[1] Pelham, B. (2004). Affective Forecasting: The perils of predicting future feelings. *Psychological Science Agenda.* https://www.apa.org/science/about/psa/2004/04/pelham.

[2] Gilbert, D., Lieberman, M., Morewedge, C. and Wilson, T. (2004). The peculiar longevity of things not so bad. *Psychological Science. 15*(1): 14-19.

[3] Perez, V., Alexander, D. and Bailey, W. (2013). Air ions and mood outcomes: a review and meta-analysis. *BMC Psychiatry. 13*(29): 1-20.

[4] Gascon, M., Zijema, W., Vert, C., White, M., Nieuwenhuijsen, M. (2017). Outdoor blue spaces, human health and well-being: A systematic review of quantitative studies. *International Journal of Hygiene and Environmental Health. 220*(8): 1207-1221.

[5] Li, Q., Otsuka, T., Wakayama, K., Katsumata, M., Hirata, Y., Li, Y., Hirata, K., Shimizu, T., Suzuki, H., Kawada, T. and Kagawa, T. (2011). Acute effects of walking in forest environments on cardiovascular and metabolic parameters. *European Journal of Applied Physiology. 111*(11): 2845-2853.

[6] Gruebner, O., Rapp, M., Adli, M., Kluge, U., Galea, S. and Heinz, A. (2017). Cities and mental health. *Deutsches Ärzteblatt International. 114*: 121-7.

[7] Steinberg, L. (2005). Cognitive and affective development in adolescence. *Trends in Cognitive Science. 9*(2): 69-74.

[8] Johnson, S., Blum, R. and Giedd, J. (2009). Adolescent Maturity and the Brain: The promise and pitfalls of neuroscience research in adolescent health policy. *Journal of Adolescent Health. 45*(3): 216-221.

Chapter 2: Find the Suffering You're Okay With in Life

[1] Baird, L. (1985). Do grades and tests predict adult accomplishment? *Research in Higher Education. 23*(1): 3-85.

[2] Harvard University report (2014). Executive summary from https://staticl.squarespace.com/static/5b7c56e255b02c683659fe43/t/5bae774424a694b5feb2b05f/1538160453604/report-children-raise.pdf.

[3] Stoeber, J. and Rambow, A. (2007). Perfectionism in adolescent school students: Relations with motivation, achievement, and well-being. *Personality and Individual Differences. 42*(7): 1379-1389.

[4] Werner, E. (1989). High-risk children in young adulthood: A longitudinal study from birth to 32 years. *American Journal of Orthopsychiatry. 59*(1): 72-81.

[5] Killingsworth, M., Gilbert, D. (2010). A wandering mind is an unhappy mind. *Science. 330*(6006): pp.932.

[6] Keng, S., Smoski, M. and Robins, C. (2011). Effects of mindfulness on psychological health: A review of empirical studies. *Clinical Psychology Review.* *31*: 1041-1056.

[7] Lykins, E. and Baer, R. (2009). Psychological functioning in a sample of long-term practitioners of mindfulness meditation. *Journal of Cognitive Psychotherapy: An International Quarterly.* *23*:226-241.

[8] New York Times, August 22, 1998. http://www.nytimes.com/1998/08/22/us/philadelphia-shaken-by-collapse-of-a-health-care-giant.html.

[9] Duckworth, A., Peterson, C., Matthew, M. and Kelly, D., (2007). Grit: perseverance and passion for long-term goals. *Journal of Personality and Social Psychology.* *92*(6): 1087-1101.

[10] Reed, J., Pritschet, B. and Cutton, D. (2013). Grit, conscientiousness and the transtheoretical model of change for exercise behavior. *Journal of Health Psychology.* *18*(5): 612-619.

[11] Suzuki, T., Tamesue, D., Asahi, K. and Ishikawa, Y. (2015). Grit and work engagement: a cross-sectional study. *PLoS One, 10*(9): e0137501.

[12] Wang., S., Zhou, M., Chen, T., Yang, X., Chen, G., Wang, M. and Gong, Q. (2017). Grit and the brain: spontaneous activity of the dorsomedial prefrontal cortex mediates the relationship between the trait grit and academic performance. *Social Cognitive and Affective Neuroscience.* *12*(3): 452-460.

[13] Hafenbrack, A., Kinias, Z. and Barsade, S. (2014). Debiasing the mind through meditation: Mindfulness and sunk cost bias. *Psychological Science.* *25*(2):369-76.

[14] New York Times, December 25, 2015. https://www.nytimes.com/2015/12/26/nyregion/reforms-to-ease-students-stress-divide-a-new-jersey-school-district.html.

[15] Jepma, N., Koban, L., van Dorn, J., Jones, M. and Wager, T. (2018). Behavioural and neural evidence for self-reinforcing expectancy effects on pain. *Nature Human Behaviour: 2*: 838-855.

[16] Business Insider, February 19, 2017. https://www.businessinsider.com/how-to-handle-sleep-deprivation-according-to-a-navy-seal-2017-2.

[17] Lo J.C., Ong J.L., Leong R.L., Gooley J.J. and Chee M.W. (2016). Cognitive performance, sleepiness, and mood in partially sleep deprived adolescents: the need for sleep study. *Sleep. 39*(3):687-698.

[18] Ghamdi, A. (2013). Sleep deprivation and academic performance of students in the collage of nursing at King Saud University. *World Applied Sciences Journal. 27*(2): 155-167.

[19] Baum, K., Desai, A., Field, J., Miller, L., Rausch, J. and Beebe, D. (2014). Sleep restriction worsens mood and emotion regulation in adolescents. *Journal of Child Psychology and Psychiatry.* February; *55*(2): 180-190.

[20] Simon, E., Rossi, A., Harvey, A. and Walker, M. (2020). Overanxious and underslept. *Nature Human Behaviour. 4*: 100-110.

[21] Youth Risk Behavioral Surveillance System (2015). Centers for Disease Control and Prevention.

[22] Volkow, N., Wang, G. and Baler, R. (2011). Reward, dopamine and the control of food intake: implications for obesity. *Trends in Cognitive Science. 15*(1): 37-46.

[23] Hung, L., Neuner, S., Polepalli, J., Beier, K., Wright, M., Walsh, J., Lewis, E., Luo, L., Deisseroth, K., Dolen, G. and Malenka, R. (2017). Gating of social reward by oxytocin in the ventral tegmental area. *Science. 357*(6358): 1406-1411.

[24] Yim, J. (2016). Therapeutic benefits of laughter in mental health: A theoretical review. *Tohoku J. Exp. Med. 239*: 243-249.

[25] Manninen, S., Tuominen, L., Dunbar, R., Karjalainen, T., Hirvonen, J., Arponen, E., Hari, R., Ja¨a¨skela¨inen, I., Sams, M., and Nummenmaa, L. (2017). Social laughter triggers endogenous opioid release in humans. *Journal of Neuroscience. 37*(25): 6125-6131.

Chapter 3: True Friends See Your Weaknesses, But Recognize Your Strengths

[1] Baumeister, R., Twenge, J., Nuss, C. (2002). Effects of social exclusion on cognitive processes: Anticipated aloneness reduces intelligent thought. *Journal of Personality and Social Psychology. 83*(4): 817-827.

[2] Baumeister, R., DeWall, N., Ciarocco, N. and Twenge, J (2005). Social exclusion impairs self-regulation. *Journal of Personality and Social Psychology. 88*(4): 589-604.

[3] Gerber, J. and Wheeler, L. (2009). On being rejected: A meta-analysis of experimental research on rejection. *Perspectives on Psychological Science. 4*(5): 468-488.

[4] Chester, D. and DeWall, N. (2017). Combating the sting of rejection with the pleasure of revenge: A new look at how emotion shapes aggression. *Journal of Personality and Social Psychology. 112*(3): 413-430.

[5] Hartl, A., Laursen, B. and Cillessen, A. (2015). A Survival of adolescent friendships: The downside of dissimilarity. *Psychological Science. 26*(8): 1304-1315.

[6] Zerubavel, N., Hoffman, M., Reich, A., Ochsner, K. and Bearman, P. (2018). Neural precursors of future liking and affective reciprocity. *Proceedings of the National Academy of the Sciences. 115*(17): 4375-4380.

[7] Steptoe, A., Owen, N., Kunz-Ebrecht, S. and Brydon, L. (2004). *Psychoneuroedocrinology. 29*: 593-611.

[8] DiFulvio, G. (2011). Sexual minority youth, social connection and resilience: From personal struggle to collective identify. *Social Science & Medicine. 72*: 1611-1617.

[9] Kruger, J. and Dunning, D. (1999). Unskilled and unaware of it: how difficulties in recognizing one's own incompetence lead to inflated self-assessments. *Journal of Personality and Social Psychology. 77*(6): 1121-1134.

[10] Chein, J., Albert, D., O'Brien, L., Uckert, K. and Steinberg, L. (2011). Peers increase adolescent risk taking by enhancing activity in the brain's reward circuitry. *Developmental Science.* 14(2): F1-F10.

[11] Gardner, M. and Steinberg, L. (2005). Peer influence on risk taking, risk preference, and risky decision making in adolescence and adulthood: An experimental study. *Developmental Psychology. 41*(4): 625-635.

[12] Weger, H., Bell, G. and Emmet, M. (2010) Active listening in peer interviews: The influence of message paraphrasing on perceptions of listening skill. *International Journal of Listening. 24*: 34-49.

[13] Isaac, A. R. (1992). Mental practice—does it work in the field? *The Sport Psychologist. 6*: 192-198.

[14] Newmark, T. (2012). Cases in visualization for improved athletic performance. *Psychiatric Annals. 42*(10): 385-387.

[15] Kajastila, R., Hamalainen, P. and Holsti, L. (2014). Empowering the exercise: A body-controlled trampoline training game. *International Journal of Computer Science in Sport. 13*(1): 6-23.

[16] Valk, S., Bernhardt, B., Trautwein, F., Bockler, A., Kanske, P., Guizard, N., Collins, L. and Singer, T. (2017). Structural plasticity of the social brain: Differential change after socio-affective and cognitive mental training. *Science Advances. 3*: e1700489.

[17] Pattanashetty, R., Sathiamma, S., Talakkad, S., Nityananda, P., Trichur, R. and Kutty, B. (2010). Practitioners of vipassana meditation exhibit enhanced slow wave sleep and REM sleep states across different age groups. *Sleep and Biological Rhythms. 8*: 34–41.

[18] Baum, K., Desai, A., Field, J., Miller, L., Rausch, J. and Beebe, D. (2104). Sleep restriction worsens mood and emotion regulation in adolescents. *Journal of Child Psychology and Psychiatry. 55*(2): 180-190.

[19] Tate, E., Anxiety on the Rise. (March 29, 2017). *Inside Higher Ed.* https://www.insidehighered.com/news/2017/03/29/anxiety-and-depression-are-primary-concerns-students-seeking-counseling-services.

[20] AAP News. Children's hospitals admissions for suicidal thoughts, actions double during past decade (May 4, 2017). http://www.aappublications.org/news/2017/05/04/PASSuicide050417.

[21] Jevning, R., Wilson, A., Davidson, J. (1978). Adrenocortical activity during meditation. *Hormones and Behavior. 10*(1): 54-60.

[22] Goldschmied, R., Cheng, P., Kemp, K., Caccamo, L., Roberts, J. and Deldin, J. (2015). Napping to modulate frustration and impulsivity: A pilot study. *Personality and Individual Differences.* 86: 164-167.

[23] Dahm, K., Meyer, E., Neff, K., Kimbrel, N., Gulliver, S. and Morissette, S. (2015). Mindfulness, self-compassion, posttraumatic stress disorder symptoms and functional disability in US Iraq and Afghanistan war veterans. *Journal of Traumatic Stress.* 28(5): 460-464.

Chapter 4: You're Lucky to Live Sad Moments

[1] Ra, C., Cho, J. and Stone, M. (2018). Association of digital media use with subsequent symptoms of attention-deficit/hyperactivity disorder among adolescents. *Journal of the American Medical Association.* 320(3): 255-263.

[2] Darcin, A., Kose, S., Noyan, C., Nurmedov, S., Yilmaz, O. and Dilbaz, N. (2016). Smartphone addiction and its relationship with social anxiety and loneliness among university students in Turkey. *Behaviour and Information Technology.* 35(7): 520-525.

[3] Hunt, M., Marx, R., Lipson, C. and Young, J. (2018). No More FOMO: Limiting social media decreases loneliness and depression. *Journal of Social and Clinical Psychology.* 37(10): 751-768.

[4] Wiersma, J., Oppen, P., vanSchaik, D., van der Does, A., Beekman, A. and Pennix, B. (2011). Psychological characteristics of chronic depression: a longitudinal cohort study. *Journal of Clinical Psychiatry.* 72(3): 288-294.

[5] Peterson, C. (1979). Uncontrollability and self-blame in depression: Investigation of the paradox in a college population. *Journal of Abnormal Psychology.* 88(6): 620-624.

[6] Benassi, V., Sweeney, P. and Dufour, C. (1988). Is there a relation between locus of control orientation and depression? *Journal of Abnormal Psychology.* 97(3): 357–367.

[7] Presson, P. and Benassi, V. (1996). Locus of control orientation and depressive symptomatology: A meta-analysis. *Journal of Social Behavioral Perspectives.* 11(1): 201-212.

[8] Archer, R. (1979). Relationships between locus of control and anxiety. *Journal of Personality Assessment.* 43: 617-625.

[9] Bonelli, R., Dew, R., Koenig, H., Rosmarin, D. and Vasegh, S. (2012). Religious and spiritual factors in depression: Review and integration of the research. *Depression Research and Treatment.* Volume 2012; 962860.

[10] Stewart, W., Wetselaar, M., Nelson, L. and Stewart, J. (2019). Review of the effect of religion on anxiety. *International Journal of Anxiety and Depression.* 2(2): 1-5.

[11] Iles-Caven, Y., Gregory, S., Ellis, G., Golding, J. and Nowicki, S. (2020). The relationship between locus of control and religious behavior and beliefs in a large population of parents: An observational study. *Frontiers in Psychology.* *11*: 1462.

[12] Erickson, T., Granillo, M., Cocker, J., Abelson, J., Reas, H. and Quach, C. (2019). Compassionate and self-image goals as interpersonal maintenance factors in clinical depression and anxiety. *Journal of Clinical Psychology.* *74*: 608-625.

[13] Edwards-Jones, G., Millá i Canals, L., Hounsome, N., Truninger, M., Koerber, G., Hounsome, B., Cross, P., York, E. H., Hospido, A., Plassmann, K., Harris, I. M., Edwards, R. T., Day, G. A. S, Tomos, A. D., Cowell, S. J. and Jones, D. L. (2008). Testing the assertion that 'local food is best': the challenges of an evidence-based approach. *Trends in Food Science and Technology.* *19*(5): 265-74.

[14] Mariola, M. J. (2008). The local industrial complex? Questioning the link between local foods and energy use. *Agriculture and Human Values.* *25*(2): 193-96.

[15] McGuirt, J. T., Jilcott, S. B., Liu, H. and Ammerman, A.S. (2011). Produce price savings for consumers at farmers' markets compared to supermarkets in North Carolina. *Journal of Hunger and Environmental Nutrition.* *6*(1): 86-98.

[16] Valpiani, N., Wilde, P., Rogers, B. and Stewart, H. (2015). Patterns of fruit and vegetable availability and price competitiveness across four seasons are different in local food outlets and supermarkets. *Public Health Nutrition.* *18*(15): 2846-2854.

[17] Bertoia M., Mukamal K., Cahill L., Hou T., Ludwig D., Mozaffarian D., Willett W., Hu F. and Rimm E. (2015). Changes in intake of fruits and vegetables and weight change in United States men and women followed for up to 24 years: analysis from three prospective cohort studies. *PLOS Medicine.* *12*(9): e1001878.

[18] Salois, M. J. (2012). Obesity and diabetes, the built environment, and the 'local' food economy in the United States, 2007. *Economics and Human Biology.* *10*(1): 35-42.

[19] De Marco, M., Gustafson, A., Gizlice, Z., Crowder, R. and Ammerman, A. (2014). Locally grown fruit and vegetable purchasing habits and the association with children's diet. *Journal of Hunger and Environmental Nutrition.* *9*(3): 372-87.

[20] Favell, D. (1998). A comparison of the vitamin C content of fresh and frozen vegetables. *Food Chemistry.* *62*(1): 59-64.

[21] Rickman, J., Barrett, D. and Bruhn, C. (2007). Nutritional comparison of fresh, frozen and canned fruits and vegetables. Part 1. Vitamins C and B and phenolic compounds. *Journal of the Science of Food and Agriculture.* *87*: 930-944.

[22] Mann, T., Tomiyama, J., Westling, E., Lew, A., Samuels, B. and Chatman, J. (2007). Medicare's search for effective obesity treatments: diets are not the answer. *American Psychologist. 62*(3): 220-233.

[23] Garner, D. and Wooley, S. (1991). Confronting the failure of behavioral and dietary treatments for obesity. *Clinical Psychology Review. 11*: 729-780.

[24] Lowe, D., Wu, N., Rohdin-Bibby, L., Moore, H., Kelly, N., Liu, Y., Philip, E., Vittinghoff, E., Heymsfield, S., Olgin, J., Shepard, J. and Weiss, E. (2020). Effects of time-restricted eating on weight loss and other metabolic parameters in women and men with overweight and obesity: The TREAT randomized clinical trial. *JAMA Internal Medicine. 180*(11): 1491-1499.

[25] Outland L.. (2012). Bringing homeostasis back into weight control. *Journal of Obesity and Weight loss Therapy. 2*: 115.

[26] Van Holst, R., Veltman, D., Buchel, C., van dan Brink, W. and Goudriann, A. (2012). Distorted expectancy coding in problem gambling: Is the addictive in the anticipation? *Biological Psychiatry. 71*: 741-748.

[27] Zastrow, M. (2017). News Feature: Is video game addiction really an addiction? *Proceedings of the National Academy of the Sciences USA. 114*(17): 4268-4272.

[28] Lemola, S., Brand, S., Vogler, N., Perkinson-Gloor, N., Allemand, M. and Grob, A. (2011). Habitual computer game playing at night is related to depressive symptoms. *Personality and Individual Differences. 51*: 117-122.

[29] Granic, I., Lobel, A. and Engels, R., The benefits of playing video games. *American Psychologist. 69*(1): 66-78.

Chapter 5: This Too Shall Pass

[1] Carstensen, L., Shavit, Y. and Barnes, J. (2020). Age advantages in emotional experience persist even under threat from the COVID-19 pandemic. *Psychological Science. 31*(11): 1374-1385.

[2] Klaiber, P., Wen, J., DeLongis, A., and Sin, N. (2021). The ups and downs of daily life during COVID-19: Age differences in affect, stress, and positive events. *Journal of Gerontology Series B Psychological Science Social Sciences. 76*: No. 2, e30–e37.

[3] Nieuwsma, J., Trivedi, R., McDuffie, J., Kronish, I., Benjamin, D. and Williams, J. (2012). Brief psychotherapy for depression: A systematic review and meta-Analysis. *International Journal of Psychiatry Medicine. 43*(2): 129-151.

[4] Cuijpers, P., Sijbrandij, M., Koole, S., Andersson, G., Beekman, A. and Reynolds, C. (2014). Adding psychotherapy to antidepressant medication in depression and anxiety disorders: a meta-analysis. *World Psychiatry. 13*(1): 56-67.

[5] Dazzi, T., Gribble, R., Wessely, S. and Fear, N. (2014). Does asking about suicide and related behaviours induce suicidal ideation? What is the evidence? *Psychological Medicine. 44*(16): 3361-3363.

[6] McNeil J., LeBlanc, E. and Joyner, M. (1991). The effect of exercise on depressive symptoms in the moderately depressed elderly. *Psychology of Aging.* 6:487-488.

[7] DiLorenzo T., Bargman E. and Stucky-Ropp, R. (1999). Long-term effects of aerobic exercise on psychological outcomes. *Prevention Medicine. 28*: 75-85.

[8] Craft, L. and Perna, F. (2004). The benefits of exercise for the clinically depressed. *Primary Care Companion to the Journal of Clinical Psychiatry. 6*(3): 104-111.

[9] Burbach J., Young L. J. and Russell J. (2006). "Oxytocin: synthesis, secretion and reproductive functions," in *Knobil and Neill's Physiology of Reproduction* 3rd Edn ed. Neill J. D. (Amsterdam: Elsevier).

[10] Petersson, M., Uvnas-Moberg, K., Nilsson, A., Gustafson, L., Hydbring-Sandberg, E. and Handlin, L. (2017). Oxytocin and cortisol levels in dog owners and their dogs are associated with behavioral patterns: An Exploratory Study. *Frontiers in Psychology. 8*: 1796.

[11] Nagasawa, M., Mitsui, S., En, S., Ohtani, N., Ohta, M., Sakuma, Y., Onaka, T., Mogi, K. and Kikusui, T. (2105). Oxytocin-gaze positive loop and the coevolution of human-dog bonds. *Science. 348*(6232): 333-336.

[12] Parletta, N., Zarnowiecki, D., Cho, J., Wilson, A., Bogomolova, S., Villani, A., Itsiopoulos, C., Niyonsenga, T., Blunden, S., Meyer, B., Segal, L., Baune, B. and O'Dea, K. (2019). A Mediterranean-style dietary intervention supplemented with fish oil improves diet quality and mental health in people with depression: A randomized controlled trial (HELFIMED). *Nutritional Neuroscience. 22*(7): 474-487.

[13] Bandelow, B. and Michaelis, S. (2015). Epidemiology of anxiety disorders in the 21st century. *Dialogues in Clinical Neuroscience. 17*(3): 327-335.

[14] Kim, Y. (2019). Panic Disorder: Current Research and Management Approaches. *Psychiatry Investigation. 16*(1): 1-3.

[15] Perna, G., Bertani, A., Caldirola, D. and Bellodi, L. (1996). Family history of panic disorder and hypersensitivity to CO_2 in patients with panic disorder. *American Journal of Psychiatry. 153*(8): 1060-1064.

[16] Sheline, Y., Barch, D., Donnelly, J., Ollinger, J., Snyder, A. and Mintum, M. (2001). Increased amygdala response to masked emotional faces in depressed subjects resolves with antidepressant treatment: an fMRI study. *Biological Psychiatry. 50*(9): 651-8.

[17] Fu, C., Williams, S., Cleare, A., Brammer, M., Walsh, N., Andrew, C., Pich, E., Williams, P., Reed, L., Mitterschiffthaler, M., Suckling, J. and Bullmore, E. (2004). Attenuation of the neural response to sad faces in major depression by antidepressant treatment: a prospective, event-related functional magnetic resonance imaging study. *Archives of General Psychiatry. 61*(9): 877-89.

[18] Thomas, K., Drevets, W., Dahl, R., Birmaher, B., Eccard, C., Axelson, D., Whalen, P. and Casey, B. (2001). Amygdala response to fearful faces in anxious and depressed children. *Archives of General Psychiatry.* *58*(11): 1057-1063.

[19] Altamura, A., Buoli, M., Albano, A. and Dell'Osso, B. (2010). Age at onset and latency to treatment (duration of untreated illness) in patients with mood and anxiety disorders: a naturalistic study. *International Clinical Psychopharmacology.* *25*(3): 172-179.

[20] Burcusa, S. and Iacono, W. (2007). Risk for recurrence of depression. *Clinical Psychology Reviews.* *27*(8): 959-985.

[21] Fournier, M., DeRubeis, R., Hollon, S., Dimidiian, S, Amsterdam, J., Shelton, R. and Fawcett, J. (2010). Antidepressant drug effects and depression severity: A patient level meta-analysis. *Journal of the American Medical Association.* *303*(1): 47-53.22. Kasser, T. and Ryan, M. (1996). Further examining the American dream: Differential correlates of intrinsic and extrinsic goals. *Personality and Social Psychology Bulletin.* *22*(3): 280-287.

Chapter 6: Disappointment Inspired

[1] Orehek, E., Fishman, S., Dechesne, M., Doosie, B., Kruglanski, A., Cole, A., Saddler, B. and Jackson, T. (2010). Need for closure and the social response to terrorism. *Basic and Applied Social Psychology.* *32*(4): 279-290.

[2] Hamid, A., Pettibone, J., Mabrouk, O., Hetrick, V., Schmidt, R., Vander Weele, C., Kennedy, R., Aragona, B. and Berke, J. (2016). Mesolimbic dopamine signals the value of work. *Nature Neuroscience.* *19*(1): 117-126.

[3] Stroebe, M., Schut, H. and Boerner, K. (2017). Cautioning health-care professionals: bereaved persons are misguided through the stages of grief. *Journal of Death and Dying.* *74*(4): 455-473.

ABOUT THE AUTHOR

Since 1995, Matt Bellace, Ph.D., has been a professional speaker and stand-up comedian. His programs encourage over a hundred thousand students and adults each year to pursue natural highs (e.g. laughter, meditation) and be resilient in the face of stress.

Dr. Bellace has a Ph.D. in clinical neuropsychology, the study of the brain and behavior. He worked at the National Institutes of Mental Health, and completed his internship at the traumatic brain and spinal cord units at The Mount Sinai Medical Center in New York City.

He's the author of the book *A Better High*, a contributing author for *National Geographic Kids*, and was a recurring comedian on truTV's "World's Dumbest." As a comedian, he's appeared in comedy in clubs and colleges across the country, including Gotham Comedy Club in New York City and the Just For Laughs Festival in Montreal.

As an undergraduate at Bucknell University, Matt founded a student prevention organization named C.a.l.v.i.n. & H.o.b.b.e.s. Over 25 years later, it is the oldest student group on campus, providing substance-free events every weekend of the school year. In 1995, the trustees of Bucknell approved funding to refurbish a former fraternity house for the group to reside. *U.S. News and World Report* heralded the move, noting, "How times have changed." Bucknell President, William "Bro" Adams referred to the group as "revolutionary."

He currently lives in Princeton, NJ and enjoys pursuing natural highs with his wife and two children. For more information visit **MattBallace.com**.

CPSIA information can be obtained
at www.ICGtesting.com
Printed in the USA
BVHW030812210821
614334BV00007B/3